ARCHITECTURAL DESIGN

EDITORIAL OFFICES:
42 LEINSTER GARDENS, LONDON W2 3AN
TEL: 0171-402 2141 FAX: 0171-723 9540

SUBSCRIPTION OFFICES:
UK: ACADEMY GROUP LTD
42 LEINSTER GARDENS
LONDON W2 3AN
TEL: 0171-402 2141 FAX: 0171-723 9540

USA AND CANADA: VCH PUBLISHERS NEW YORK INC, SUITE 907, 220 EAST 23RD STREET
NEW YORK, NY 10010-4606
TEL: (212) 683 8333 FAX: (212) 779 8890

ALL OTHER COUNTRIES:
VCH VERLAGSGESELLSCHAFT MBH
BOSCHSTRASSE 12, POSTFACH 101161
69451 WEINHEIM
FEDERAL REPUBLIC OF GERMANY
TEL: +49 6201 606 148 FAX: +49 6201 606 184

Architectural Design is published six times per year (Jan/Feb; Mar/Apr; May/Jun; Jul/Aug; Sept/Oct; and Nov/Dec).Subscription rates for 1996 (incl p&p): *Annual subscription price:* UK only £68.00, World DM 195, USA $142.00 for regular subscribers. *Student rate*: UK only £50.00, World DM 156, USA$105.00 incl postage and handling charges. *Individual issues:* £16.95/DM 42.50 (plus £2.40/DM 6 for p&p, per issue ordered), US$28.95 (incl p&p).

For the USA and Canada, *Architectural Design* is distributed by VCH Publishers New York Inc, Suite 907, 220 East 23rd Street New York, NY 10010-4606; Tel: (212) 683 8333, Fax: (212) 779 8890. Application to mail at second-class postage rates is pending at New York, NY. **POSTMASTER**. Send address changes to *Architectural Design*, VCH Publishers New York Inc, Suite 907, 220 East 23rd Street, New York, NY 10010-4606. Printed in Italy. Origination by Media 2000, London.
All prices are subject to change without notice. [ISSN: 0003-8504]

CONTENTS

ARCHITECTURAL DESIGN **MAGAZINE**

Battle McCarthy *Multi-Source Synthesis: A Breath of Fresh Air* • ***Christian Brensing*** *Berlin: Young Architects Today II* • ***Katherine MacInnes*** *An interview with Fernando Castillo* • *Academy Highlights* • *Exhibitions*

ARCHITECTURAL DESIGN **PROFILE** No 123

INTEGRATING ARCHITECTURE

Neil Spiller • *Michael Sorkin* • ***Richard Goodwin*** • *Michael Webb* • ***William Alsop*** • *Pete Silver and Peter Fluck* • ***Ted Krueger*** • *Neil Denari* • ***Ben Nicholson*** • *Mark Titman* • ***Sixteen* (makers)*** • *John Andrews* • ***Shin Egashira*** • *Lab – Bates + Davidson* • ***Paul Ursell*** • *Nat Chard* • ***Alison Sampson*** • *Rachel Armstrong*

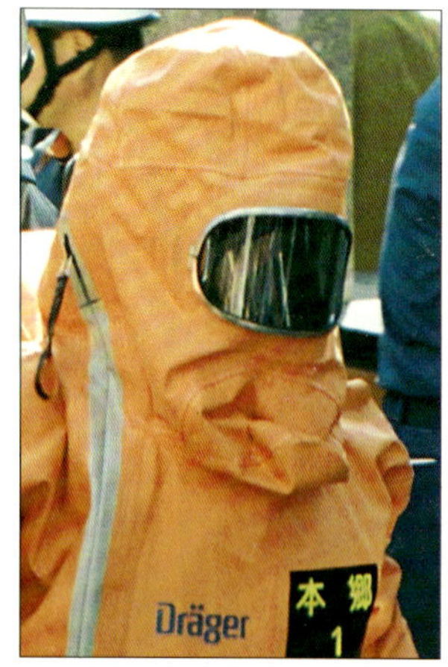

Police in protective clothing during the Tokyo gas attacks

Becker, Gewers, Kühn & Kühn, model of the Volksbank Headquarters, Berlin

Nat Chard, *The Hall and The Staircase*, detail, 1994-95

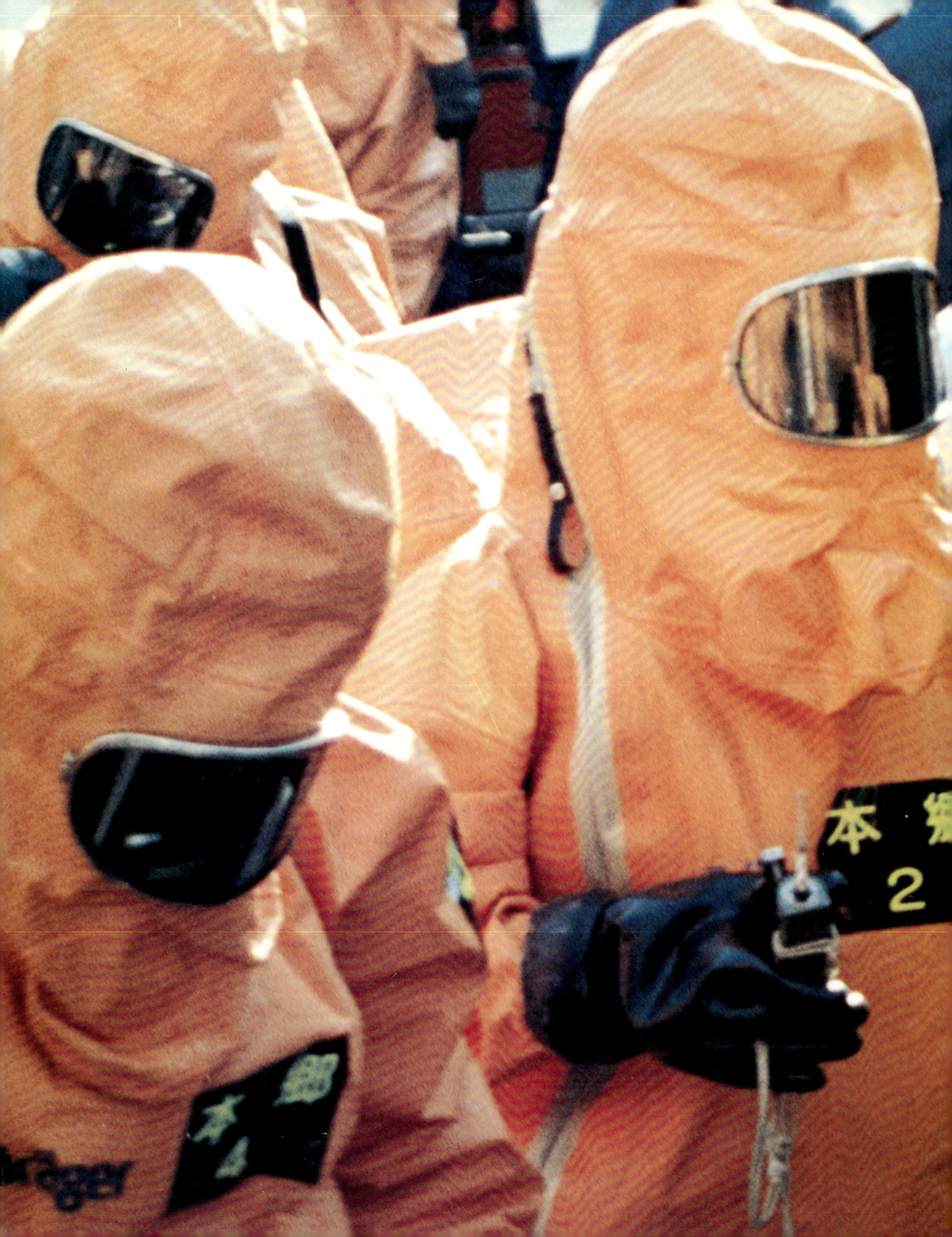

BATTLE McCARTHY

MULTI-SOURCE SYNTHESIS

A Breath of Fresh Air

It has long been accepted that buildings can make people sick. Yet it may be that the real issue in the future is what buildings can do to make you well – by protecting occupants from the extremes of outside air quality. Most of the problems of ill buildings are now understood and can be avoided with good design. But the problem of air pollution – the atmosphere in which buildings dwell – is posing a threat from outside which is very difficult to master.

Many buildings designed and constructed today will suffer from increasing air quality problems in the future. If the siting, orientation or servicing strategy of the building exacerbates rather than improves the quality of air and affects occupant health, will it be the responsibility of the developer, the architect or the engineer?

Poisoned air

Over the past three years, a series of pollution peaks in world cities, mainly as a result of petrol and diesel fumes, has caused death and controversy. In May, June and July 1995 for example, ozone levels in European cities exceeded EU and World Health Organisation (WHO) limits in more than 2,800 cases, with high pollution levels being reported in 76 major cities. The results are not purely academic: 170 people died in London in November 1991 as a result of the smog, according to *New Scientist*. Meanwhile the world's ecosystems are suffering major damage, and certain species are facing extinction due to poor air quality.

The anatomy of atmospheric pollution

High pollution levels occur when it is very hot, or when it is very cold; when windless conditions or a temperature inversion allow ground-generated pollution to build up, and when hot sunlight causes pollutants to react in the air. The effects vary: ground-level ozone causes stinging eyes and breathing difficulties; carbon monoxide renders red blood cells useless; and particulates lodge in the lungs causing respiratory disease.

Not everyone is sensitive to environmental pollution, and those worst hit tend to be those with respiratory diseases or asthma. However the number of people who are sensitive seems to be increasing, as in the case of asthma. More than three million people in the UK now suffer from asthma and nine million suffer from breathing problems, according to the National Asthma Campaign.

Design team response

Air pollution is just one issue among many – one source requiring design synthesis – and statistics are only partially useful without context. There is no doubt that London air is cleaner by far than in the days of coal, when as late as the 1950s not hundreds but thousands of people were dying each year in coal-smoke smog.

It is not a question of the presence of pollutants or poisons – which abound in nature – but in their concentration. Design teams can no longer design in ignorance of site air quality when the means of measurement are available at moderate cost and the links between poor air quality in buildings and poor health are generally accepted. Building design should now include the measurement of existing air quality from site surveys, historical data and medical records, and the establishment of guidelines for acceptable air quality related to exposure periods.

Sniffer buildings

Future buildings will be able to sniff the air around them before deciding which way to breathe. This will not mean the end of natural ventilation (air conditioning makes no difference to air quality and filtering can break large safe dust particles into small dangerous particles). It means an extension of building control intelligence to include air quality, and the development of different ways of dealing with the problem. Buildings may change inlet positions, switch to mechanical ventilation, or use electrostatic precipitation to remove particles. They will even use plants to purify and perfume the air in response to changing requirements (research by NASA has revealed how some plants can be used to absorb certain pollutants – for instance spider plants have an affinity for formaldehyde).

The important factor is that the list of critical environmental design issues: daylighting, acoustics, ventilation, thermal comfort, and the aromatic environment must now be extended to include air quality – at least until our transport systems can be revolutionised.

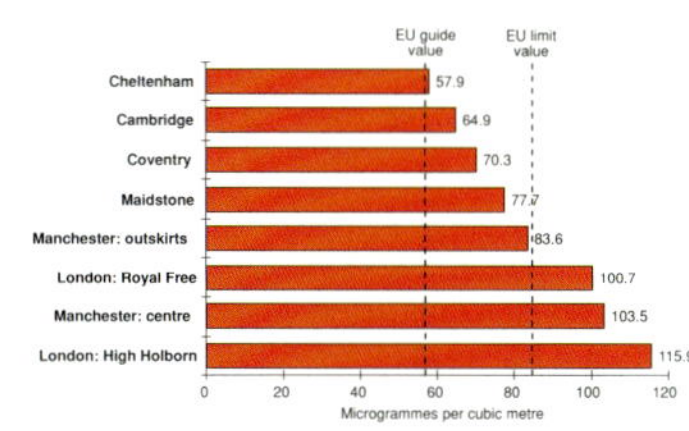

Levels of Nitrogen Dioxide in UK cities

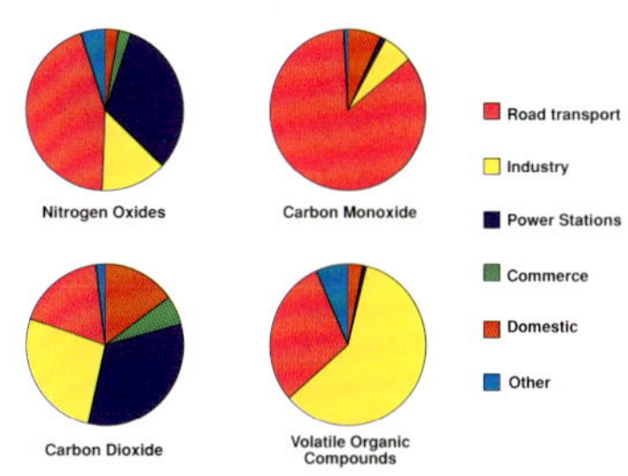

Breakdown of UK air pollution by source

Data from DoE for 1988

OPPOSITE, MAIN PICTURE: Police in protective clothing during the Tokyo gas attacks; FROM ABOVE: Designers are only as good as their ability to allow for future change; typical levels of nitrogen dioxide in UK cities exceed both EU guide levels and EU legal limits; the major cause of air pollution is road transport

The authors would like to thank Professor Patrick O'Sullivan and Robert Webb for their assistance in the preparation of this article

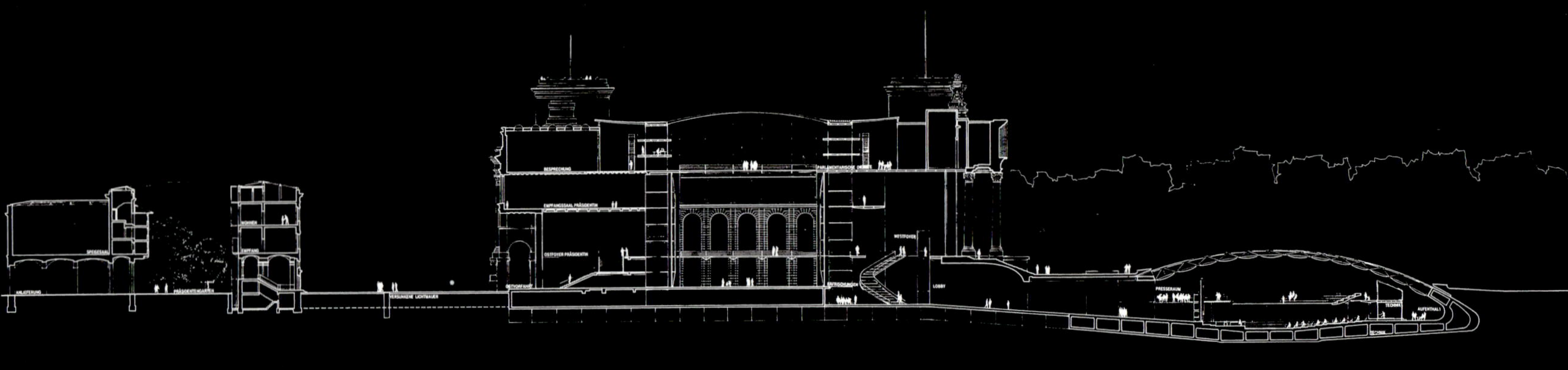

CHRISTIAN BRENSING

BERLIN: YOUNG ARCHITECTS TODAY II

Grüntuch/Ernst: Tomorrow's World

Throughout the 80s until the fall of the Wall, the career options for young architects in Berlin had largely been channelled by the all pervasive system of competitions for public projects. Countless projects for schools, kindergartens, day nurseries, sports halls and the occasional public swimming pool had provided a reliable and stable source of income. Private investors or developers did not play any major role before 1989. This changed dramatically when the Wall came down. The market quickly improved, yet left young offices few chances of securing a significant share of the market. The big commissions, for example Potsdamer Platz, went to international architects and the mundane German investors had more faith in the established Berlin architectural quartet of Kleihues, Kollhoff, Sawade and Dudler. This left little room for architectural experiment and innovation.

The alternatives left to young architectural practices were nevertheless not so scarce. Either they specialised in small and unique projects or, due to the international pedigree which most of them enjoyed, they became contact architects for the 'stars' who had won large projects in Berlin. Other options included the participation in the major international competitions for Berlin, such as the one for the Reichstag, or to advocate specialised aspects of architecture such as ecology or that of the 'intelligent building'. These two subjects in particular are persistently gaining more and more attention in environmentally aware German society.

Since their move from Cologne to Berlin in 1991 Armand Grüntuch and Almut Ernst have gained experience in the whole range of the options outlined above for young architects. One of their first commissions was to redesign the foyer and canopy of a hotel in western Berlin (AD Profile no 122). The historic building had not been refurbished since the 60s and the entrance area, in particular, called for an entirely new solution. The existing canopy, of corrugated plastic sheeting, was replaced with a new stainless steel construction with an all glass roof, made of 130 by 130 centimetre sheets, spanning across the entire pavement. High-tech filigree steel members rest on cantilevered stilts and provide a contemporary antidote to the ornate facade. The success of the entire concept is determined by the balance of old and new and by the extent to which daylight has been brought into the previously dark entrance.

A far greater challenge in the combination of old and new, and the handling of daylight has been the Grüntuch/Ernst competition entry for the refurbishment of the Reichstag to house the German Parliament when the government moves to Berlin in the year 2000. Most significantly the debating chamber, metaphorically the heart of democracy, is located outside the Reichstag building. The section reveals a futuristic looking shell half submerged in front of the Reichstag main entrance with just a glass lense as roof visible; a stark contrast between the heavy load-bearing brick walls of the Reichstag and the slender beams forming the cupola of the column-free debating chamber. Though mainly underground, the construction principle is reminiscent of airport hangars with strong anticipation of the 21st century.

The prize-winning scheme for a school for children with learning difficulties in Berlin Hellersdorf (AD Profile no 122) demonstrates a more evenly balanced equilibrium between design and advanced technology. The design brief asked for a building in which the pupils benefited as much as possible from their environment: naturally ventilated rooms with maximum daylight. It is the sensitive arrangement of the building masses which is the key to the entire concept. The three similar sections – the southern sports complex, the central garden and the northern wing of classrooms – are positioned to exploit the sun's movement.

The ecological design solutions put forward by Grüntuch/Ernst are examples of the increasing emphasis on green issues by the German planning authorities. In combination with an excellent architectural style, the future of ecologically aware building could at the same time achieve cost effectiveness, operational simplicity and still be aesthetically pleasing. One of the greatest potentials for young architects in Berlin lies in this particular formula of a successfully integrated construction.

OPPOSITE, FROM ABOVE: The Reichstag – front elevation with debating chamber; longitudinal section; model

Pysall/Ruge: Transit and Transitory Spaces
Potsdamer Platz before the war had the reputation of the busiest traffic intersection in Europe. It was equipped with the first set of traffic lights in Germany. Not dissimilar, Alexander Platz was depicted in Alfred Döblin's 1927 novel of the same title as an urban place undergoing permanent transformation: a place that few people called their home because of the restless pace of change. Berlin was a national and international hub with millions of people and goods milling through its urban fabric.

Nowadays Berlin is at pains to revitalise its former central position among German and European cities. The role it played so well during the Cold War, that of the charming but neglected capitalist outpost, has to be reversed into one of an expanding international city. The protective qualities of the Wall have vanished once and for all and they are gradually being replaced by expanding links all over the world.

However, few architects in Berlin seem to have taken notice of this relentless development as far as their work is concerned. Their projects are largely untouched by the extent to which public life has been changing since the fall of the Wall. The speed, volume and variety of traffic, communication, construction, trade and people, in other words, the globalisation of Berlin, has not yet been properly absorbed and reflected by local architects. The return to traditional facade cladding such as stone and the demure obedience to the 22-metre eaves height restriction suggest a rather anachronistic behaviour.

This inward looking attitude, however, has little to do with the aims and the architecture of Justus Pysall and Peter Ruge. Their respective careers have taken them around the world before they opened their own practice in Berlin. Metaphorically, the circulation and fluctuation of large numbers of people in one place has turned into a recurrent theme in their choice of projects.

The proposed roof extension for an Art Nouveau complex of buildings and courtyards in the city centre of Berlin is a perfect example of how Pysall/Ruge succeed in opening up traditional structures and turn them into con-

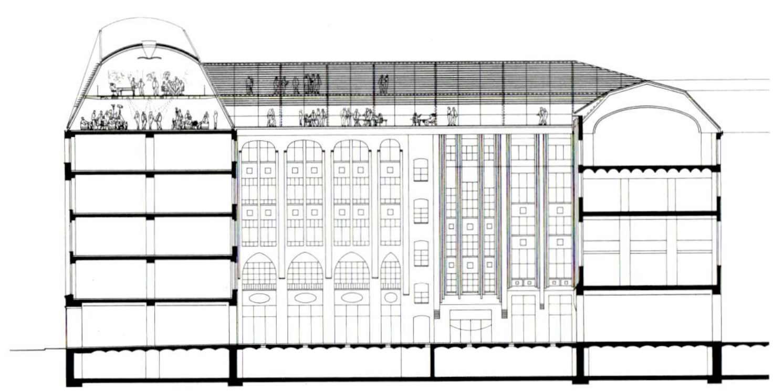

FROM ABOVE: Hackesche Höfe, Berlin – perspective view; bird's-eye view; longitudinal section through first courtyard building

temporary public spaces. Their goal is further supported by the history of Hackesche Höfe as a mixed development including workshops, theatres, retail and housing. This plurality of use is being extended by the present owner who wants to add three floors on the roof as office and exhibition spaces.

Pysall/Ruge designed a bold roof construction, following the shape of the destroyed historic roof line, thus adding a new dimension, of transparency, openness and accessibility. The suspended floors behind slanted louvres, as substitute for traditional roof tiling, seem to float like a cloud above the building mass. The entire weight and elaboration of the Art Nouveau courtyard facade of glazed bricks is counterbalanced by the lightweight roof. At night the entire volume of the roof space will be visible from the street and courtyards. The open plan will enable visitors to experience the full dimensions of this unique assembly of architectural spaces. The uninhibited circulation in the attic would be a continuation of the stream of people strolling through the courtyards.

The subject of material and historic transition, as reflected in the movement of people, is also the inspiration for two further competition submissions by Pysall/Ruge: the Yokohama Port Terminal in Japan and the extension of Erfurt Railway Station for German high-speed trains. Both competition entries bear a resemblance to the Berlin roof concept. In all three cases we are dealing with a de-materialisation of architecture. In other words, the curvilinear language of the architectural frame becomes an instrument which is adapted to the type and frequency of its usage. Like a musical instrument the inherent architectural qualities are not revealed until a skilled individual performs a set piece.

At best the architectural language blends effortlessly with the strict demands of functionality and efficiency, as is demonstrated in both public buildings. It provides a flexible envelope which in itself is pliable enough to respond to the various role models. The architectural transformation thus goes far beyond the mere visualisation of day and night; it is a permanent diurnal process of evolution.

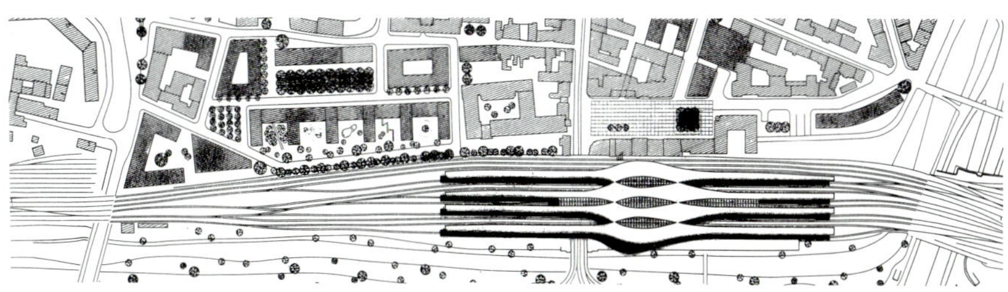

FROM ABOVE: Erfurt Main Station – perspective of platform by day; perspective by night; site plan

Becker, Gewers, Kühn & Kühn: Orchestrated Intelligence

Without doubt the future of Berlin will be designed and determined by the uncompromisingly global and interdisciplinary design approach of the architectural practices presented so far. The trend was established by the Berlin housing association GSW in 1991 when it awarded the London/Berlin-based architects Sauerbruch/Hutton the first prize for its daring high-rise for the new GSW headquarters in central Berlin. It took three more years, until May 1994, for the client to announce with some confidence that he was likely to receive full planning permission for this 22-storey tower with its striking ecological double facade.

However arduous the arguments might have been about the pros and cons of allowing a tower of glass and steel in the middle of Berlin, so obviously violating the building regulations prescribed by the Senate, Sauerbruch/Hutton widened the scope of the Berlin architectural debate. In hindsight the fight for the GSW headquarters, now under construction, was a signal for architects as well as clients that the struggle for excellent architecture can be won despite an officially endorsed anachronistic spirit.

A year after the momentous decision in favour of the ultra-modern Sauerbruch/Hutton scheme, the Berlin practice of Becker, Gewers, Kühn & Kühn won first prize for its design of the new Berlin headquarters of Volksbank. As in the GSW competition, a young team from Berlin beat an international field of architects. Significantly, the design is for a 21-storey round tower featuring an all-glass double facade. It is the second high-rise since the GSW competition (apart from the autarchic situation at Potsdamer Platz and an outrageous skyscraper scenario at Alexander Platz) which has been awarded first prize and the assurance of realisation. The building will feature as a landmark in the vicinity of the Berlin Radio Tower and the International Congress Centre (ICC), and will be clearly visible from a busy neighbouring highway. In many ways the project represents a clever compromise. On the one hand, it closes the Berlin block structure on two sides with buildings of the traditional height; on the other, it places a dominant high-rise in the centre of the block. A link between the two extremes is provided by an inner courtyard and an atrium between the tower and the modern blocks facing the street. The result is a homogeneous urban situation which meets the common consent.

The BGKK scheme for the Volksbank headquarters begs the question of how a young practice of four strong individual architects can achieve such results? Their common experience in the London construction boom of the late-80s does not account for their uncompromisingly inquisitive nature and their persistent probing. The willingness to experiment and to seek the cooperation of not just architecturally related partners, result in the startling effects of their architectural end product. A small building in Zossen just outside Berlin provides some interesting insights and clues.

Walking along the main street of Zossen one notices one facade in particular: that of the regional agricultural bank. Its seamless

BELOW, L TO R: Verbundnetz Gas Headquarters, Leipzig – model, cross-section of north wing; cross-section

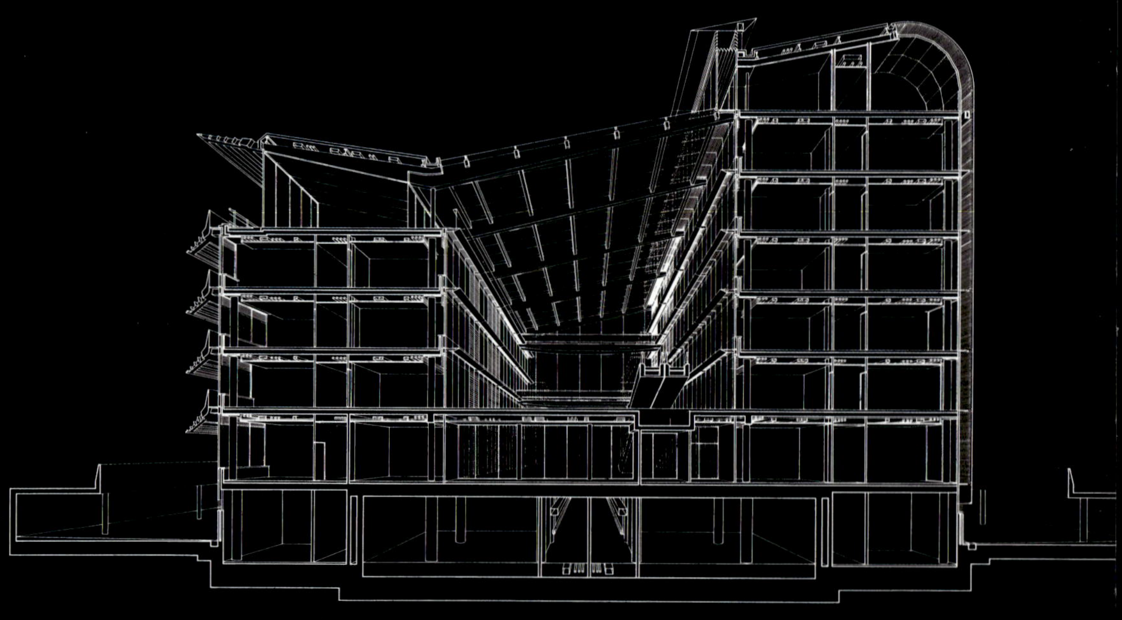

uncluttered facade of perfectly fitted windows, fair-faced concrete and aluminium radiates an air of control and perfection. On entering the building, all impressions of a local parochialism are left behind. The interior is pervaded by an aura of unpretentious purity and elegant simplicity.

The central atrium, with its glass roof and the surrounding frameless glass walls of the two top floors, displays best the BGKK office philosophy of transparency. The invisible joints, the meticulous fitting and the denial of obtrusive construction details remind one more of a well-designed and manufactured machine than a building. Analogies with advanced technical products, for example, from the car industry, could be made: special product research and development of the 2.5 by 2.1 metres low-emission glass for the roof glazing, understated mechanical and structural details (like the external roof fittings) and the aesthetic of linear and spatial proportions. The end product, in other words, the building completed in February 1995, is a model worthy of the highest distinction.

The headquarters building for the gas company Verbundnetz Gas in Leipzig will demonstrate an even higher order of architectural refinement and environmental sophistication. The sheer length of the two parallel wings of 125 metres each indicate that we are moving in a different scale from the Zossen building. However, the distribution of volume and of the different functions receives the same utmost consideration. The size and volume are counterbalanced by the highest possible degree of transparency and structural understatement.

A degree of abstraction dominated the scheme from the early design phases. Its consequent de-materialisation took a further step during the model stages to reach its conclusion on site during the current fitting out.

A perfect way to comprehend the building and its concept would be to compare it with a microprocessor. The all-pervasive logic of its internal organisation becomes apparent in the rational ground plan, the cascading atrium space with its gas distribution centre underneath, or details such as the double facade glazing. On all levels of planning one perceives the building as a harmonious unity. The more the construction process advances towards completion in late 1996, the more one gains awareness of the combined forces at work in their nevertheless gentle totality.

Berlin as a seedbed for architectural talent and inspiration? The stormy and somewhat jagged development of the city since unification holds plenty of promises for anyone who is prepared to observe patiently as well as critically. The young German architects introduced here belong to an increasing number of internationally experienced practitioners of the young generation who not only see themselves less rooted in their parochial traditions but demonstrate a global awareness and responsibility for architecture and the environment. The final years approaching the Millennium and beyond will reveal whether their projects and solutions will be awarded the public approval they already deserve.

Christian Brensing works for Ove Arup & Partners, Berlin

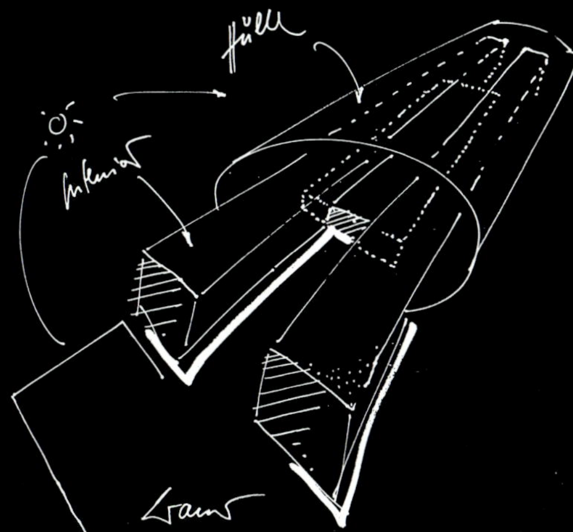

FROM ABOVE: Verbundnetz Gas Headquarters, Leipzig – atrium facade; internal facade details; BELOW, L TO R: Model scheme design; concept sketch

KATHERINE MACINNES

AN INTERVIEW WITH FERNANDO CASTILLO
The last four decades of Chilean architecture

Fernando Castillo is an architect from the old school. As rector of the Catholic University of Architecture in Santiago, the capital of Chile, from 1968, he tutored many of the country's best known architects practising today. Castillo is a passionate believer in the essential goodness of man. His family owned a valuable area of land within the city boundaries which he divided into plots to enable those less well off to build themselves homes. These pioneering self-build projects led him to be chosen for the cabinet of a government that preceded General Pinochet's military coup and subsequent dictatorship in the 1970s and 80s. During the 80s Castillo brought his family to safety in England and taught at Cambridge University where he introduced his ideas of the community into the curriculum of the architectural school. On his return to Chile before the end of Pinochet's dictatorship in 1989, his family suffered and he lost his son. Unusually, this magnetic man has retained the loyalty of his former pupils from the Right as well as the Left and his positive, community-based ideology has influenced generations of Latin America's architects. Now in his late 70s, Fernando Castillo lives with his wife and family in La Reina, the peaceful, green community architecture project in Santiago that he started over 30 years ago. He can only whisper as a result of an operation to remove cancer of the throat. This interview was done by answering my questions on a computer. Despite his age and disability, Castillo has a lively interest in new technology, an impatience with tradition and an extraordinary level of generosity which involves providing every stranger with a bed, a meal and a *traigo* of the local Chilean spirit: *pisco sour.* He is a living testimony to the essential 'goodness' of man, around which his philosophy is based.

Katherine MacInnes: Community architecture has been a central theme in your career. You seem to have adopted different solutions to the problem however. Your early buildings such as the Unidad Vecinal Portales (1956-60), are based clearly on Corbusian ideas of living. Latterly, in the La Reina project your solution approaches the problem from the opposite angle. Instead of the architect leading the way, the people dictate the process. Please could you explain how your ideas have evolved to incorporate these extremes?

Fernando Castillo: In the past, being a young architect I thought it would be of use to me to satisfy my own curiosity. I saw architecture like the game piece and myself as the player. With time I understood that architecture was an expression of the dreams and aspirations of the people. I knew, therefore, that my work should contain the hallmarks of the life of the people and my task was to try to be their interpreter.

KM: Which points of Le Corbusier's 'player' philosophy do you still feel are useful for architects today?

FC: Le Corbusier's great contribution was his concept of the city; when he clearly defined the functions that it should comply with, and how one should order urban space. Also, he contributed enormously to the development of new architectural forms whilst demanding that these would be true expressions of the intrinsic quality of materials and the functions which they have within architecture. His works of steel reinforced concrete are, to this day, a model for architects.

KM: Do you think that scale is important in housing developments? Corbusier's work is on a very large scale. Once projects lose their human scale they seem to lose the feeling of domestic security and can become threatening.

FC: It is not the human scale of works that is important. Before that there is the transcendence of the 'play' or the 'game'. And the relationship between the constructed and the not constructed which must form a whole, harmonious and indestructible. Architecture doesn't happen just like that. It forms an integral part of the landscape that surrounds it. However scale, that is to say, the relationship between the constructed work and the man who occupies it, makes it possible for architecture to be a blanket that covers and protects human activities. In the case of the dwelling this human scale allows that a house might be an intimate refuge and a secret of man and the family.

KM: The idea of the family unit seems to be at the centre of your philosophy. At the beginning of your career your father set you up in an office and commissioned work from you?

FC: As a young man, my father set me up both in the field of passionate inspiration on the one hand, and to confront reality just as it is on the other. During my first year of studying architecture at university he told me that in order to be an architect one had to build and so he contracted me to design a building. On the other

ABOVE: Fernando Castillo; OPPOSITE, FROM ABOVE: Community Andalucia, Santiago (1992); El Bosque, Santiago (1987); Fernando Castillo's house, La Reina, Santiago (1975)

hand as town mayor I have been able to perceive that the strength of the family unit or groups of families can multiply ten times man's capacity to do things. The will to share and solidarity are the great motors of the human capacity to achieve.

KM: Some community-based philosophies involve separating the family. What do you feel about the kibbutz idea in Israel, for example, where children live separately from their parents. Would this work in Chile?

FC: I understand that the kibbutz does not intend to separate people spiritually but rather it tries to form one larger family, made up of many families; where the children of all these families live together, although somewhat separate from their parents as happens in any large household. The kibbutz is a beautiful experience that could happen in Chile or in any other country. I don't understand the fundamental reasons for its demise.

KM: Do you think that the idea of community differs according to the country in which the idea is being applied?

FC: Yes, I think that community life is something that is instinctive to man but this coexistence can adopt many varied forms of expression, depending on race and culture.

KM: Why do you think that President Frei Montalva chose you to be Minister of Housing? And what did you hope to achieve?

FC: I suppose that President Frei Montalva thought that it was good to assign the office to an architect who had been a member of the community since birth and who also was a comrade of the political party.

KM: In 1968 you were elected rector of the Catholic University. Why do you think that the people voted for you? And how would you describe your time as rector?

FC: The Catholic University had gone through a tremendous crisis. The students had rebelled and triumphed. They had questioned the relevance of the Pope appointing the rector of an architectural school on the other side of the world and had been heard. I understood them. I was a relatively successful professor at that time, a town mayor and an architect, but it was my apparent ability to empathise that made the students choose me. The existing rector suggested potential candidates and a 'committee' of students interviewed us one by one. They asked us 'what we would do if we were made rector?'. The other candidates presented

good ideas but when the committee asked me, I just asked them what they would do in my position. So we developed a conversation-like approach. Not just my ideas. And I was elected then and many times subsequently. My time as rector was the most rewarding and passionate time of my life. Chile was changing dramatically. We were on the crest of a wave. People needed my support and in the majority of cases I was able to guide them so that the University went from strength to strength and realised its most ambitious goals.

Most universities want to create an intellectually stimulating climate consummate with their place in time. They want to consider the past with hindsight, interrogate the present and to investigate a pattern to allow the truths of the future to manifest themselves. I tried to create a place in which the students could do this.

KM: You say that Chileans are individualistic which, in the communes, you have found to be a bad thing. How did you find the British during the time you exiled yourself to Cambridge, England in the early 1980s and why did you choose England?

FC: The military coup, by President Pinochet in the early 80s made my situation dangerous. The British Ambassador to Chile invited me to come to Cambridge in the capacity of a visiting professor. The welcome my family and I received from the architectural community was amazing and it seemed to last for the four years we were there. The British have a reputation for 'splendid isolation' but I only encountered warmth; like the Chilean people, who have a reputation for being proud but are also generous.

KM: You say that during your time in Cambridge you tried to absorb many of the ideas of old Europe. Which ideas were these?

FC: With respect to the aesthetic – I realised that in England, simple form and clear lines in speech, thought and vision, have a long history. Also it is a land which believes in the 'word'. The Chile that I had left had forgotten the meaning of trust. In England people seemed to assume responsibility and try to simplify things to reach a solution. The Latin mentality is to create enough links in an administrative chain to ensure that you can always blame someone else. I tried to absorb some of these admirable traits of the British into my architecture and my life without losing the openness, forgiveness and energy of Latin America.

KM: How did you feel that these values were expressed in European architecture?

FC: European architecture reads like a social history book. It always adjusts to its time. When times were bad creativity was sometimes at its height. But always a huge gulf existed between the client and the craftsman. Clients can be creative and craftsmen are rich in many ways. The architecture of Europe is a testament to the skill of men.

KM: Referring to your first architectural partnership with Bresciani, Huidobro and Valdes, you say that 'We embraced the modern style as a moral principle – perhaps we were mistaken but even more mistaken were the architects of that generation who wanted to rehash the works of the past'. How did you use the knowledge of historical architecture that you had acquired in Europe once you returned to Chile?

FC: I think that my years with Bresciani, Valdes and Huidobro were the most productive of my life and we established the principal foundations of our individual working lives. Each of them was my tutor and I hope I was a tutor to them too. We achieved an extraordinary balance through like-mindedness and through concentrated focus on our aims. We were very clear about what we wanted to achieve and the Modern Movement seemed to offer us a vocabulary through which to realise our intentions. During my time in England I became aware of the quality of timelessness and modified my ideas. Europe is more cautious when it approaches change because of the fabric of history which is its reference. My country is young. It is more malleable and accepting of dramatic solutions when they are derived from pure ideas. But unlike you, we do not have the foundations from which to be sure where we have come from and where we are going. So we need to develop shapes and forms of our own.

KM: The houses you designed before you went to England seem to be predominantly unpainted concrete. How do you feel about this material now?

FC: I am a passionate believer in the potential of this material in architecture. For a country where right-angles do not exist philosophically or aesthetically, it is the very thing.

Advances in reinforced concrete have helped us to build safely here, in an area of occasional earthquakes but frequent tremors. It enables us to build high to avoid urban sprawl and retain the countryside. One of the advantages of being a young country is that we have the opportunity to learn from older country's mistakes in time to avoid making them ourselves.

KM: Post-Cambridge, your work is characterised by the use of brick. Please could you describe the relation between the use of brick and the architecture you returned to Chile to construct?

FC: There are three reasons for my fondness for brick: firstly my memories of domestic architecture in England; secondly, the principle of hundreds of bricks making one building, rather as with people, their coming together

FROM ABOVE: Construction on a self-build project; model of new construction at La Reina (1994); OPPOSITE, FROM ABOVE: Cau Cau, a worker's holiday camp near Valparaíso on the Pacific Coast (1988); 'Casas Entile Medianeros' community, Santiago (1977); BELOW, L TO R: La Reina, Santiago; Santiago as it was in 1910

Colourscape

Michael Lancaster

With this invaluable handbook, Michael Lancaster seeks to clarify the place and meaning of colour in our surroundings. The complex subject matter is explored thoroughly – from the biological nature of colour and colour perception to the contemporary concerns of colour planning and control – to provide a solid base for the author's prime concern: the use of colour in the context of the environment. Taking examples from a wide range of townscapes and landscapes, Michael Lancaster identifies the confusion that has arisen from the recent colour revolution, and the increasing possibilities for colour pollution. Such negative examples contrast sharply with the detailed analyses of town planning in which harmony of colour and context is sought.

The wealth and diversity of illustrations throughout vividly brings to life the issues raised by the author, providing readers with a highly accessible source of reference from which to re-evaluate their understanding and experience of colour.

Michael Lancaster is an architect, landscape architect and colour consultant and has lectured extensively on the use of colour. His published works include *Britain in View: Colour and the Landscape* (1984), *The New European Landscape* (1994) and contributions to the 'Colour in Architecture' issue of *Architectural Design* (1996). He also co-wrote and presented the film *The Colour Eye 5* for BBC 2.

Paperback 1 85490 451 5
246 x 225mm, 128 pages
64 pages of colour, and 64 pages of b&w illustrations
£21.95 DM57.00 $38.00

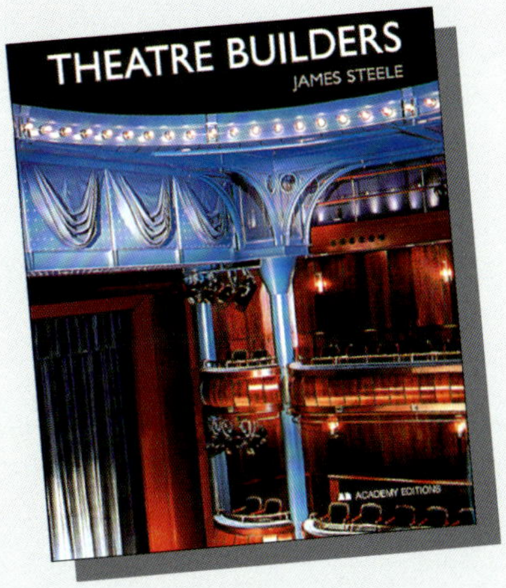

Theatre Builders

James Steele

Theatre design is one of the most complex and challenging tasks faced by contemporary architects; it represents an area where art and science collide, where the harsh realities of construction, such as the search for the perfect acoustic environment, must be resolved within an ephemeral space where the magic that is theatre may unfold. It is this conflict which James Steele defines in his introductory essay, where he shows that the most memorable and engaging theatres are those that forge the mechanical and artistic into a coherent whole to produce an ambience greater than the sum of its parts.

Similarly, the expansive profile on Ove Arup – one of the world's most successful engineering partnerships – explores the relationship between the technical and architectural from an engineer's perspective, and is illustrated by two technical studies, detailing the design of the Cerritos Performing Arts Center, California, and the International Convention Centre, Birmingham. This section also incorporates a detailed history of Arup's extensive involvement with theatre design.

Theatre Builders presents nearly 50 of the best and most innovative contemporary theatres, through illustrations and project descriptions which include incisive analyses of their contribution to this most intriguing of genres. Amongst the prominent architects and projects featured are Tadao Ando, Kara-za Theater, Tokyo; Mario Botta, Palazzo del Cinema al Lido, Venice; Frank Gehry, Walt Disney Concert Hall, Los Angeles; Michael Hopkins, Glyndebourne Opera House, Lewes; Arata Isozaki, Kyoto Concert Hall, Kyoto; Eric Owen Moss, Vesey Street Theater, New York; Jean Nouvel, Opera House, Lyon; Aldo Rossi, Carlo Felice Theatre, Genoa, and James Stirling + Michael Wilford, Singapore Arts Centre.

James Steele is an architect, prolific writer and Associate Professor of Architecture at the University of Southern California. He is the author of many titles for Academy Editions, including *Hassan Fathy*, *Museum Builders* and *Charles Rennie Mackintosh*. He is also co-author of the recently published *The Architecture of the Contemporary Mosque* and the author of *How House*, part of the Historical Building Monographs series.

Hardback 1 85490 450 7
305 x 252mm, 224 pages
Over 400 illustrations, mostly in colour
£45.00 DM147.00 $70.00

Reviewing 'The Desiring Eye: reviewing the Slow House'

Diller+Scofidio at the Ikon Gallery, Birmingham (31 January - 9 March 1996)

'Do you like it?' *(a – s l u g s move s l o w l y)* No need to speed, and chase with two sexes in one; no battles in the bedroom, no domesticity at war – bliss, oh, to escape from all that theory and frustration. There are many orifices into the work of New York architects **Diller+Scofidio**; they digest the latest techniques and content of geography, film, literature and art, (channel) hopping, (lane) weaving, and surfing the slugs' trailways, hungry for words, images and questions. The installation, '**The Desiring Eye: reViewing the Slow House**' inserted into the basement of Birmingham's Ikon Gallery, revealed the deep cultural baggage D+S carry when they pack their pieces into the Samsonite and travel to the still unfinished house for the Long Island sea-view. *(b – l'escargot are more appetising)* Isn't it a slug, so why the shell? Surely they aren't referencing Gaston's phenomenal delicacy as it could cause the belly of the dillio serious post-structural failure. The House appears like a slug ingesting, digesting and exuding the view of late twentieth-century life. The car, TV, video camera, the dominant bodily extensions of our lifestyles, are consumed by the architects to create a vision of reality seen through and on our wind- and TV screens every night. **'What's "like" got to do with it?'** *(c – are you allowed to have sex on the table . . . the bedroom's normal)* All this lot seem to think about is sex, violence and the TV, well, society gets what society deserves, this pair of flesh bums prefer beds to buildings. They share a sixteen-year age gap like Peter and Cynthia. Internally the house is dominated by eating disorders, talk show hosts and serial killers stalking the house. Indeed half-way through the house at the section/point at which the table sits over the bed, the architects become psychiatrists, advising their clients not to eat in bed in order to release the dining table, on the floor above, from their problematic sexual passions. The Ikon exhibition, displays the background and foreground to the design of the house set within 24 panels of liquid crystal. *(x – it's too well referenced)* I can't even criticise that it all uses the same sterile comments, as that is just a 'good post-structuralist series'. Couldn't it come down to whether you like it or not – no it just depends whether you know all the references or you've read the right review. **'A gut reaction?'** Overlaid text and images weave an intricate performance; the panels switching from solid text to text and actual model. The panels emerge from a plywood floor on telescopic rods. The 24 mini-installations start with a TV image of a s l o w l y moving snail. Every element of the house is explicitly revealed with exquisite models and drawings: a section through a plaster and metal model of the garage and car; or the revolving front door. Each panel leads you more deeply into the house, arriving at the picture window and TV. D+S work across many media revealing the social political and economic space within which their constructions exist. The clarity and humour in their explanation is accessible at many different levels. Their work shows a different view of creating an architecture, not expressing the vision of a better world but exposing the conditions of reality. **'Where's the bathroom?'**

(00–D+S The space between two sexes – a hermaphrodite)

(01–D+S Visions through the windscreen)

(02–D+S Birmingham Ikon)

Text – Ed Frith, Moving Architecture (with choreographer Caroline Salem) is a lecturer at UCE Birmingham School of Architecture. He has worked with Diller+Scofidio in New York. Project images – Kevin Singh, a visiting lecturer at UCE.

INTEGRATING ARCHITECTURE

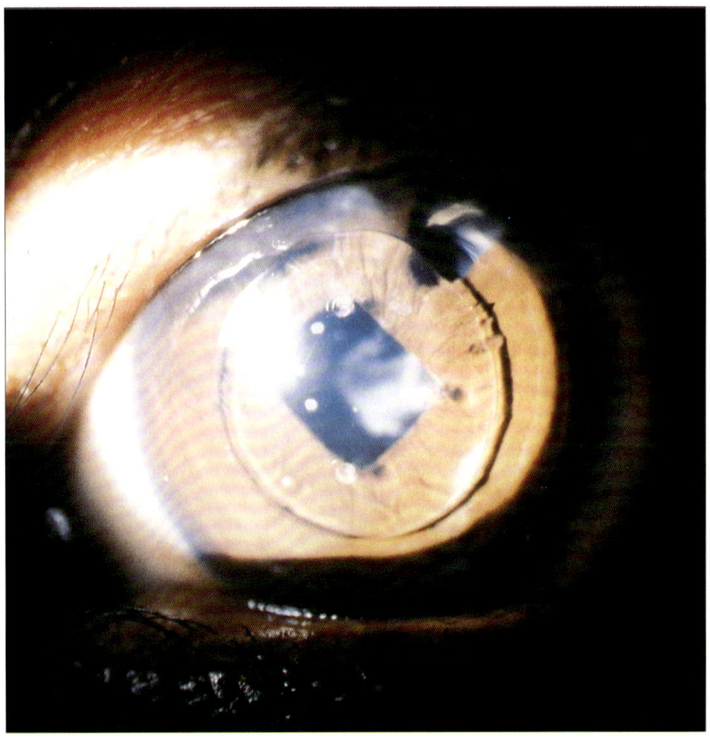

PAUL URSELL, 'IRIS CLIP IOL' IN HUMAN EYE

Architectural Design

INTEGRATING ARCHITECTURE

NAT CHARD, DURATION PHOTOGRAPH OF TWO PEOPLE WALKING, 1994-95
OPPOSITE: RICHARD GOODWIN, THE CORVETTE MEMORIAL, GARDEN ISLAND, SYDNEY, STAINLESS STEEL, FIBREGLASS, GLASS, CLOTHING, 1995

ACADEMY EDITIONS • LONDON

Acknowledgements

All material is courtesy of the authors and architects unless otherwise stated. We are grateful to the architects for their enthusiasm and interest in the project. **Neil Denari** credits the following for their work shown in his article: project assistant (Territorial Recodings on the Worldsheet),Georg Kolmayr; drawing assistants (Design Studio), David Hsu, Benny Chan; project assistant (Massey Residence), Andrew Waisler. **Ted Krueger** would like to thank Neil Garrioch and Jean Krueger for their thoughtful review of drafts of his paper and regrets that he has not yet been able to answer the numerous issues that they have raised. **Ben Nicholson**, as director of the Loaf House project, extends thanks to the following team at the Illinois Institute of Architecture: co-director, Catherine Wetzel; chief designer, Peter Ippolito; structural engineers, Majoub Elnimeri, Joe Burns with Johnathan Block; drawings and collages, Simon Chan, Boris Cubas, Greg Delaleurs, Serhan Gurkin, Jason Kerwin, Nate Lindsay, Issa Sherzad, Kristina Yu, Lane Zabala; model construction, John Kriegshauser, Tim Burke, Amy Berka, Carly Carlson, Simon Chan, Winai Chairakpong; Mike Cippriani, Oh Moon Cho, Fritz Head, Saori Hisano, Peter Ippolito, Jason Kerwin, Chit-tin Montatupalin, Veronica Pazaran, Beate Schiltmeyer, Ralph Schopen, Scott Skipworth, Mat Snethen, Asli Velidedeoglis; computer design and production, Peter Ippolito; computer lighting, Ralph Schopen; computer colourwork, Laura Foster Nicholson; photography, Ralph Schopen; sponsorship, Dr Graphx, Chicago, M Bohlke Veneer Corp, IIT. **Sixteen* (makers)** extend thanks to Stephen Groâk, Acting Head of Research and Development of Ove Arup and Partners, London. The views expressed are the personal views of the author. **Michael Sorkin** (principal) credits Andrei Vovk (partner) and Michael Sorkin Studio, Jim Wilson, Caroline Lichtenberg for the Brooklyn Waterfront project; Michael Sorkin Studio, Andrei Vovk, Yukiko Yokoo, Rebecca Parker and Celine Condorelli for the Governor's Island project; Michael Sorkin Studio, Andrei Vovk, Peter Kormer, Doug Bergert, Matthew Mueller, Silva Ajemian, Patrick Clifford, Zingg, Dominik Schwarzer and Jeffrey Johnson for the Weed, AZ project. **Paul G Ursell FRCOphth**, Cataract Surgery Research Fellow at St Thomas' Hospital, London and practising ophthalmologist, is grateful to the following for providing the illustrations: Mr DJ Spalton, Consultant Ophthalmologist, St Thomas' Hospital; Prof DJ Apple, Director Centre for Research on Ocular Therapeutics and Biodevices, Medical University of South Carolina; John Crellin, Alcon Laboratories (UK), Ltd; Dr Swaranjit Singh Bhatti, Hon Prof and Head, KJ Somiaiya Hospital and Medical College, Bombay. **Michael Webb** acknowledges the following at the Massachusetts Institute of Technology for the images accompanying his article: Marios A Christodoulides, Chia-Chang Hsu, Kent Larson, Takehiko Nagakura, Priti Paul – all images © Massachusetts Institute of Technology.

Photographic Credits: All material is courtesy of the authors and architects unless otherwise stated. Attempts have been made to locate the sources of all photographs to obtain full reproduction rights, but in the very few cases where this process has failed to find the copyright holder, our apologies are offered. S Adjemian *p34 (above left)* Marq Bailey *p3*; A Browell, *pp12, 15*; D Burger *p34 (above left)*; Emma Darwin *p28*; P Ippolito *pp38, 40 (below), 42 (above right)*; J Johnson *p34 (above left)*; Caroline Lichenberg *pp32-35 (below)*; M Mueller *p34 (above left)*; Michael Sorkin *pp32-35*; Andrei Vovk *pp32-35*; Jim Wilson *pp32-35 (below)*; Yukliko Yokoo *pp32-33, 35 (above right)*; K Yu *p43 (below left)*; Zingg *p34 (above left)*

Front Cover: Ben Nicholson, *Cat Walk*, 1996
Inside Covers: John Andrews – *An Erratic Machine for Recording the Movements of Ghosts*, detail, pencil and ink, 1996; *An Instrument to Turn Love into Lust*, pencil and ink, 1996

EDITOR: Maggie Toy
EDITORIAL TEAM: Lucy Ryan, Jane Richards, Iona Baird, Stephen Watt
ART EDITOR: Andrea Bettella CHIEF DESIGNER: Mario Bettella DESIGNERS: Marie Carter, James Powley

First published in Great Britain in 1996 by *Architectural Design* an imprint of
ACADEMY GROUP LTD, 42 LEINSTER GARDENS, LONDON W2 3AN
Member of the VCH Publishing Group

ISBN: 1 85490 258 X (UK)

Architectural Design Profile 123 is published as part of *Architectural Design* Vol 66 9-10/1996
Architectural Design Magazine is published six times a year and is available by subscription

Distributed to the trade in the United States of America by
NATIONAL BOOK NETWORK INC, 4720 BOSTON WAY, LANHAM, MARYLAND, 20706

Printed and bound in Singapore

Contents

WILLIAM ALSOP, GRONINGEN PAINTINGS, *WIGWAM*, 1996, OIL ON CANVAS, 83 X 39CM

ARCHITECTURAL DESIGN PROFILE No 123

INTEGRATING ARCHITECTURE

GUEST-EDITED BY NEIL SPILLER

Neil Spiller Editorial *6*
Michael Sorkin Trip *8*
Richard Goodwin Artist as Collaborator *12*
Michael Webb Depicting the Drive-in House *16*
William Alsop The Context for Practice *20*
Pete Silver and Peter Fluck Non-linear Dynamical Systems *26*
Ted Krueger Like a Second Skin, Living Machines *29*
Neil Denari Interrupted Projections, Another Global Surface *33*
Ben Nicholson War and Peacefare at the Loaf House *38*
Mark Titman Stretch City *44*
Sixteen (makers)* Board Games *48*
John Andrews Nova Mappamundi, Drawings and Designs *52*
Shin Egashira Forming Enclosures *60*
Lab – Bates + Davidson Architecture After Geometry *66*
Paul Ursell The Evolution of Prosthetic Intraocular Lens Design *72*
Nat Chard Architecture of Our Interior *76*
Alison Sampson Inside Out: Clinical Procedure Relating to Caesarean Section as Practised on Bodies, Objects and Buildings *82*
Rachel Armstrong The Body as an Architectural Space – From Lips to Anus *86*
Neil Spiller Leaving Nadir *92*

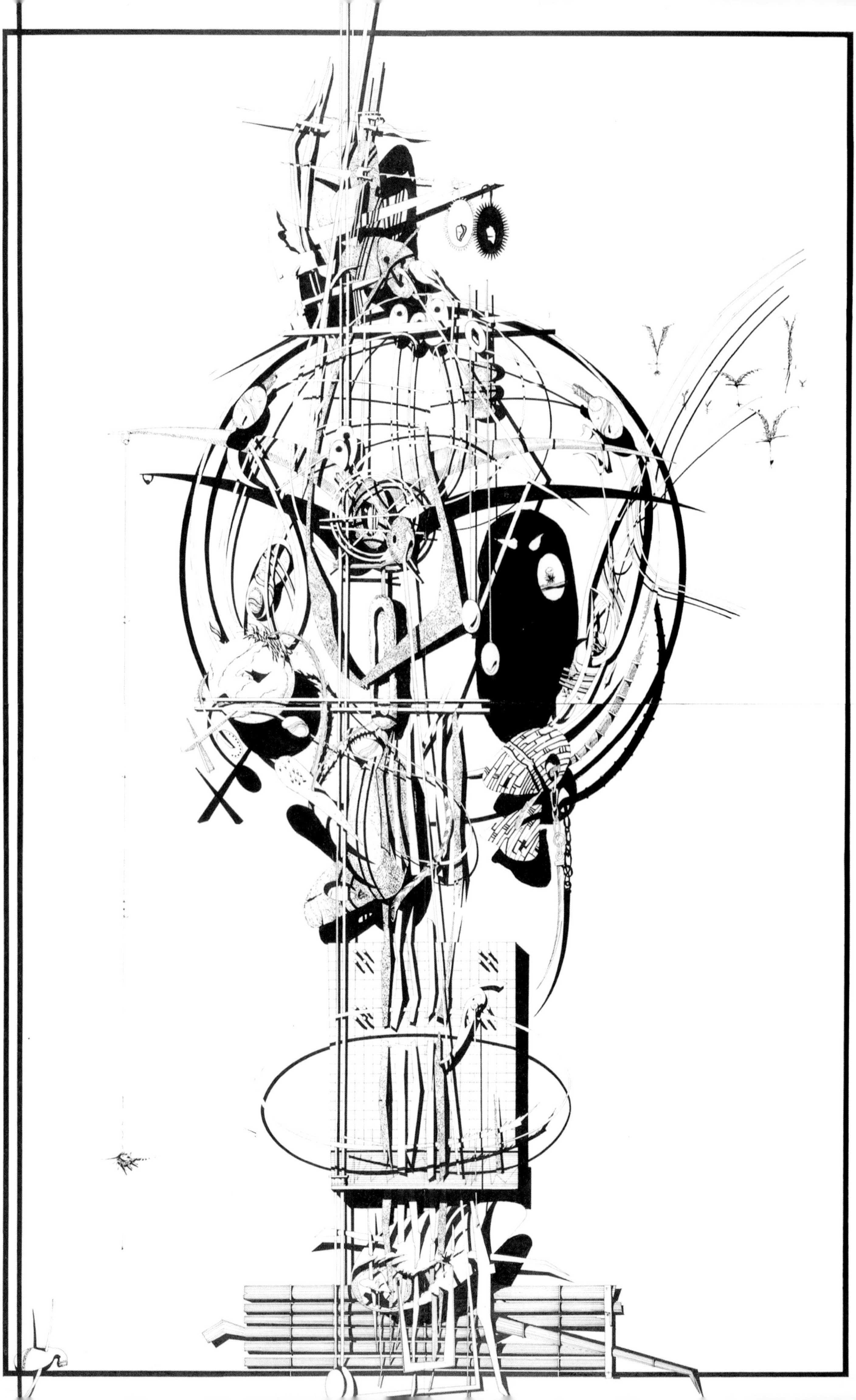

NEIL SPILLER

EDITORIAL: GAMES WITHOUT FRONTIERS

The old adage,'Before studying history, study the historian' might be equally well-employed in the context of this issue of *Architectural Design* as, 'Before studying the issue, understand the Editor'. As an architect and educator, I have always found interest and solace at the periphery of the practice of architecture. The central ground of the profession has always seemed both conservative and pessimistic about the future. Whilst I would describe myself as a modern architect, I do not subscribe to the Modern Movement's superseded dictums. There seem to be two sides to the contemporary Modernist coin. One of these sides I believe to be a way to proceed: the other, I consider a fruitless stylistic cul-de-sac. The architects in this issue were invited to contribute because of their explorations of the first side of the Modernist coin. Their work is based on an optimism about the continuing central role of architecture as a catalyst for the further evolution of civilised society. This optimism is conditioned by a belief in technology. This is my side of the coin. The other side is the restrictive practices and dogma of the Modernist canon; folklore such as 'Form Follows Function' and 'Truth to Materials', which is inappropriate in our alchemic technical age.

This issue seeks to illustrate some of the more original thoughts on architecture at the periphery of the profession. Some may view this work as *fin-de-siècle* decadence or simply misguided, but I see them as beacons in a sea of potential for architecture's future. The type of future and the way in which it is couched is the first choice of any creative architect. Many of the projects are very different in relation to one another; quite rightly so, for any designer worth the name has an idiosyncratic aesthetic that is a byproduct of his individual preoccupations and *modus operandi.* His/her 'style' is a result of a way of thinking, a way of doing and a way of expressing. This brief, and by no means definitive, survey of some of the more thought-provoking and talented architects of our time seems to focus around some fundamental notions.

The symbiotic relationship between technological bodily invasion and architecture is crucial to many of the architects in this issue, regardless of how it is expressed. Different approaches to this shifting terrain are put forward by Nat Chard, Alison Sampson and myself, among others. It is here, at the point of this collision, that the distinction between architecture and medicine melts, and, indeed, two of our contributors are medical physicians – Dr Rachel Armstrong and the ophthalmologist, Paul Ursell, whose article explores the evolution of a particular form of prosthetic eye surgery. Such surgery not only rescues the patient from accumulating blindness, but is also dependent on highly inert prosthetics, specific placement and accurate and minimal incision. These are all architectural tactics of the future, as the site of the body becomes the site of architecture.

Much of the work shown in this collection is also highly poetic. The projects of John Andrews, Sixteen* (makers) and Ben Nicholson achieve striking effects to create worlds of strangeness and charm. Andrew's hauntingly beautiful drawings, the Dartmoor interventions of Sixteen*(makers), and the enigma of Nicholson's *Loaf House* are evocations of architecture's otherness. Such enterprises have distinguished precedents, including Libeskind's *Chamber Works,* Michael Webb's *Temple Island* and Hejduk's *Masques*. Enigma could be big in the 21st century.

Other practitioners have more interest in the near future, such as Shin Egashira and Neil Denari. We can see the manifestation of their machinic desires and their fascination with the metallic armature, its products and its loci. Some of the participants would suggest that their output is not concerned with the future of architecture, but the here and now. Such a comment immediately leads one to ask why so few of these architects are building. Is it because building is now controlled by a tyranny of sophist non-creativity and capitalist corner cutting with its doleful paucity of understanding for the human condition and its search for the sublime? Or is there some other less innocuous reason that has left our building stock so inert, ugly and non-responsive?

Many of us demonise technology by quoting bombs, oil slicks and holes in the sky (while basking in its 'white heat' in air conditioned cars and offices). As technology evolves, it becomes cleaner, smaller and increasingly ubiquitous. All this demands a radical rethinking of our relationship with ecological concepts and our interaction with the city. Work by Mark Titman and Michael Sorkin illustrates some of the research undertaken in this particular arena. The inhabitants of the city and its suburban hinterland have rights to safety, definable domains, varying spatial and cultural topologies and flexibility for personal registration of physical, metaphysical and educational aspirations, and in this respect, we introduce some of Richard Goodwin's imaginative work.

As part of our post-modern condition, much of what is included within this issue is difficult to pin down to a specific professional genealogy. Many of the architects here look outside the turgid ranks of traditional architectural theory in a continuing search for factors, inventions and philosophies that will influence the future of architectural production. They hope to re-establish architecture at the forefront of human endeavour. Architecture is becoming more and more a game without frontiers.

Spiller Farmer Architects, From Genesis to Genocide, *1996. This drawing is the first in a series of three. This series seeks to explore the notions of the 'New Flesh' whilst using the traditional language of the religious triptych. 'New Flesh' is the expression used to describe the changes that technology inflicts on the body. Technologies expand our limited natural bodily dexterity, allowing us to perceive and manipulate scales of matter far larger and smaller than could be done naturally. This first piece depicts the 'Hell' of our contemporary existence on an inert, polluted planet in fear of bodily decay and finally death*

MICHAEL SORKIN STUDIO

TRIP

These projects are amphibians – riffs on the land-water gradient. The Brooklyn Waterfront and Governor's Island projects both return soon-to-be-derelict sites to public use; parks of a sort, but predicted on intense and variegated use: recreational and cultural universities.

Weed, AZ – situated along an artificial lake produced by a dam on the Colorado River – is a proposal for a new town, based on post-technological means of production, great personal diversity and a high degree of sustainability. Both Governor's Island and Weed, AZ are on territories reclaimed from military use – a theme of ongoing interest to the Studio.

FROM ABOVE, L to R: Governor's Island – sketch detail; tiny sketch model: Brooklyn Waterfront, detail; OVERLEAF, FROM ABOVE L to R: Weed, AZ; Governor's Island, plan; Brooklyn Waterfront, detail

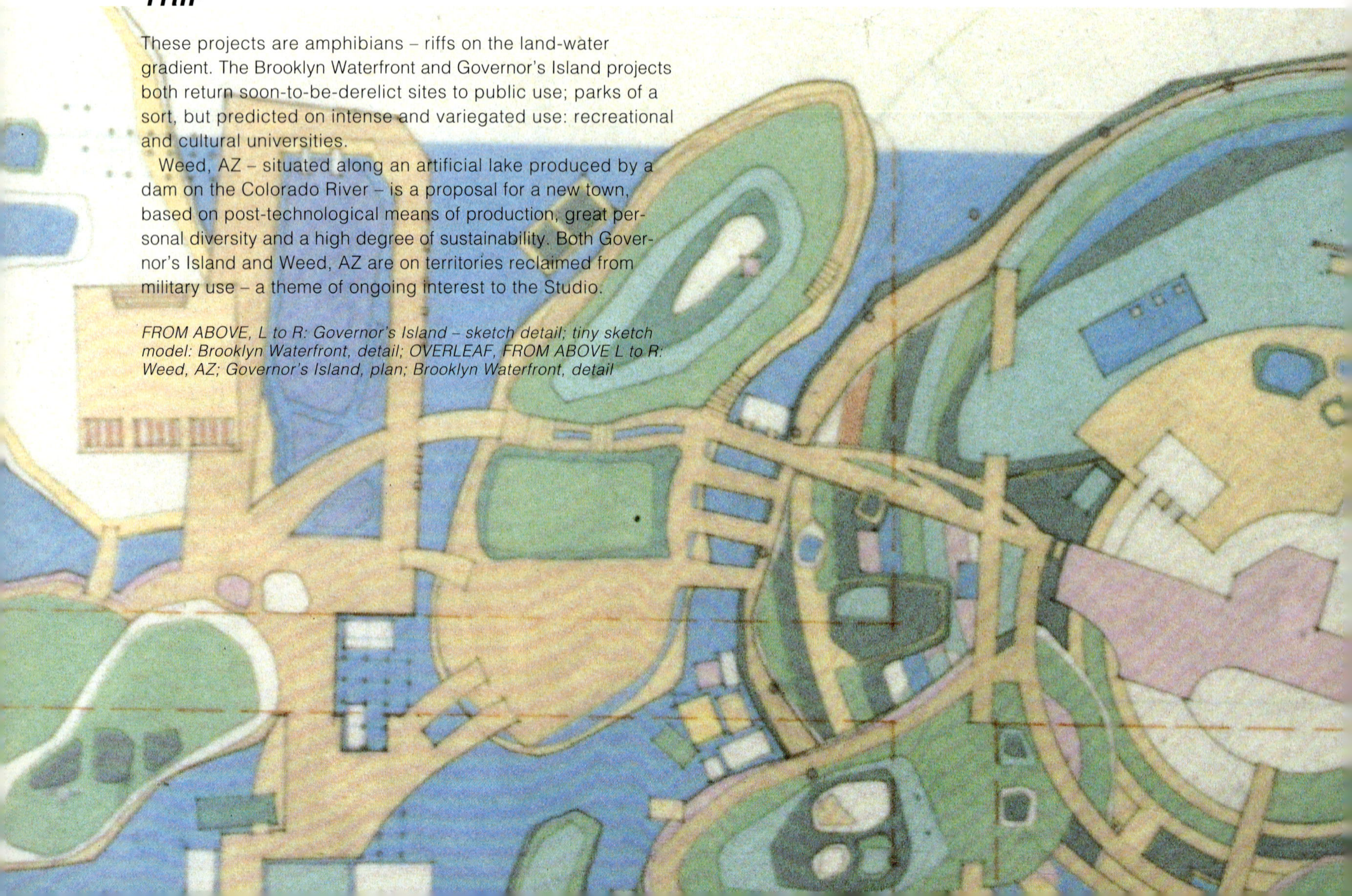

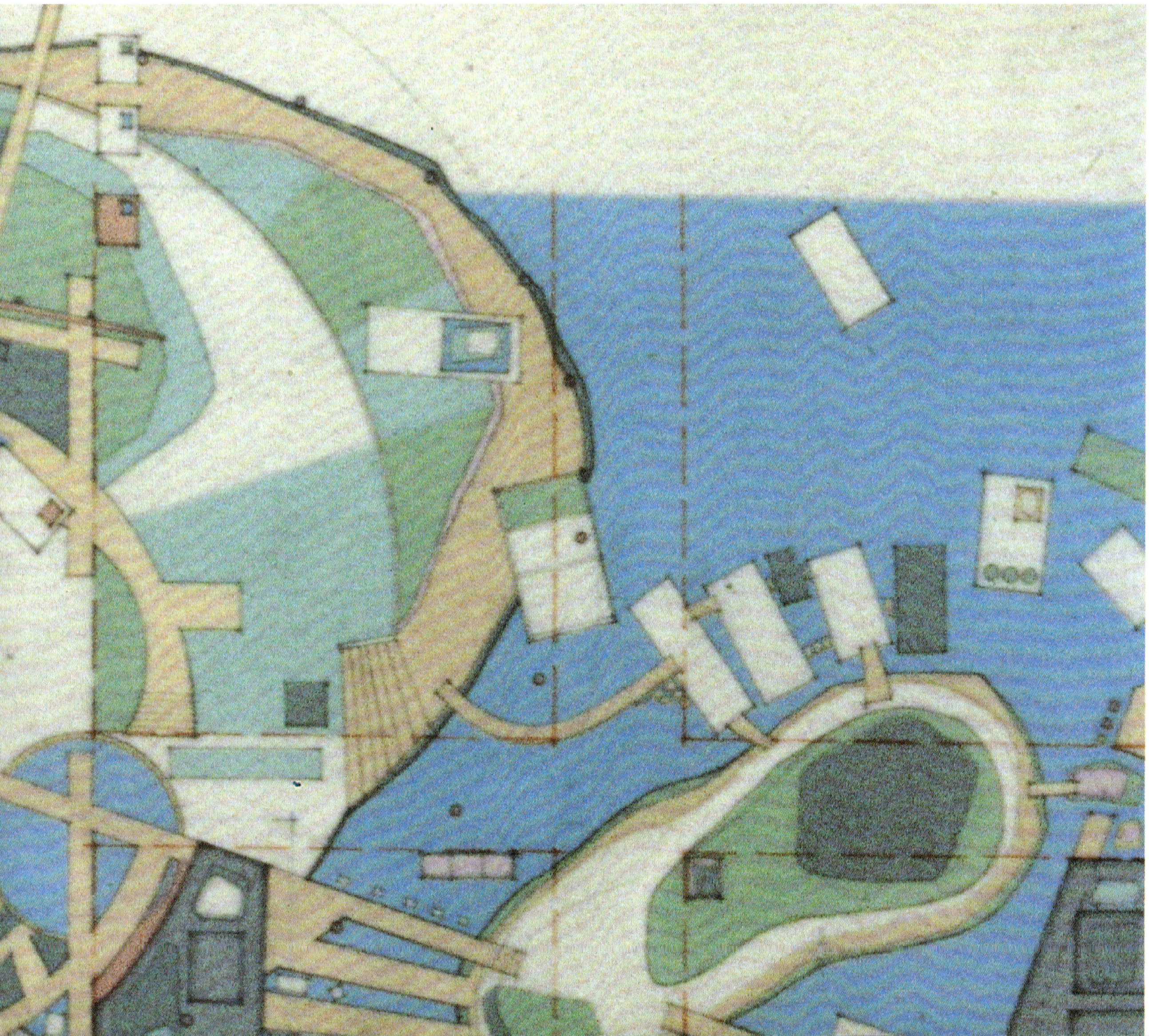

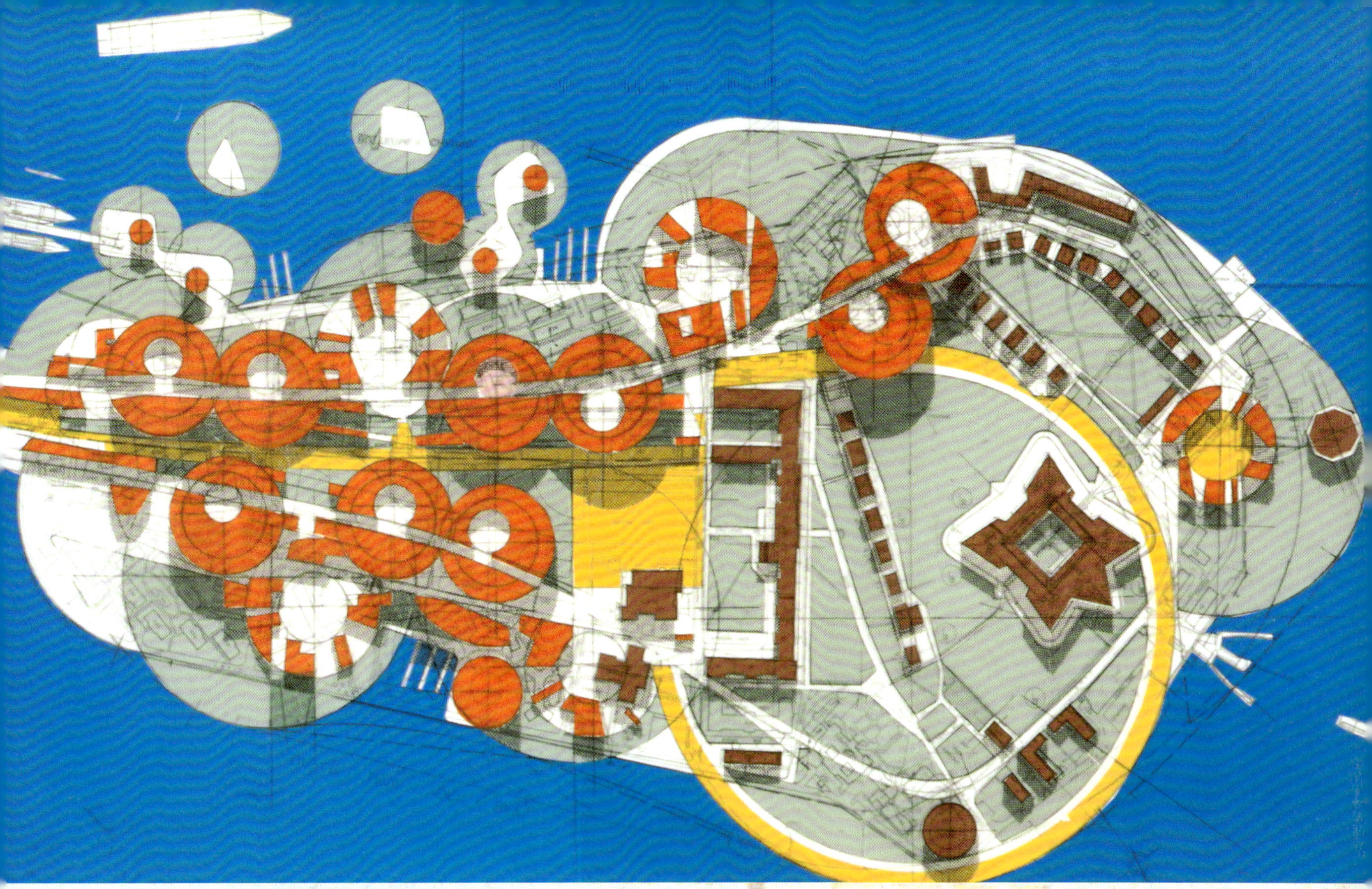

RICHARD GOODWIN

ARTIST AS COLLABORATOR

In 1977, I graduated with a BArch to pursue a career in art and, specifically, sculpture. In the last ten years my practice has involved work in public space, both outside and within the gallery system. Gradually, I am experiencing an evolution back to architecture and urban or city planning with a different perspective – that of an artist. Underpinning the public projects, my gallery work is currently exploring the body in relation to architecture or exoskeleton – prosthetic architecture or prosthetic sculpture; 'the point above zero at which architecture begins,' as Michael Sorkin puts it. This work has its roots not only in my architectural training, but also in my practice in the 70s – ie, performance and *arte povera*. From this point, the evolution was via figuration and installation to a position from which I can now springboard into the debate and practice of collaboration with architects and planners, on work which is of truly hybrid form.

The first step in understanding the process of collaboration is to perceive the built environment in terms of its unbuilt space or potential energy bank – 'public space'. If one took the city as a whole and, upending it, pushed it into the sand, the resulting imprint would represent the totality of 'public space'. I call this the reverse envelope; a vast labyrinthine structure of spaces – the city's true 'other'. What are the politics of this space? Is it equal to the capitalist political structure with which it has an awkward symbiosis, or are its politics naturally feral?

Strangely, in this zone of the homeless, one key difference is obvious – a lack of toilets. The political ramifications of this phenomenon are complex. I define architecture as an elaborate way of connecting the body to the sewer. The structures of public space need no such connection. Belonging and ownership are continually and ritually blessed via this system in a communion linking people with the soil and ocean via the vast umbilical system of the sewer. To be an outcast from the system is to experience the humiliation of being detached from this communion and the right to restore one's dignity and demeanour via the toilet.

I advocate the dissolution of architecture and all our current thinking about architecture in order to really comprehend the dilemma and opportunities of our 'public space'. In other words, collaboration is about equal partners from the beginning. Artists need to psych themselves up as they leave the gallery, and architects and bureaucracy need to lift the veil to relinquish their hold on power before it is taken away by force.

I wish to contend, as others have, that architecture is art and that otherwise, it is merely building. Furthermore, I wish to argue that architecture may provide a site in which artists can engage; that art is a possible site for other art. This is not achieved through adornment, as most architects are prone to think, but in a more invasive way, allowing a symbiosis between the creators of our urban fabric. When Gordon Matta-Clark carved into and cut open architecture, the relationship between these two prongs of the art world forever changed. Today, we are seeing the manifestations of the first hybrid forms of gallery art/architecture art. When the artist Olaf Metzel carved a swastika in the wall of a building in Berlin in the 80s, the true psyche of the built environment was again susceptible to the invasive scalpel of the art world. The dissolution of what we perceive as architecture today, by this action of invasion, has become necessary in the city if we are to address the massive problems not solved by our planners and politicians.

The grandstanding of individual buildings, within the organism or cancer which is the city, is simply absurd unless the sites have island qualities such as the Sydney Opera House. Only architects perceive such buildings in their minds as autonomous entities. Architecture within the city is becoming, as Paul Virilio has stated, 'continuous habitable circulation space'. Deyan Sudjic has said in his book *Hundred Mile City,* 'In the final analysis, it is in its role as an engine for change that the city is most alive'.

Joseph Beuys was the artist-prophet who pointed to the 'wounds' in our urban fabric which led the way for action within the interstices of our reverse envelope. In 1977, he made the work *Tallow.* The city of Munster staged an open-air sculpture exhibition in which artists were asked to select a site. Beuys chose a dead corner, a deep wedge-shaped area under a concrete overpass in which nothing could collect but dirt. The implication was that the trauma within our urban fabric must be demonstrated before healing can begin. He made a mould of the space and cast it in animal fat – a negative space was hence transformed into a positive form. More important, however, is the legacy left regarding the way in which we think about the urban fabric in terms of the organism and wounds. Beuys work is critical as an example of the proactive approach to site specificity; the artist chooses the site and heals the wound.

My first public commissions were site-specific and architecturally scaled, but were nevertheless essentially objects in space. In 1990 I became involved in a series of think tanks with our state road transport body, the RTA (Roads and Traffic Authority). The object of these discussions was to formulate ways in which artists and others could contribute to healing the wounds inflicted by our freeway systems, and ultimately become involved in the design and placement and potential of these arteries. To collaborate on such projects confronted me with the dilemma of being both collaborator and decorator, whose designs ran against gallery practice. However, I believe it is possible for artists to lend their thinking to such difficult and challenging positions in order to help heal the wound without damaging their integrity or the critical range of their work.

My first major project with the RTA was the Gore Hill Freeway in Sydney. This project involved collaboration with landscape architects on the mapping of the walls and environmental planning for the area. I then designed the sound attenuation walls and a language of design which related to the *genius loci.*

Specifically, Aboriginal rock engravings from the area were traced on plastic and then chipped into the ribbed concrete retaining walls at the freeways' gateways. Aboriginal land councils and archaeologists were involved in this sensitive translation. The wall designs consisted of Walter Burley Griffin tile designs from Pyrmont in Sydney – a relevant choice on account of Griffin's historic incinerator being situated alongside the road. An abstract design derived from a mapping of the freeway itself then completed the family. The sense of a particular place was thus reinforced subliminally by a range of designs and their placement within the journey. My collaboration was consolidated by the fact that I designed the architecture of the walls and their support systems.

Subsequent freeway design projects for which my collaboration was sought, include Glebe Island Arterial and Chinderah Bypass on the New South Wales border with Queensland. In each case, the designs are derived from the location and context of the freeway.

Closely associated with the Glebe Island arterial sound walls was a joint project with the architects Conybeare Morrison and the landscape architects Context, which required the redesign of an enormous undercroft space – a forest of columns in a typical leftover space under the freeway. This urban planning and sculptural exercise was made more significant by the fact that the RTA was prepared to transform such an area at its own expense, without a functional imperative. The result comprises a reorchestration of the forest of columns into a language of shapes which mould a new experience in terms of material and sculpture. Here too, we were able to change roads layouts and in one case eliminate a giant roundabout for more pedestrian-friendly zones and crossings. Clearly more than decoration, the works draw on the history and culture of the area. Previously an area of industry and stone quarries, the materiality of the place was easy to access. A rich pattern of stone, fig trees, inner city communities and fiery metal foundries became a language of fire, earth and water, reflected in the materials zinc, stone and climbing plants on steel frames. These materials have been employed to encase 9-metre columns, in a composition on the same scale as the freeway, which transforms the experience of both motorists and pedestrians, and creates the sense of a unique place in what would otherwise have been a leftover urban wound.

In Chinderah, at the border of New South Wales and Queensland, a new freeway bypass crosses the Tweed River. Although not the true border, the river figures in the psyche as the true line of demarcation. Trudging around on site, I found myself confronted with the obvious theme of mangrove swamps. Marking the crossing, I designed four beacon-like towers with steel root structures, like mangrove trees. The sound wall designs also use the mangrove motif, and on the reverse side, canoe shapes are expressed in steel. Local aborigines used the river extensively for food and, of course, the means of crossing was the canoe.

Such designs are obviously far-removed from my studio practice in that they are more design than art. The point of being involved in such design and urban planning projects, however, is simply to provide the perspective of an artist: to heal a wound.

In the process of working on such projects I have graduated from the role of consultant to partner. Successful collaboration can only really occur when the artist is on an equal footing from the commencement of work. This requires a quantum leap in the thinking of both artists and architects. Artists need to prepare themselves. In my case, it involved becoming a company and getting properly insured, for example. Taking responsibility for major projects is the only path to a true synthesis of practices. Of course, architects resent the invasion of artists who are tacked onto the process of constructing architecture. Any architect worth his salt would protest that his work is already art and that even the placement of paintings and conventional sculpture is demeaning. Architecture is art. The point I wish to make is that architecture can be changed through collaboration. This also applies to urban planning.

When I do collaborate, I want my contribution to be genuine, not ersatz. Too much lip service is being paid to superficial collaboration, the results of which are resentful architects and a programme of kitsch additions, such as patterns in the floor plane, furniture, gates, murals and fountains, all of which are merely dressing. Dressing can be effective and appropriate, however, I would rather the accretions of time and occupancy satisfy these needs, and not that they be prescribed prior to occupancy.

In most cases architects should be left alone to practice their art. They will, however, on specific work, be made to compete with collaborative teams of artists and architects who not only change architecture but build into its very fabric the thinking of an art community usually confined to the gallery. The result will be an immediate translation of thinking and ideas which have traditionally taken many years to trickle down. Architecture is an effective vehicle to bring art of the highest order to the people.

Recently, a design forum was held in Sydney for the impending Olympic Games. The key task of this forum was to explore and generate ideas for the Homebush Bay site which currently exists as a wasteland in the demographic heart of Sydney. Artists, architects, planners and landscape architects worked together with visiting architects such as Jean Nouvel to come up with design solutions. Other offshoots in the lead up to the Olympics included *Sydney Spaces,* a project which required teams of artists and architects to solve key problem areas in the heart of Sydney. I was involved in both of these initiatives as an artist. The Olympic site is, of course, an enormous ongoing design issue, but at least this initiative took place and artists were included in the discussion process.

Sydney Spaces points to problems that I am now keen to

solve. I worked with Grose Bradley architects on a major leftover intersection at the foot of the Sydney Harbour Bridge. The issues of such spaces are now familiar to me; for example, the residual spaces left by freeways, the allied pedestrian zones and the need to identify and consolidate a unique place out of a zone of alienation and disinterest. We came up with a series of designs to solve these problems, but what hope does such a project have of realisation when city councils have such limited budgets? The idea of such an initiative in the first place was to attract funding. But this is one of many projects. Private money for public space is the issue. How do we lure developers to help improve our cities' public spaces and see the benefit? This is the great challenge. Currently, we are pursuing this major project with our own team and are determined to gain private funding for it. The result will be close to what I think should be happening more; that is, artist/architect/planner teams choosing sites within the fabric of public space and initiating a process which will then involve councils and all relevant planning bodies. We simply cannot wait for competitions, for example, before projects can be pursued. The existing system of planning has failed. It is a key role for artists to select the wounds and heal them, or at least lick them.

In 1992, John Barrett-Lennard curated the seminal exhibition 'Working in Public' for Artspace, Sydney. My role in this exhibition was to address a specific and typical wound in Sydney's urban fabric. The Art Gallery of New South Wales is the cultural heart of the city, but it exists in a nineteenth-century cloud, separated from 'the place' of the city, which is best represented by its working waterfront and hilly sandstone terrain. With the sculptural installation *Exoskeleton Cord,* I linked the Art Gallery of New South Wales with the Finger Wharf, an extraordinary timber building on the harbour at Woolloomooloo embodying the sense of Sydney's true place. The cord crossed a 300-metre city space laced with freeways and overhead wires. This was 'taboo architecture' in taboo space, as indicated by the reluctance of the relevant authorities to sanction the action. The linkage was critical to this wound, denying the obvious need to link culture with place. Ideally, this line would be replaced with a simple suspension bridge for pedestrians. I produced preliminary designs for such a bridge and had their feasibility tested. This is the site-specific, culturally potent sculpture of tomorrow.

PAGE 12: *Gore Hill Walls*, sound attenuation walls for the Gore Hill Freeway north of the Harbour Bridge, Sydney, concrete, 1992; *FROM ABOVE*: *The Corvette Memorial*, Garden Island, Sydney, stainless steel fibreglass, glass, clothing, 1995; *Follicle*, site-specific sculptural installation for the new Children's Hospital, Sydney, stainless steel, clothing encased in fibreglass, 1995; *Parasite/Follicle*, exploring the public and private space of the Art Gallery of NSW, steel, timber, clothing, 1994

MICHAEL WEBB

DEPICTING THE DRIVE-IN HOUSE

Note from the author: when a word appearing in the text is followed by a bracketed numeral, eg, 'deiform (2)', the reader is encouraged to refer to the New Shorter Oxford English Dictionary *for the precise shade of meaning intended.*

The decorum of the 'crit' at Columbia University's new 'paperless studio'[1] is somewhat an inversion of its more traditional counterpart, ie, in the days when the visual medium – the *lingua franca* for discussion – was the steam[2] drawing. Consider the students' passion (1): two nights without sleep, and on the third day, to stand, flayed before the critters . . . that student now sits behind a monitor, hidden except for occasional glimpses of garishly illuminated temple, bringing forth wonders projected on a giant overhead screen. Power now rests with the student. The form of interaction is similar to that of being at JFK; you're pleading with a surly, indifferent booking agent, likewise hidden behind the deiform (2) monitor . . . you'll do anything, anything, if only the agent can get you on a flight to Heathrow!

Here are reasons given for failure to present work:

Paperless studio crit: 'my project is lost in the hard drive'.

Steam drawing crit: 'my pen broke'.

For one whose work[3] has so much concerned motion and depiction, and who has figured, reluctantly, that the still (4) or series of stills may convey the mathematics of motion, but never its grace or its beauties, the opportunity of having computer animations made of the work was bemusing. Such was the case when MOCA, the Museum of Contemporary Art in Los Angeles, in preparation for its 'End of the Century' show asked the New York based architect Kent Larson to supervise the preparation of computer animations of certain twentieth-century projects, among them the 'Drive-in House'. Under his guidance, and my needling, and with the help of MIT Professor Takehiko Nagakura and three MIT students (Chia Chang Hsu, Priti Paul and Marios Christodoulides), work was started on three separate manifestations of the project.

The Drive-in House (written 1976)

'My maiden aunts, now long gone to their reward, referred to the automobile as a 'horseless carriage', even as late as the 1940s. And well they might have, for, as old Buckminster Fuller loved to tell us, the car is still a coach and four . . . just with different styling and more horse(!) power: which didn't mess the village up too much when only the squire had one, but when everyone wanted one it led to the planning and ecological disaster that is America today.

So, if the basic programme of the car were to be extended to cover social issues, such as the journey from dining table to driver's seat, what happens to the car when left alone . . . were the architect's purview (2) to be extended beyond the limits of the site . . . ' (here the fragment ends).

Addendum (from 1966)

'The motivating force, behind the Drive-in House, was the observation that facilities existed such as movie theatres, restaurants or churches with drive-in options, where the management would provide the movie, food or the peace that passeth all-understanding, and you BYO mini auditorium, dining area or pew. What if a house were thought of in the same way? You might have as a fixed locus, the stuff that's too heavy to move: bathtub, stove, family heirloom, but the rest (that which is needed for the journey) could be folded down into the auto and driven away'.

Storyboards were prepared for three manifestations of the project: the '25 x 25' House of 1964, the Sky-rise Slab Block, and the Wankelhaus of 1988.

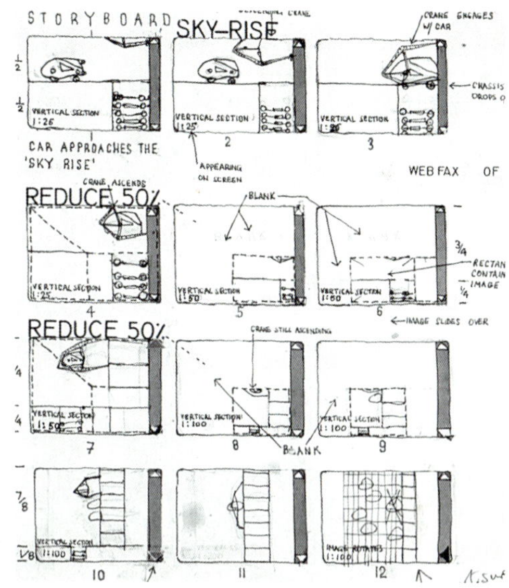

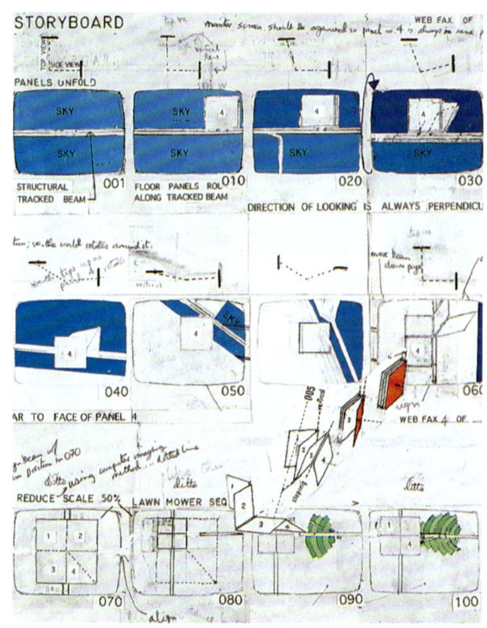

OPPOSITE: Drive-in House, detail; FROM ABOVE: Sky-rise 'storyboard'; '25 x 25' House 'storyboard'; PAGE 18: Wankelhaus, detail; PAGE 19, FROM ABOVE: Sky-rise, electric runabout cars; '25 x 25' House, lawn mower detail

The '25 x 25' House

Perspective projection 'privileges' (a popular locution among critters in the USA), a singular point, the location of the observer, and if there be no compelling reason within the scope of the overall projects for the existence of such a point, then the appropriateness of the choice of projection should be in doubt. Most students working with the computer, it seems to me, are blissfully free of such doubts. So, in my storyboard, the projection is orthographic, the direction of looking always perpendicular to the face of panel four. Stainless steel floor panels roll along a structural track system, each hinging open like a petal – a metal petal. Also shown is the lawn mower sequence.

The Sky-rise

Special electric runabout cars arrive at the base of the Sky-rise, at which point the body and chassis separate, the chassis to be stacked in subterranean racks and the body to be hoisted up via a travelling crane to the appropriate apartment in the sky, or perhaps more interestingly, to the inappropriate apartment. The devices developed by Macintosh to move text and/or images up and down (the scroll bar) or to change size (the dotted rectangles) were appropriated here to allow vertical scanning and scale changes.

The Wankelhaus

The Wankel rotary engine as exemplar of the miracle of the rotor (a quasi-triangular form) rotating within the cylinder (a quasi-circular form), yet maintaining constant contact at four sliding points. 'Epitrochoid' is the arcane word that describes this. In the Wankelhaus, the car as energiser and activator of the house (which is an empty shell when the car is gone), rotates the space – metal panels unfolding and sliding past each other so as to maintain a seal against external inclement weather. A nocturnal plan projection reveals slits in the metal panel skin, the shape of the car's lights and windows, illuminated as the car rotates.

Notes

1 Columbia University in New York has a computer-only studio

2 It was considered that the spread of television during the 1950s in England would mean the end of radio. At the same time, British Rail was eliminating its fleet of steam locomotives and replacing them with diesel power, so naturally, radio began to be referred to as 'steam radio'.

3 What pretensions are contained within this world. The US Internal Revenue Service classifies it as a 'hobby'!

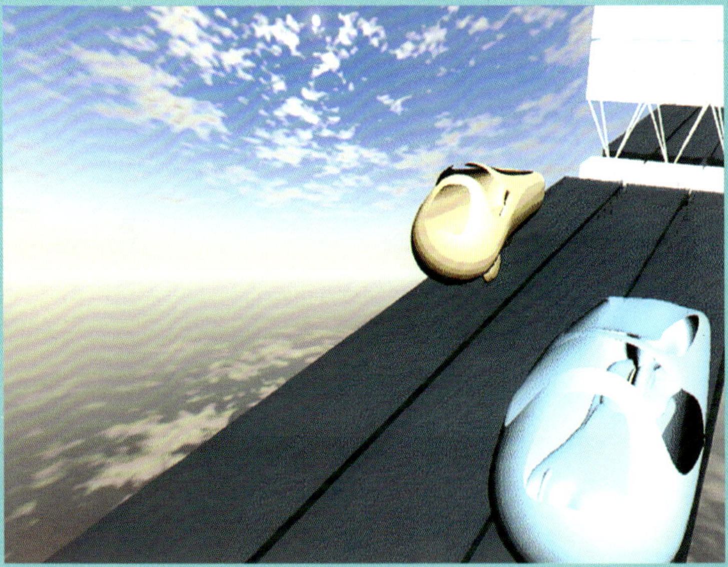

THE CONTEXT FOR PRACTICE

WILLIAM ALSOP, ALSOP & STÖRMER

In traditional terms, architecture is concerned with function, form and space. These three elements interact together resulting in an object (or objects) of BEAUTY.

Terms such as SPACE, FUNCTION, FORM and BEAUTY are highly subjective and are transformed by different cultures in different periods into different meanings, of different importance. The history of architecture is the tracking of these attitudes; these attitudes create the climate or context in which architectural objects are allowed to exist.

Architecture demands public consent in order to exist, which at various times has resulted in many architects being 'condemned' to the ranks of the unbuilt 'avant-garde'. Today, there is no avant-garde in ART. This is due to a much more open attitude towards the nature of acceptable practice. This battle was fought in the first 60 years of this century, resulting in a questioning of the art itself – not its right to be considered as ART. ART could always be produced and untested before the 'public' gaze.

Architecture has far to go in order to advance to the same state. Until the idea of an avant-garde is irrelevant, the architect is forced to make a division between exploration of the edges, forming an enquiry into the nature of the subject itself, and accepting the practice of the art of compromise (which in itself is not uninteresting). The question in architecture of how to bring the edge to practice leads to a schizophrenia that most architects cannot cope with. They end up making a choice between the rigours of practice or the discipline of academia (usually to fund their exploration). The relationship between academic life and that of practice has moved further apart in the UK since 1979, which exacerbates and perpetuates the idea of the avant-garde.

This gap, I believe, acts to the detriment of both architects and architecture alike. What are the conditions that could prevail to allow say, Frederick Kiesler to build his Endless House, today. The idea of context is fundamental to this question.

Architecture does not kill people, and yet there is more heated debate regarding buildings and their right to exist, than their is about medical practice, law or ethics. This is not to say that the latter are not debated, but the significant difference is the arena in which it takes place. Everyone is touched by architecture and, as a result, everyone has a view which can be articulated. This view is formalised in planning committees, royal parlours and newspaper columns. The level of the debate is generally outside the concerns of architecture in its pure sense and, usually, is rooted in historic precedent. It is very rare indeed for a new building to be approved because of what it represents.

The medium of language used as a means of representation of a project is more potent than the images which describe it. Unlike other disciplines, architecture at this stage is a judgement on a prediction of the future. For many, including the architect, the idea of accurate forecasting is not possible, and yet important decisions are made with the aid of rough approximations of the future. This process keeps architectural concerns in the same essential state as it was in the Renaissance.

The use of perspective drawings as a means of ordering the visual experience has kept architecture as a simplistic object-making discipline.

Brunelleschi would recognise the processes that today's architects follow. Our way of representing form and space controls both the debate and the eventual object. This is the context in which we work. To see beyond the context is extremely dangerous, as well as difficult; dangerous because you risk alienating the status quo, condemning both you and your project to the realms of the avant-garde (ie, terribly interesting, but easy to ignore), or difficult because an even greater act of prediction is entered into. The problem arises from the idea that we have to be right. Very often the requirement for certainty strangles the interesting possibility.

Bricks and mortar are the epitome of certainty, and yet they do not respond to the changes brought about by the electronic age. I do not believe that the architectural response to the electronic age has a tangible effect on the material of architecture itself, but rather, that the behaviour it allows will. The mechanical age created new techniques of creating objects and conditioning them, and I have no doubt that development will continue, albeit informed by new shifts in behavioural patterns.

Climate can be moderated through materials and design, or alternatively, it can be avoided by occupying different areas of the earth's surfaces to suit one's tastes. The electronic age permits a global connectivity. The idea of cultural displacement will undoubtedly put pressure on society's ideas of context and the local vernacular. The universal house, which can contain the same contents and spaces in different locations, is an interesting issue. Not mobile architecture, but mobile people.

The dispersal of the family unit will be taken to further extremes due to global spread; the parent (single or married) must expect a satisfaction of contact through electronics.

The unification of global areas, for trading reasons, makes mobility more simple. The passport becomes an antique.

It is predicted that more than 50 per cent of the world's population will live in URBAN conglomerates by the year 2000.

The city of Vienna 'imports' material into itself, adding 36,000 tons to its weight every day.

London requires an area of 50,000,000 acres to support its population living in an area of 400,000 acres.

Males in Bangladesh have a better chance of living to the

Northampton Millennium Sky, 1996

age of 65 (Bangladesh is the twelfth poorest country in the world) than the average male living in Harlem, New York. Does our perception of 'CITY' life, mean a high density?

Why is China building new towns at an alarming rate, without the use of architects, urbanists and environmentalists?

Does all we 'know' count for nothing when faced with commercial opportunity?

How long will the businessman, when criticised for placing people out of work or creating pollution, be allowed to throw up his hands and say 'business is business', as though it conforms to an independent set of rules?

All of these facts and questions are the context in which we operate as architects. Some of the questions are so huge that we feel impotent in the face of them, but they remain a potent background to our 'architectural thinking, or at least they should. This context tends to find no space for architecture. Architecture is seen to be too elite or too expensive. Architecture is seen to be irrelevant as it is only a question of money, speed and practicality. And yet Jamie Lemer (architect) has succeeded, as MAYOR of CURITIBA in BRAZIL to address and solve many of the problems associated with urban life. He is celebrated as a mayor, not an ARCHITECT.

'Great Architecture is good for you.' It has the ability to relieve stress, empower the individual, and be beautiful, and yet, it is undervalued everywhere.

Architecture is not merely BUILDINGS.

ARCHITECTURE=BUILDING +
Plus what?
The 'what is' thing, like time and space, has no actual physical properties. It should not be confused with the architectural object. It is the subject of architecture which has properties that transcend the physicality of the object.

The subject of ARCHITECTURE is aesthetic perception.

Some architects talk of the subject requiring rigour. It does, but not in the constipated form of their interpretation. It is not a discipline that reduces elements down to a mannerist set of principles. It is the discovery of architecture through inquiry which requires rigour.

ARCHITECTURE IS NOT CONCERNED WITH IDEAS. ALL ARCHITECTURE PAST, PRESENT AND FUTURE EXISTS – IT IS THE PRACTICE OF ARCHITECTURE TO DISCOVER IT.

ROBERT IRWIN, the American artist, has, for me, always been a relevant source of reference. His identification of separate frames of reference as a context for art practice can equally apply to architecture. I substitute the word ARCHITECTURE for ART:

1 ARCHITECTURE is a positive of aesthetic enquiry, the perceptual/conceptual recognition, construction and ordering of individual reality. ARCHITECTURE as ARCHITECTURE.

2 ARCHITECTURE is a process of cultural innovation, the interdisciplinary articulation and argumentation by means of which novel ideas and forms achieve cultural validity. The ARCHITECTURE of ARCHITECTURE.

3 ARCHITECTURE is a communicative interaction with social need, the fostering of those 'meaningful' overlaps of form for social practice and function. The ARCHITECTURE of SOCIAL CONCERN.

4 ARCHITECTURE is a compounded historical development. This historical process is the grounds for art as a sophisticated cultural discipline. The ARCHITECTURE of CIVILISATION.

If these four frameworks are the basis for the practice, acceptance and criticism, it seems clear to me that architectural practice, as characterised by an office with employees marketing and building, is perhaps not the model for practice that should exist. The conventional model cannot afford to 'indulge' in aesthetic inquiry. It cannot devote the time to achieving cultural validity for new realisations. Because of these two restrictions, it pays only lip service to 'social concern' and the development of a sophisticated cultural discipline. A new form of practice must emerge, moulding academic and conventional practice principles into one.

This practice must be total and must not use social or environmental concern as a marketing tool; it must be concerned with the discovery and effective communication of what it does. It will promote the abolition of the avant-garde. This realisation has emerged over a number of years; the process started with a concern for getting beyond the idea of ideas.

Technique has always been a confusing issue to me. It is the essence of craftsmanship, where a necessarily narrow range of skills is developed to a high level of technical proficiency. Many art schools and architecture schools indulged in this idea of teaching. The problem is that when a technique is mastered, it tends to determine the decision making of the artist or architect. They are constrained by what they know. The development of welding in sculpture at St Martin's School of Art was a prime example of this limitation in action. In architecture, some have developed a similar attitude towards glass technology. This type of expertise tends to breed the idea of ideas. In the absence of an open inquiry, the author tends to study possibilities within a certain limited range. This results in the idea only ever remaining an idea, as a means of extending the known technique.

My own work from the beginning has studiously avoided this trap. In the early 70s, it was concerned with invisibility. This

FROM ABOVE, L to R: Groningen paintings – Gourmet; What; Wigwam; Interflora; Wheels; Swanky Modes, *oil on canvas, 1996, 83 x 39cm*

FROM ABOVE L to R: Groningen paintings – Dolce Vita; Friction to the Jurisdiction; Agitprop; Big Grass; Gastric Picnic; Memory Voids, *oil on canvas, 1996, 83 x 35cm*

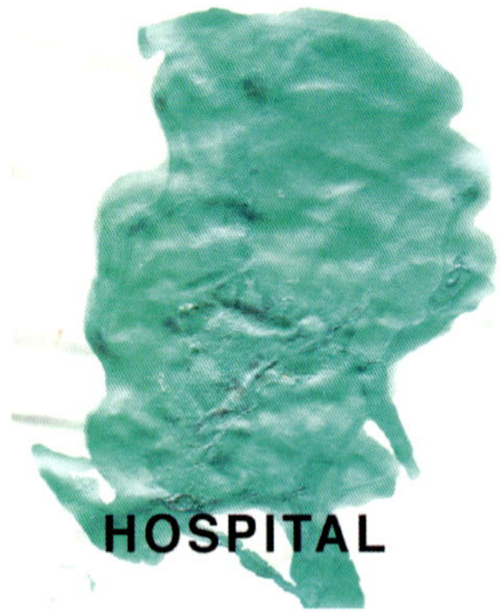

HOSPITAL

MATERNITY HOME

inquiry ranged from the study of illusion through to the questioning of why buildings exist. It became obsessed with the idea of 'occupying' the landscape and effective control of house prices through planning restriction. Decentralisation of cities seemed to me to be a viable alternative to cities as well as a method by which to study the aesthetic of rural locations. In all these areas, the essential ingredient was the aesthetic perception of the propositions. What of course it did not achieve was any notion of cultural validity. All the propositions lay outside the possibility of acceptance by society and, in this way, they belonged to the AVANT-GARDE. Exploration continued into the specifics of function. Was it possible to create space that was particular in its programme and yet open enough to allow many behaviours to inhabit the space? From this exploration emerged works like the house with six identical rooms, which posed more questions about the nature of behaviour. From this I substituted the word function, which locks people into a narrow bend of activities, with 'behaviour'. This line of inquiry continues and, as one gets older, one realises that everything ever thought or done is current. The idea of a progression which invalidates all the work that went before, is a self denial of one's own history and it is history which is the grounds for a sophisticated cultural discipline. If we look back at the claims for the death of Modernism, or the virtues of Post-Modernism – and all the other 'isms' for that matter – we can see the futility of them. The evolution of the inquiry is the important element – what others may choose to call it is irrelevant.

NO TECHNIQUE, NO TITLES, NO FUNCTIONAL LABELS

Beyond the idea lies the unknown. The architecture of air developed by KLEIN and WERNER RUHNAU led to the concept of the VOID and the selling of acts of performance. The dematerialisation of the work led beyond what was known. The context of each sequence of an architect's or artist's inquiry changes as the world changes. The ideas of mobility, explored as an idea by Archigram, have a different meaning today. Historically, it is very important not to peg concepts of one generation in a particular time. The mobile theatre at GRONINGEN, for example, is a current project, seen today in a very different light to Instant City of 1969. There is a poetry which today emerges above the celebration of technology.

The theatre is composed of a series of elements that can be assembled in different ways. It has a permanent summer location at the confluence of two canals. The object will act as theatre when there is no performance. It allows people to create dreams for limited periods of time. Each arrangement represents one possibility realised, which then becomes the history of the piece. The accumulative history becomes the ARCHITECTURE. The proposal, currently under construction, fits into the concept of the non-determined function. It is there to promote unknown behaviours. Society accepts this proposition because it is practical and contributes to the 'equipment' of the city. It extends the range of possibilities.

Our proposal for the TATE at Bankside was also an opportunity for ART. It is not to be confused with the idea of architecture. It is not consumed by notions of style or design, it is a direct inquiry into the nature of placing a series of containers for ART into and onto another former container of machinery: a clear expression of one proposition transforming another. It was clear to me that such a gallery should not only be there to contain a known collection, but also to promote new art activity (inquiries). The form of artist's behaviour to come is unknown and should not be confined by architecture. This proposition failed. It did not find favour with the Tate management or their advisors. Instead, they chose a minimalist statement from Herzog & de Meuron which will cause least offence.

It is clear that the 'IDEA' of a Museum of Modern Art is already an archetypal building type that has acquired rules and a particular image. This institutionalisation has occurred very quickly, since we must remember that Museums of Art are a recent invention. WHAT SHOULD BE INFORMAL has become FORMALISED. This occurrence is a part of the nature of society which requires buildings that can be named to contain a particular image. This process inevitably inhibits the AVANT-GARDE. It is the architect's job to offer visions of new possibilities, and yet society has disenfranchised the ARCHITECT. The architect must change the nature of his practice. Obviously the idea of two works of architecture occupying the same site at Bankside was, on a formal level, unacceptable. This is a failure on my part as an architect – not the client.

The transformation of existing patterns of behaviour and geography is a central theme in the work of the practice. In Bordeaux, we changed the geography by conceptually straightening the river. The river Garonne curves round as it passes through the city. This curve gives the name of PORT DE LA LUNE. As ships no longer enter the city, it is possible to capture the surface of the river as a part of the city, while at the same time creating a link to the North Bank. This is achieved with a floating semi-submersible link which is large enough to contain a variety of functions. This link becomes invisible at high tide to allow the existing separation of north and south banks to manifest itself, whilst at low tide the physicality becomes apparent. The captured segment of water becomes a random theatre of floating subjects which respond to each other. Sails of political paintings respond to the wind along the line of the intervention. This project does not differentiate between patterns of old and new use. It

NURSING HOME

SURGERY

gives equal importance to the whole of the earth's surface. The project was commissioned and made public by the city of BORDEAUX as a means of stimulating a debate. This is part of the job of the architect in redefined practice. This project does its job by changing the perception of the city for the people living in the city. IT LIVES.

In NORTHAMPTON, we are engaged in the development of a new URBAN PARK as a Millennium bid. The project itself is, of course, interesting, but certainly of equal interest is the way the project came into being. I was invited by the TOWN to give a lecture at the Town Hall as a part of its 800th anniversary celebrations. I decided not to talk about architecture and my work, but rather to concentrate on the problems of Northampton and possible ways of addressing them. (I was born and bred in Northampton, which gave me the right to be critical.)

The town, in common with many others, was subjected to the creation of an inner ring road in the 1960s when the population stood at 10,000. The population by the year 2000 will be 200,000 ie, a doubling over a 35 year period. The constraints imposed by the ring road meant that the provision of new shopping and working opportunities leapt over the ring road into the beyond, thereby putting pressure on the future of the town centre. One such development is an industrial/business park called BRACKMILLS. BRACKMILLS has almost as many people in it during the working day as the town centre area which is approximately 1.25 miles away. It certainly has almost the same area. In the day BRACKMILLS does not contribute to the life to the town centre at all as there is no transport link. This link, which is the subject of the urban park, also follows the line of the RIVER NENE, which has been consistently forgotten in all planning of NORTHAMPTON. The project is to bring BRACKMILLS into the town centre by the formation of a DUMBELL. This strategy acts as a potential model for many waning town centres.

The response to the lecture was very positive and created a sense of excitement among politicians and citizens alike. This gave the opportunity for me to work with Roger Zogolovitch, who is a brilliant financial and political support. The project is still developing, into one that works in every way. This could only be achieved by the architect in the guise of a new form of practice, being in control. There are virtually no mechanisms within local government to allow visions for their towns to see the light of day. It is easier not to do things, than to change. The advantage of our new practice is that we are organised in a way that provides answers, solutions and positive responses to all the problems that usually sink any initiative. THIS is RADICAL by necessity but cannot be downgraded to the ranks of the AVANT-GARDE.

THIS action brings together the overlaps between form, social practice and function – THE ARCHITECTURE OF SOCIAL CONCERN to what is normally seen as too radical in set of actions.

The role of the community has always been problematic to me. On one level, a sense of community is vital to individuals: it gives a sense of involvement, as well as self direction and self policy; it reduces stress and involves the elderly. The dynamics of a community, on the other hand, are such that it has to develop fixed values in order to become one at all. This makes it resistant to change and adaptation, and it is this quality that destroys it as it ceases to be relevant in a changing world. The new practice has to deal with the truth. Meaning has no tangible definition; it is a question of individual and collective perception, which has to include AESTHETIC PERCEPTION. The new practice has to carefully communicate the nature of any proposal. It has to involve and engage the people of the community.

This is more easily said than done. Ambitions of this nature in the past have diluted architectural intent in order to gain acceptance: this is not good enough. The new practice must use workshops as a device for widening the perception of the issues beyond the lowest common denominator often found in a democracy. An engagement in the joys of potential change must be disseminated, as opposed to protection of the status quo as the safest route forward.

Conventional architectural practice is in danger of being ignored. It has not responded to the idea of taking responsibility for what it does, or being pro-active. Indeed, it has shrunk from responsibility wherever it looked dangerous, which has allowed other disciplines, including those of the politician, to step in. The new practice engages a multi-disciplinary team that can mould together all aspects of a project, and is also active in being proactive. The architect is only ever as good as the clients and we cannot afford to wait for the good clients to find us. It is an OPEN practice attempting to mould a sophisticated cultural discipline.

THE ARCHITECTURE OF CIVILISATION

Projects and proposals must not be afraid of lying outside the terms of RECOGNITION AND COMPREHENSION of the client and society. It is our job to see beyond those limitations through the process of AESTHETIC INQUIRY. It is the ARCHITECT'S task to bring the work into a value system that will enable society to allow it to exist. This inevitably means compromising in some form to reach an agreement, but this process can be dynamic and creative. If this is not achieved, the work will only exist in the mind of the architect and will be called the AVANT-GARDE. This is a different reality that ultimately does not help create the more open attitude towards the built environment that makes the AVANT-GARDE irrelevant.

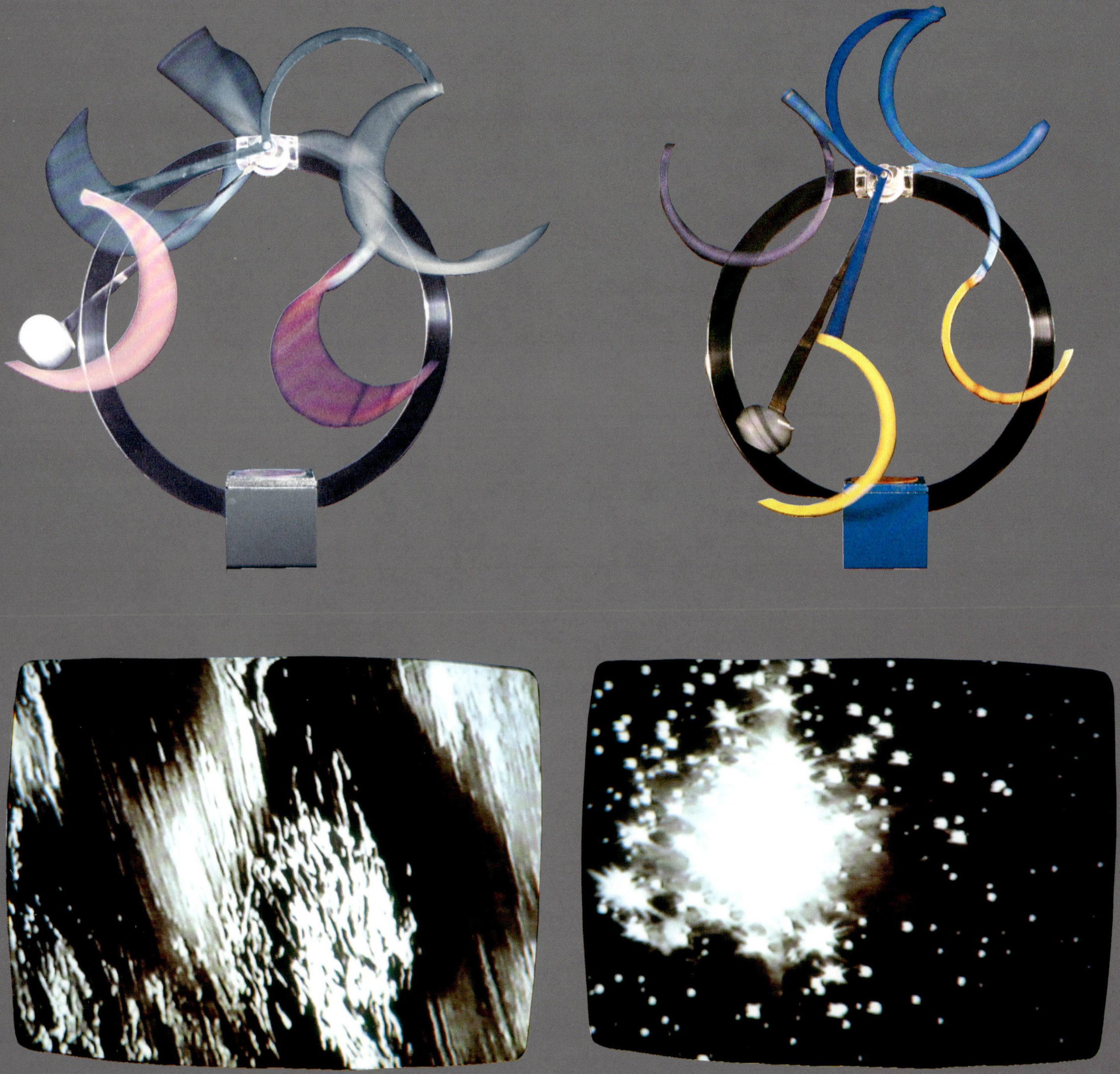

ABOVE: Long exposures showing characteristic movements of chaotic mechanism; BELOW: environmental data in digital form. The images here show the effect of sunlight reflected off waves

PETE SILVER AND PETER FLUCK

NON-LINEAR DYNAMICAL SYSTEMS

PETE SILVER

Abstract
Chaos theory is concerned with a new understanding of dynamics – the way in which systems behave in time.

It concerns the realisation that certain types of deterministic systems, ie, ones that obey fixed laws, can exhibit unpredictable behaviour. This may be described as nonlinearity – the relationship between things when viewed on a graph is not just straight lines. Similarly, the theory of fractals is concerned with a new understanding of geometry based on a realisation that there exists a large class of geometric objects that are not encompassed by traditional Euclidian geometry. Fractal objects have dimensions that are not integers and take the same form when viewed on different scales – a property known as self-similarity.

The theories of fractals and chaos overlap with the concept of a strange attractor – an object in state space to which trajectories are pulled. It is itself a fractal, and hence a geometric object that embodies the dynamical behaviour of a chaotic system. In their most primitive form, these systems are mathematical equations which may be viewed as a graph wherein the variables are plotted over time. When the system's parameters are changed, there is a corresponding change in the form of its attractor – a process known as bifurcation.

In electronic systems, the first transformation is often to make a small signal larger by using an amplifier. In analogue form, the attractors can then be viewed as wavelengths. A digital coding will produce a stream of binary particles. Any further transformations are by design; as Gordon Pask would say, 'It is the process of turning data into information that gives rise to knowledge, and pleasure'.

The three projects illustrated are exploring the phenomena of non-linear dynamics through various electromechanical devices.

Project 1: Bowstring Structure
The mechanisms that are being used to create the attractor are employing one of the fundamental principles of Cybernetic systems, that of feedback. The Cybernetic model permits any dynamical system to be viewed as a flow of information: feedback then refers to the process in which part of the output is fed back in order to regulate the operation. When the feedback system reinforces the trend of the system, it is said to be positive. When it opposes the trend of the system, it is called negative feedback. In living organisms, biofeedback is used to control physiological processes.

Tiny switches, known as tilt switches, consist of a sealed cup of mercury and make a contact when rotated beyond a particular angle. These switches control electromagnetic solenoids. Two solenoids support a rigid structure from which elastic rods are used to carry the mercury switches. The tension in the rods is tuneable so that the sensitivity of the switches to any movement in the system can vary. Once the system is triggered by any amount of extraneous noise, it rapidly begins to feed back upon itself. While the system is tensioned symmetrically, the structure falls into a pattern of regular oscillation. When it is out of balance, it becomes unpredictable in its behaviour, often pausing, immobile for long periods before suddenly being triggered once again into chaotic activity. With too little or too much tension, it simply ceases to function.

Project 2: Mapping Turbulence
The ability to retrieve environmental data in digital form through electronic sensors and transducers has an implication that any mapping can be reduced to a universal coding of zeros and ones and, hence, may be transformed into a range of outputs.

A video camera is an example of such a system: the original image is stored as bits, and reproduced line by line as

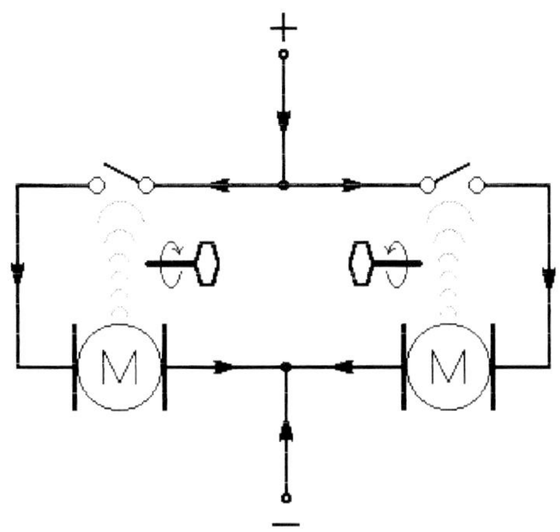

Bowstring structure demonstrating fundamental principles of cybernetic systems – feedback

animated *bit maps* on a monitor screen.

Activity in nature is often either too small, too large, too slow or too rapid for conscious human senses to digest its patterns of order and chaos. The notion of *making the invisible visible* is nevertheless common to both art and science. The artist will frame a subject, and, in doing so, will draw the viewer's attention to a hitherto unseen moment. The scientist will amplify and dissect his subject so that it may be offered up in a form that can be subjected to analysis. The images seen here are a tiny sample of the effect of sunlight reflected off waves.

PETER FLUCK

Project 3: The Wrotz Pendulum

A collaboration with Dr Tony Myatt of University of York Music Department has created a project seeking to integrate kinetic sculpture and musical compositions produced by the application of computer and video technologies.

The computer systems are used, through a colour recognition program which monitors and tracks the sculptures, to generate sounds and musical structures which directly correspond to their movement.

Initial experiments to find a suitable form of movement were focused on the Wrotz pendulum – designed to illustrate Chaos theory. The Wrotz pendulum is constructed from a set of three pendula, which hang from the extremities of a T-shaped construction. The 'T' is pivoted at the junction of its upright and cross pieces. When spun around its central pivot, the three smaller pieces, which are fitted with adjustable weights, will spin independently. This motion constantly changes the distribution of weight in the system, influences the behaviour of each element and of the whole assembly, and causes it to slow down, to stop, to restart, accelerate and reverse its rotation.

The motion of the device is chaotic and defies prediction. As with all chaotic systems, the Wrotz pendulum is extremely sensitive and difficult to tune. Interestingly, laughter caused by its frenetic movements often indicates that it is correctly balanced. The demands of this project have led to adaptations and developments of the Wrotz device in order to achieve a continuous form of movement exhibiting a slower, more flowing and varied behaviour.

To cause a pendulum to swing continually, a coil or electromagnet is actuated by a Hall-effect switch which introduces a current that repels a permanent magnet mounted on the bob of the pendulum, when it passes through its vertical position. This maintains the momentum. A slipping clutch was constructed using four magnets at the top of the pendulum, either side of its pivot. Two permanent magnets repel a further pair mounted on a separate shaft on the same axis.

The pendulum is able to drive a large disc which replaces the 'T' of the Wrotz pendulum, producing a drive system which can rotate clockwise or anticlockwise according to the positioning of the four magnets and the speed and momentum of the disc. To provide variables that influence this central drive, pivoted elements are mounted on the disc. These function as the three small arms of the Wrotz pendulum.

These assemblies are carefully balance forms comprised of three or four pivoted elements, to overcome unwanted gravitational effects. Magnets are used on these 'limbs' to reintroduce rotational movements and to allow the sculpture to develop visual dialogues, individual characters, and relationships between different elements of the piece.

Using these mechanisms, the frenzied behaviour of the Wrotz pendulum can be converted into a soft, flowing chaotic choreography of shape and colour.

The Wrotz Pendulum (The Beast), *designed to illustrate Chaos theory*

TED KRUEGER

LIKE A SECOND SKIN, LIVING MACHINES

In *Erehwon,*[1] Samuel Butler characterises technology as an extension of the human – more or less remote senses, limbs and intellects that amplify our innate capabilities. Certainly architecture, as a built enterprise, fits comfortably into this description. Architecture is our collective epidermis, dressed roughly as a blacksmith, or in the *haute couture* of the moment. Architecture emerges out of a functional substrate. At its most basic level, it serves to moderate the environment at a social scale. It is a body that we inhabit together.

Is this only a metaphoric operation? We make architecture out of the most inert and durable materials available: stone, glass, steel, reinforced concrete or wood; we are unsure about plastics. To speak of a body, especially in the context of epidermis, is to recall almost the opposite quality on every count – infirm,

perishable, mutable and frequently anti-inert.

Yet, there is no requirement that the two kinds of body be identical. Could it be that we build in one the exact qualities that we find missing in the other? Or is it more likely, that we make our architecture out of what is available to us? While there is much to recommend the materials currently in use, there is always more that could be done if we had access to the proper substances.

In this paper, I argue for the possibility of an intelligent and interactive architecture conceived of as a metadermis, referencing recent work in the fields of mobile robotics, intelligent structures and skins, and interactive materials. These developments can serve as both a source of technical information and as a methodology by which architecture may develop qualities currently considered to be available only within the organic realm.

The investigation of fields outside architecture that may have common technical interests is justified in that architecture has few resources to devote to basic research. It is possible, however, to review disciplines that are more liberally funded by culture, and to appropriate developments as they occur.

One such area is the aerospace and defence industry. The rigours of high performance aircraft and space vehicles have led to the generation of sophisticated sensing and control technologies that are applied to the structure of the vehicle. In an effort to understand the integrity of structural components during manufacture, installation and use, techniques for embedding sensors in structural components have been developed. Fibre optic strands have proven to be particularly useful for measuring, *in situ,* a wide range of forces and environmental conditions.

Optical fibre, as used in the telecommunications industry, has been carefully engineered to be immune to distortions of the signals due to environmental conditions.[2] In sensing applications, however, the character of these distortions is analysed to determine the nature, magnitude and location of the forces that have produced them. 'Structurally integrated optical neuro-systems' have been developed which are presently capable of sensing position, orientation, rotation, displacement, deformation, liquid level, temperature, pressure, strain, velocity, acceleration, impact, structural damage, frequency, vibration, acoustic waves, electromagnetic fields, current, voltage and magnetic fields.[3]

The reference to 'nerves' is to the point. The sensing systems are closely modelled on those of biological systems. It is commonly understood that many involuntary reactions in the human take place without involving the brain. Signals travel, perhaps as far as the spinal cord, before a reaction is returned.

In the same way, complex sensing systems in structures may benefit from parallel and distributed computation. The large array of sensors envisioned in these applications would produce a sufficient quantity of data to overload a centralised computer. Consequently, dispersed systems capable of a more tight coupling of sensing, evaluation and response are being analysed.

Optical networks can be used to determine a 'baseline signature' for a structure to which it can be compared during use and over the life of a component. It may become unethical to design structures that fail to give warning of impaired capability or impending failure.[4] This health monitoring strategy is particularly attractive for implementation in civil structures. At the University of Vermont, Huston and Fuhr have installed optical fibre sensors (in concrete and on steel substrates) on a university medical building, a hydroelectric dam[5,6] and a highway bridge[7]; the resulting data is being collected.

There are several benefits to civil applications in addition to the safety issues. These and future studies will inform analytic models with empirical data and provide direct insight into complex shapes that cannot be solved by contemporary analytical tools.

This has the potential to reduce the required safety factors, resulting in smaller structural members, decreasing material quantities and, therefore, costs.[8,9] On-site monitoring and evaluation will reduce the risks involved with incorporating new materials or innovative techniques into buildings. The combination of safety and economy will drive the incorporation of sensing technologies. What is of interest here is the probability that they will be installed.

Despite their versatility, sensor technologies useful in architectural applications are not limited to fibre optics. Thermal sensors, motion detectors, and photosensors are already commonplace. Low cost radar,[10] accelerometers,[11] ultrasonic range finders, humidity sensors, mat switches, opto-electronics, for example, are available to track a wide range of parameters that may be environmental or programmatic, as well as structural.

Parallel to monitoring the state of components in advanced structures is an interest in using that information to take action. In the context of composites used in aerospace, it is possible to embed reactive materials or actuators which act as artificial muscles within the same component housing the sensors. Shape memory alloys, piezoelectric ceramics, magnetostrictive materials and electrorheological and magnetorheological fluids have been proposed for use.[12] With these techniques, it is possible to modify the structural properties of the material, altering its geometry or vibrational characteristics[13] in reaction to information obtained through the senors.

While many of the techniques that are under investigation in the aerospace field are not yet relevant to civil structures, there is substantial investigation into active[14] as well as passive[15] structural control techniques applicable at this scale. Active strategies include active bracing and tendon systems, and active mass dampers and drivers which, when coupled to sensor technology, yield an adaptive system.

It is this element of adaptation[16] – whether applied to the structural, mechanical, circulation, communication, or control systems – that differentiates the possibilities that architecture can draw from other technical disciplines from those it now possesses. Adaptability is also one of the distinguishing characteristics of the organic. The process of embedding our intelligence in the environment makes this adaptability possible.

Ubiquitous Computing, as developed by Mark Weiser at Xerox PARC[17] has the objective of rendering the computer invisible. It would disappear into the woodwork (or wallboard) yet be continuously present and available; it becomes part of the environment. It is possible to consider another aspect of an intelligent architecture. Rather than having an architecture that contains smart bits, we might consider an architecture that possesses intelligence. I will reference recent work in mobile robotics to illustrate this possibility.

An intelligent architecture in the present context is only distantly related to the discussions of 'smart' buildings or 'intelligent' buildings as found in the literature of builders and developers, or engineers and architects. In these contexts, an 'intelligent' building is one that affords:

> productivity and cost effectiveness by means of optimally designed and interrelated structures, systems and subsystems, and services and management.[18]

The objective of these integrated and centralised systems is an economy of building construction, operation, maintenance and management. These are discussions about efficiency, hierarchy, optimisation and control. Intelligent, in these cases, does not refer to the building, but is an opinion about the quality of the design solution.

There is no necessary link between optimisation and intelligence. It is possible that they are antagonistic. By inspection, one finds that many systems occurring in nature are not optimised, but are rather a collection of apparently redundant and residual processes. One could think of the quantity of 'junk' DNA in the human genome or the appendix as examples. These overlapping layers result in a robustness that is very difficult, if not impossible, to achieve in optimised systems. In highly optimised systems, robustness is generally provided by the complete duplication of the system to run as a backup. Robustness is simulated by the duplication of fragile systems.

Here, the interest is in an understanding that the building itself may have intelligence in the same way that we understand biological phenomena to have intelligence.

To precisely define the concepts of 'intelligence' or of 'building' lies beyond the scope of this paper and the inclinations of the author. I recommend such an infinite series of regressions to the cafe theoreticians.

While the intersection of architecture, intelligence and mobile robotics may seem to be an artefact of the surrealist dissection table, it may be helpful to begin by linking the latter pair, then follow with the former.

Much of the research in the field of mobile robotics is undertaken at the Mobot Lab at MIT. The subject matter in the Lab is, in fact, not robots, but machine intelligence. This Lab is part of the larger Artificial Intelligence Laboratory at MIT. Robots are simply the platform on which intelligence is studied, though not one that was arbitrarily chosen. Autonomous mobile robots as a methodology grew out of a critique of the state of academic AI research as it had developed through the mid-80s. In *Achieving Artificial Intelligence through Building Robots*[19] Rodney Brooks, director of the Mobot Lab, considers abstraction to be a method of self-delusion.

Much of the carefully crafted research that had been undertaken in the academic laboratories was incapable of making the transition out of it.[20] In part, this was due to the desire to achieve human level intelligence. In order to do so, researchers started with what they 'knew' about the human experience of intelligence through introspection. They began by emulating what is a higher order phenomenon (consciousness) without first building the appropriate substrate. Systems were delicately balanced; fragile constructs that did not adjust well to incomplete, unanticipated or contradictory information. Brooks proposed insect robots as a starting point; human level intelligence could wait.[21, 22]

The model for artificial intelligence was altered from one based on thinking processes to one grounded in behaviours. Rather than create a system that would move through a 'sense-model-plan-act' (consciousness emulation) sequence, a number of rudimentary, but tightly-coupled, sensor-actuator behaviours were run in parallel with simple asynchronous communications established between them. This was a stroke of pragmatic genius, for it allowed for the testing and debugging of a number of simple behaviours which, once perfected, could be left untouched. Meanwhile, attention could be turned to higher order structures which were concerned with mediation or coordination between simple behaviours to produce a more complex activity.

It was assumed that there would be conflicting information, missed communications, and the occasional failure of a mechanism or behaviour module. However, the failure of a single element would not bring the whole robot to a halt, although it would have to revert to a more primitive level of behaviour or adjust itself to the loss of a sensor. Modularity and robustness are central to this approach.

The layering of behaviours, or Subsumption Architecture,[23] was used in conjunction with a learning algorithm[24] to develop a robot that could walk.

Simple behaviours such as leg movements and a monitoring of the state of adjacent legs, were used as input into a behaviour activation strategy that, after a few minutes of uncoordinated flailing about, resulted in the development of the alternating tripod gait. This six-legged robot was not programmed to walk. The control of an individual leg movement was programmed and debugged, but the coordination of activity between them was an emergent phenomena based on the learning algorithm.

In *Intelligence without Reason,*[25] Brooks clarifies the approach developed in the Mobot Lab, citing 'situatedness, embodiment, intelligence and emergence' as key ideas.

Situatedness is the state of being in the world and is related to the rejection of abstraction, as noted above. In particular, it rejects 'toy' worlds – custom-built environments for the study of a specific behaviour – as the basis for research. In contrast, actual conditions should be used as they provide the most comprehensive description of themselves, are constantly available for direct reference, are updated in real-time, and thus, do not require representation. Rather than modelling a simplified world, the robots could directly react to a complex one.

Embodiment is the method by which situatedness is achieved. It proves the actual functioning of the system in ways that simulation cannot. It is ruthlessly efficient at exposing wishful thinking. Embodiment allows for behaviour.

Intelligence grows out of the conjunction of situatedness and embodiment, and may be defined as the relationship between behaviours and the environment. Emergence is the development of unprogrammed higher order behaviours resulting from the interaction of simpler behavioural components of the system and/or their interactions with the environment.

The fact that situatedness and embodiment flow quite easily from the study of mobile robots in a real environment should not obscure the fact that mobile systems are not unique in supplying these requirements. A dynamic relationship with an environment is necessary. The sensor cannot understand mobility, but only a change of state. This may be provided by a change in the environmental or programmatic conditions of a fixed object. What becomes clear is that the development of intellect as an artefact or project is conditioned on a dynamic field.

In the Mobot Lab, work is being undertaken with the objective of producing intelligent behaviours. In biology, no such objective directed this development. It is entirely emergent. It is possible that intellect could also emerge undirected in non-biological substrates; architecture may be among them.

These ideas should be of interest to the development of intelligent systems in architecture, one of which is the methodology used in subsumption architecture[26] whereby an incremental and iterative strategy yields useful behaviours at regular intervals. Once a behavioural module is perfected, it is exportable to another context. Higher level behaviours assume the existence, but not the authorship of more simple behaviours.

Some of the lowest level sensor-actuator couplings are already developed and in place in mechanical and security systems, and other, more sophisticated systems exist within most appliances. Standards are being developed to allow these devices to intercommunicate.[27] Fibre optic networks and active materials, as noted above, could supply the architectural 'body' with a measure of self-awareness and reactivity. There would be no need to integrate all systems into a unified network, but only to establish communication between them as the need arises. This sets a context in which higher levels behaviours can be developed. The fact that useful behaviours result from each layer of integration

provides a motive for an increase in sophistication. An ideology of utility and the entrepreneurial imperative in contemporary economics guarantees this kind of development.

It has been argued previously that a comprehensive biological model for architecture may develop out of research into sensing, active control systems and interactive materials that has been under development in the aerospace and defence industries during the last decade.[28] It seems probable that, as these control schemes increase in sophistication and complexity, we may experience some forms of emergent phenomena within the field. As with all non-linear dynamics, we cannot predict with any precision the scale or scales at which they may occur, or the forms that they may take.

As a discipline, architecture is oblivious to these possibilities and so may be unable to recognise them as they happen. As there may be no direct formal implications, many architects will not be interested and need not concern themselves. However, given some probability that intellect will arise, there may be those who would attempt to engage it and to take a hand in its development. In this case, the locus of design shifts away from form to concentrate on the behaviours and the interface required for intelligent and interactive environments.[29]

At another point in *Erehwon*,[30] Butler characterises technology as something independent, on its own developmental trajectory; one with the possibility of overtaking and surpassing human development. One need not attempt to choose between these two interpretations. It may be that we are in a feedback loop with the products of our culture. We experience them within a kind of perceptual Doppler-effect. They develop and go out as extensions of our selves and return to us, subtly shifted, as an 'Other'.

The research cited above has led Brooks to conclude that thought and consciousness are emergent epiphenomena of the process of being in the world. So to those who wish to ask: 'For what purpose would architecture develop thought or even consciousness?', one may reply: 'For what purpose did humans?'.

Notes

1 Samuel Butler, Erehwon, *The Book of the Machines*, chp 25, first published, 1872.
2 Brown, 'Materials Get Smarter', *Aerospace America*, pp30-36, March 1990.
3 RM Measures, 'Smart Structures with Nerves of Glass', *Progress in Aerospace Science*, vol 26, pp289-351, Pergamon Press, 1989.
4 Ibid.
5 Robinson, 'Smart Structures', *Civil Engineering*, Nov 1992.
6 Huston et al, 'Installation and Preliminary Results from Fibre Optic Sensors Embedded in a Concrete Building', *Proceedings of the 1st European Conference on Smart Structures and Materials*, Glasgow, SPIE, vol 1777, 1992.
7 Intelligent structures from Vermont include a railway bridge, dam, and five-storey building, *Optical Engineering Reports*, November 1994, available at: http://www.spie.org/web/oer/november/smart_structures.html.
8 Mendez, Morse and Mendez, 'Applications of Embedded Optical Fiber Sensors in Reinforced Concrete Buildings and Structures', *Fiber Optic Smart Skins and Structures II*, SPIE, vol 1170, 1989.
9 Wright and Lloyd, 'Monitoring the Performance of Real Building Structures', *Proceedings of the 1st European Conference on Smart Structures and Materials*, Glasgow, SPIE, vol 1777, 1992.
10 Stover, 'Radar on a Chip: 101 Uses in Your Life', *Popular Science*, vol 246, no 3, March 1995.
11 Carlson, 'The New Backyard Seismology', *Scientific American*, vol 274, no 4, April, 1996.
12 For an overview, *see* Rogers, 'Intelligent Materials', *Scientific American*, vol 273, no 3, Sept 1995.
13 Wada, Fanson and Crawley, 'Adaptive Structures', *Mechanical Engineering*, Nov 1990.
14 Housner et al, 'Recent Developments in Active Structural Control Research in the USA', *Proceedings of the 1st European Conference on Smart Structures and Materials*, Glasgow, SPIE, vol 1777, 1992.
15 Webster and Vaicaitis, 'Application of Tuned Mass Dampers to Control Vibrations of Composite Floor Systems', *Engineering Journal*, American Institute of Steel Construction, Q3 1992.
16 Spillman, 'The Evolution of Smart Structures/Materials', *Proceedings of the 1st European Conference on Smart Structures and Materials*, Glasgow, SPIE, vol 1777, 1992.
17 *See* http://www.itptsoa.nyu.edu/~review/current/focus2/open00.html and: http://www.ubiq.com/hypertext/weiser/UbiHome.html.
18 Gordon Friedlander, 'Smart Structures', *Mechanical Engineering*, October 1988.
19 Rodney Brooks, 'Achieving Artificial Intelligence Through Building Robots', *AI Memo* 899, MIT Artificial Intelligence Laboratory, May 1986.
20 I am avoiding a digression on architectural theory and the state of the academy, etc. I hope that my restraint is appreciated.
21 But not for too long, Brooks has founded the 'COG Shop' where platforms for the development of human-level cognition are under construction. *See* http://www.ai.mit.edu/projects/cog.
22 Brooks and Stein, 'Building Brains for Bodies', *AI Memo* 1439, MIT Artificial Intelligence Laboratory, August 1993.
23 Rodney Brooks, 'A Robust Layered Control System for a Mobile Robot', *AI Memo* 864, MIT Artificial Intelligence Laboratory, Sept 1985.
24 Pattie Maes and Rodney Brooks, *Learning to Coordinate Behaviors*, AAAI-90, Boston Ma, 1990.
25 Rodney Brooks, *Intelligence Without Reason*, AI Memo 1293, MIT Artificial Intelligence Laboratory, April 1991.
26 Ibid.
27 Stauffer, 'The Smart House System: A Technical Overview', *Computer Applications Journal*, no 31, Feb 1993.
28 Kaplan and Krueger, 'Artificial Life – Artificial Personality', *Oz 15*, Kansas State University School of Architecture, 1993.
29 Krueger, *Futur. Visionary Architecture and the Concept of the Future*, Marc Mer, Thos Feuerstein, Klaus Strickner, Triton Press, Vienna, 1994.
30 Butler, op cit, chps 23-25.

NEIL DENARI

INTERRUPTED PROJECTIONS, ANOTHER GLOBAL SURFACE

Territorial Recodings on the Worldsheet
Sited just above the Nogizaka Subway Station in Tokyo, Gallery MA is a ten year old space devoted to exhibiting architecture. This project by Cor-Tex Architecture will be inserted into the third floor of a six-storey building. On this level, half of the ground floor footprint stops to provide a courtyard bounded by concrete walls and the buildings beyond. A glass membrane divides the interior space from the courtyard and allows total visual invasion into the inserted project. The space is approximately 6.5 x 11 metres in plan and 2.45 metres in section. With a critical nod to early Baudrillard, the project is based on the following premise:

• The system or matrix of objects constitutes the material production of the world. In theory, objects have a use value or an instrumental nature, and are developed out of various existing or potential needs/desires of culture. Despite the utilitarian value of most objects, the possibility exists for any object to signify a status of itself or its user. The exchange value of an object is determined in the market system of all related objects. Here, the object is a commodity. What follows from this is the symbolic or signform value of the object where performance, need, or utility fall away in the face of another, more superficial iconography of value such as the image or the logo.

• Mass production of consumer objects is deployed producing corporate wealth and identity. The logic of capitalism is primarily a cultural logic. Product and company identity, usually manifest through advertising and graphic design, operate as a type of saturated code whereby the logo appears over and over again in all corners of the world.

• The signform overtakes/occludes the object as referent. The stretchy, 'logo-ised' FABRIC is invented – worldsheet. The logo or identifying symbol merely becomes a sign, or further, a code in the move from an object-based to a graphic-based culture. Like DNA or computer codes, the graphic sign codes may be mapped out and programmed to carry out certain tasks or performances. In the case of the graphic, the task may be that of *seduction,* or of infinite reproduction. It is possible, then, to imagine how the fluid plasmas of economics, communications, entertainment, etc collapse onto a single homogeneous worldskin. The code for printing is the CMYK strip. It is the code that comes before the logo. The code for video projection is the trio of RGB lenses. They together conspire to make the images readable.

• This produces 'ANOTHER GLOBAL SURFACE' of practically homogeneous signforms. (NB, the IBM rain forest commercial where the guide goes on-line to get a map to locate the lost safari.) Through technology, the concept of the local site or real ground is changed. Digital technology is especially indifferent to location (electricity can be everywhere a battery can go!) The world in terms of technology is then more like a map than a real sphere. Perhaps it could even be called a graph where information such as GNP is more important than how many square miles of land a country or city has.

• MAP comes from the Latin word for 'sheet'. Its origins are not in information, but in the geometry of the FLAT SURFACE. As a 2D plane, the sheet must be bent in order to architecturally spatialise a phenomenon. Its flatness is overcome by the powerful ability of architecture to momentarily intensify the graphic surface of seduction.

• GOODE'S INTERRUPTED HOMOLOSINE PROJECTION depicts the world in 2D in a series of sheared ellipses. This projection system is a combination of the Sinusoidal and Mollweide grids. These grids are interrupted and combined so that land masses can be projected with a minimum of shape distortion by positioning each section on a separate central meridian.

• ERASE geographic information on the interrupted projection. We are left with a *silhouette du monde* (outline of the world). Fill in with logos and text for a realigned world. Projections of all kinds proliferate, criss-crossing and interrupting, flowing on and cancelling out.

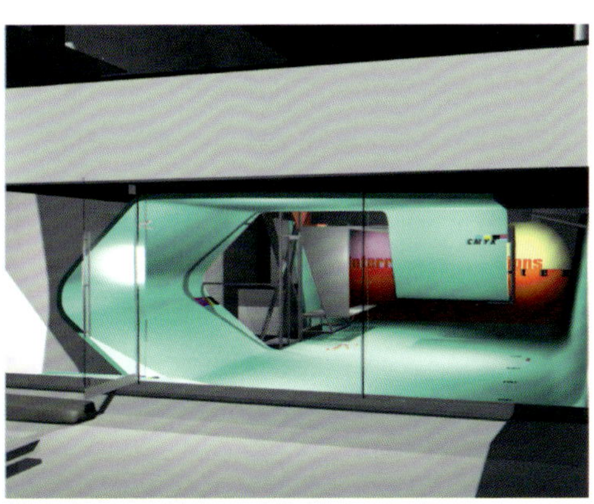

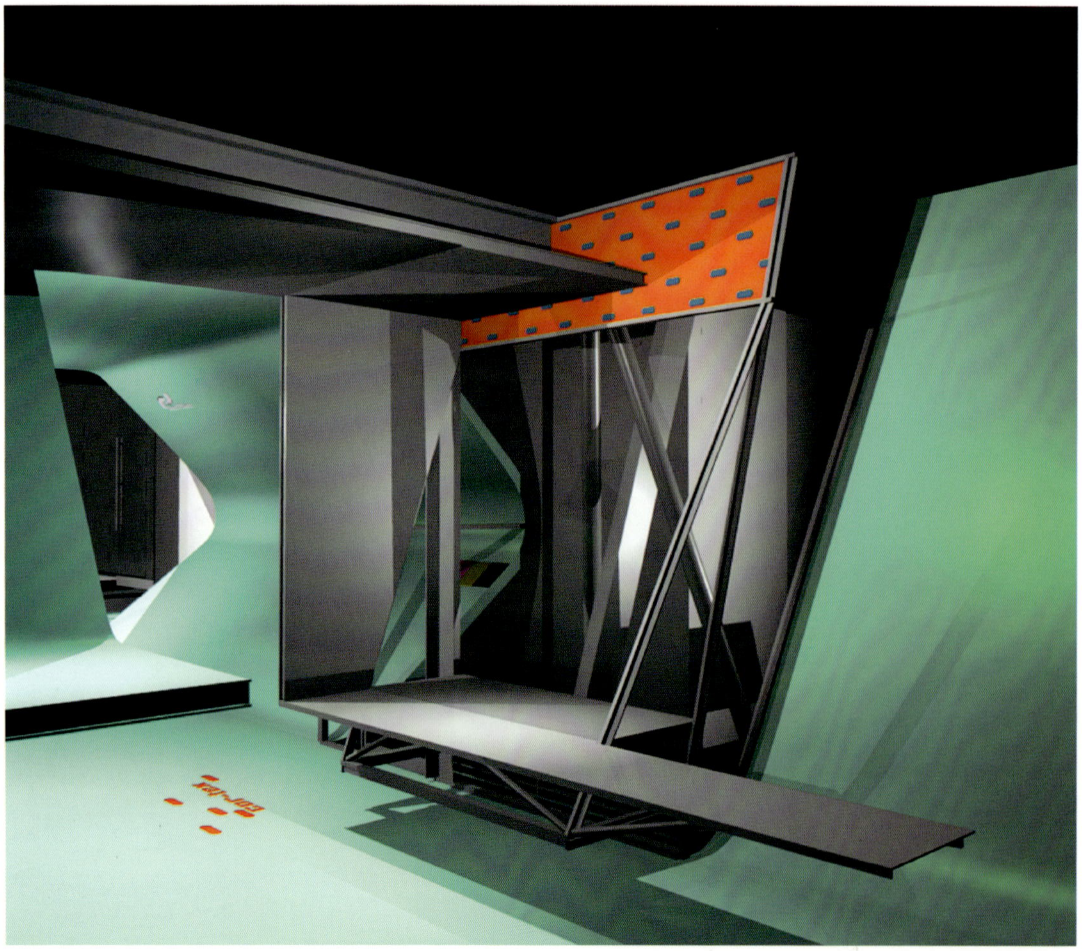

Design Studio, 1993

Originally commissioned in 1990 by a new subdivision of Steelcase, this project is the result of five schemes developed over a three year period. The company named Details asked for a 'wall' which would divide a large (1,858 square metres) loft space in Soho, downtown New York into two distinct spaces, each of which would have a different but related function. One space is defined as clerical, the other as a design studio.

The function of the wall, beyond its own properties of bisection, serves as storage for books and prototypes; one end houses a work table underneath the fibreglass skin.

The project operates as an information cypher or vapour trail which passes through the space becoming reified in form within the room itself. The room, however, is considered to be insignificant and serves only to cut the information vapour which is wafting through the entire Euclidean matrix of Manhattan. The wall, therefore, is not site driven and accommodates entry by merely making functional cuts into the white skin.

Structurally, the moulded, curving skin supports itself. It is made in 10.2-centimetres wide sections which bolt together. It sits on top of a welded and bolted aluminium structural tube frame which supports the floor and table.

nyc:SO-HO

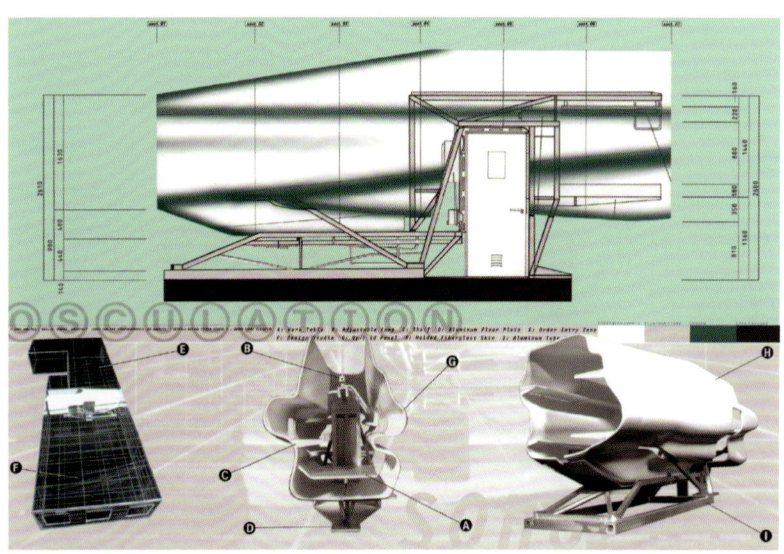

Massey Residence (Schnitt-Haus)
This house is for a young graphic designer in Los Angeles. The house is located on a typical LA site: 15.24 x 45.7 metres, proportionally a triple square. It is the client's wish to explore the basic conditions of the North American Suburban Subdivision through a typical flat site and a typical programme of three bedrooms and two bathrooms. However, the house itself, though accommodating these ordinary factors, promises to be extraordinary.

Like many smaller multi-unit apartment buildings in Los Angeles, this house has one level below ground and two above, thus disguising its size. Essentially, the house sits in an excavation with the driveway sloping down to -2.6 metres. The experience and concept of the house is developed from the SECTION CUT. The front and rear elevations show the roof skin and the basic extruded form of the overall volume. Inside, the circulation space revolves around a stair which connects seven different levels, each one shifted in height to create half levels and splintered views of adjacent spaces.

So, the living experience exposes the tectonic and constructional aspects of the house and allows the inhabitant to be *in* the space being formed as well as being able to *see* the shearing effect caused by the stepped floor plates. Perhaps this is like looking simultaneously at a sectional view (drawing or image) and a perspective view of a building: *the section is external and analytical, whereas the perspective is internal and experiential.*

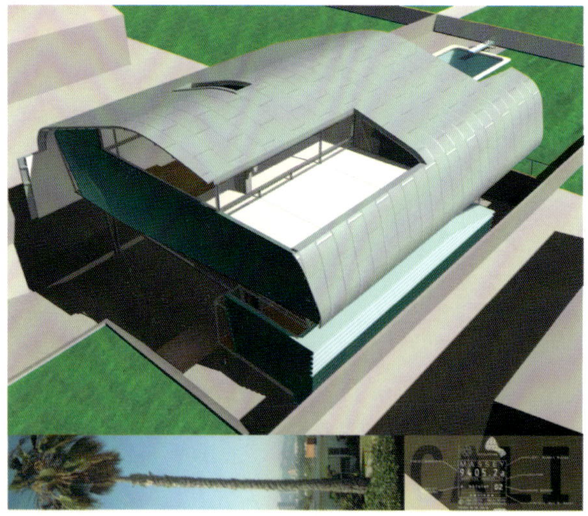

Central Glass Competition: Museum of the 20th Century, 1993

The 20th century is summarised in this project by the twin phenomena of flight and quantum physics. Since 1901, humans have been liberated from the ground by aircraft, leaving behind the weight and monumentality of the 19th century. Lifting off into the sky, we poetically dwell in the clouds. But since 1945, with the advent of nuclear weaponry, the politics of science and technology have created an ominous sense of liberation, wholly different from that of flight. So, as the century closes, we again, albeit more humble and wise, return to the ground to study the effects of our own progress.

The project symbolically refers to these phenomena by placing in the ground a gridded network of circulation/simulation spaces which link ten cloud-shaped spaces. The (formal) dialectic between the systems reveals the (apparent) conflict between the Newtonian world of the ground and the non-Euclidean quantum world. At the end, the building for the final decade of this century 1990-99 emerges from the ground only to be connected again to a raised artificial ground-plane which symbolises our need to study NATURE in a new way.

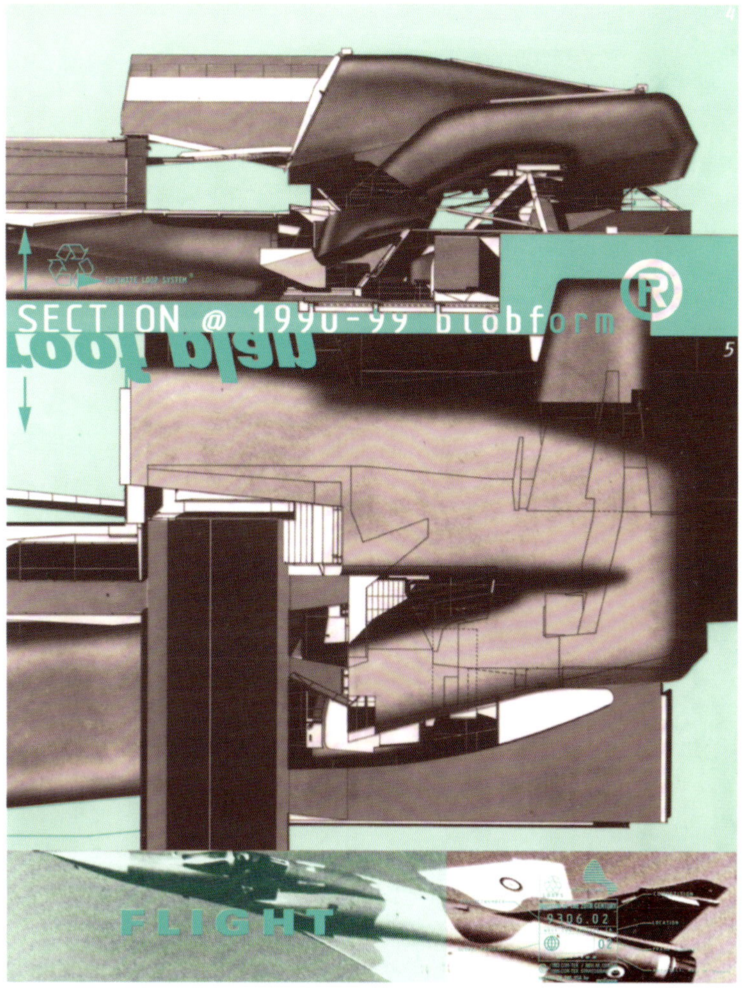

BEN NICHOLSON

WAR AND PEACEFARE AT THE LOAF HOUSE

An American nuclear family, the Loafers, has constructed a three-bedroom home within the city limits of Chicago. It is designed for a standard, homely interpretation of everyday activities, but is a place where the uncanny foibles of human nature have plenty of room to move. The rooms are configured to permit the many components of domestic life to drift across each others' paths with impunity. The parts are encouraged to form a spatial collage between the empirical and propositional aspects of home life.

The Loaf House exists in a number of forms, each a slightly different version of the same, and each requiring a different discipline to make the concept of homeliness complete. A series of drawings and collages work as multi-layered maps and, like all maps, suggest ways to locate the spaces in the house. The mahogany model functions as the palimpsest for the Loaf House, yet is restrained from committing to the actualities of the programme. The text 'The Loaf Notes' is a sequence of vignettes and propositions that form an apparition of life for the inhabitants. These three aspects of the Loaf House are then consummated in the virtual space of the computer, giving rise to a minutely described and fully programmed home, detailed to include everything from its overall structure to the form of the doorknobs.

In the context of computer design, the fiscal limits of actual construction have evaporated in the face of a raw determination to conceive a place that responds more accurately to the complexities of domestic intrigue. The computer allows the Loafers to wander at will in a place that is well beyond the pocket book of the average family. The Loaf House, as CD-ROM or on the Internet, could become a fully animated place for the domestic traveller to test life (without having to foot the bills) in a place that comes face to face with the modern daylight nightmare of irresolvable complexity and intrigue – laced with liberal doses of the ordinary.

The design has been undertaken by a team of over 30 people, working in relays of between two and eight, over a period of five years at the Illinois Institute of Technology. At each stage of its development, the Loaf House represents a discrete entity, be it in drawing, modelling, animation or construction. The intricate process of programming and three-dimensional computer design has created a very tempting apparition.

Were it to be built, the multi-storeyed house would take on the full spectrum of architectural method – of which the animated realm would then be its shadow. Every step of the design has been done to serve the worldly desire of construction and bodily intervention, where the virtual becomes actual, and where the Loafer comes to the giddy realisation that life itself is more potent than virtuality. Yet, as the poets have always told us, unless the virtual is experienced, the proposition of the actual might just pass by unnoticed.

OPPOSITE: Loaf House, upper plan, 1996; FROM ABOVE: Chocolate bar, for mold and smell; Bread tag, for plan-shape and iconography, 1989: B-52 wheel well flap for technique and door, 1995

THE LOAF NOTES (EXCERPTED)

Addiction

What is so reassuring about the artistic temperament is that when the artist does not work, extraordinary melancholia sets in – which can be remedied by working again. The craving and ranting of the addicted draughtsman is reduced by the drug of drawing. Is addiction necessarily bad? Cigarettes or drawing both take you away from what you ought to love, to the same degree.

Animals

Should a house have insect screens on the windows? Differentiate between butterflies and mosquitoes. Is the discomfort to the eye, in seeing the world through a wire screen, greater or lesser than the discomfort to the ear caused by the noise of buzzing flies bumping into light bulbs? See Gardens.

Architecture

Architecture stretches the faculties in every

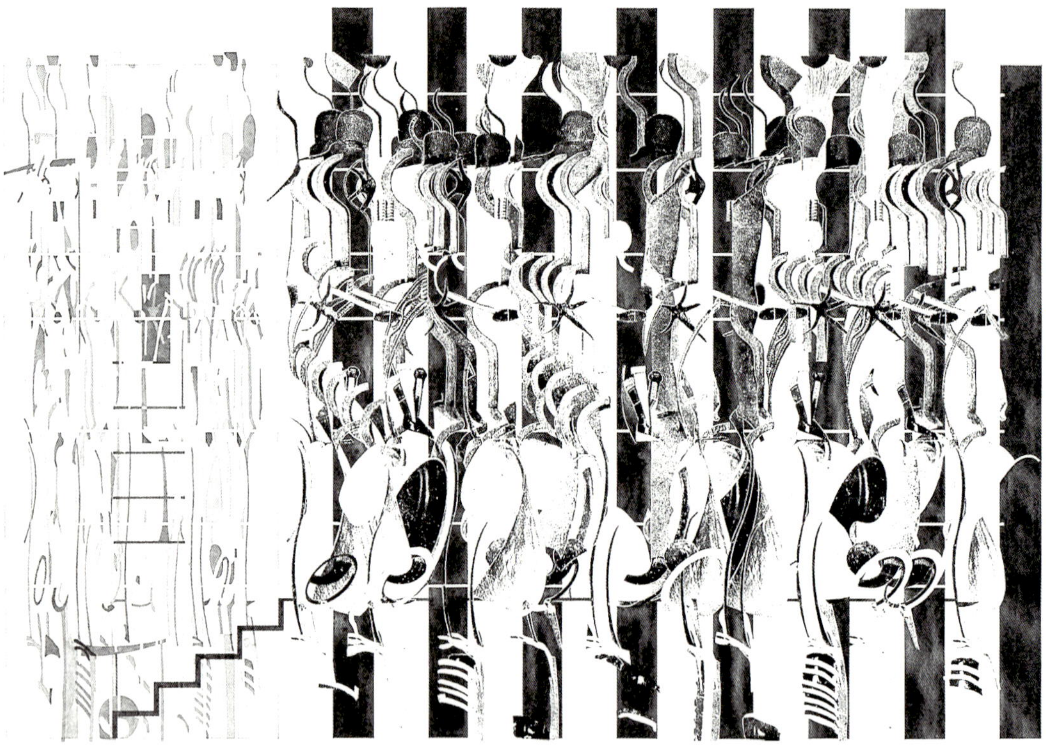

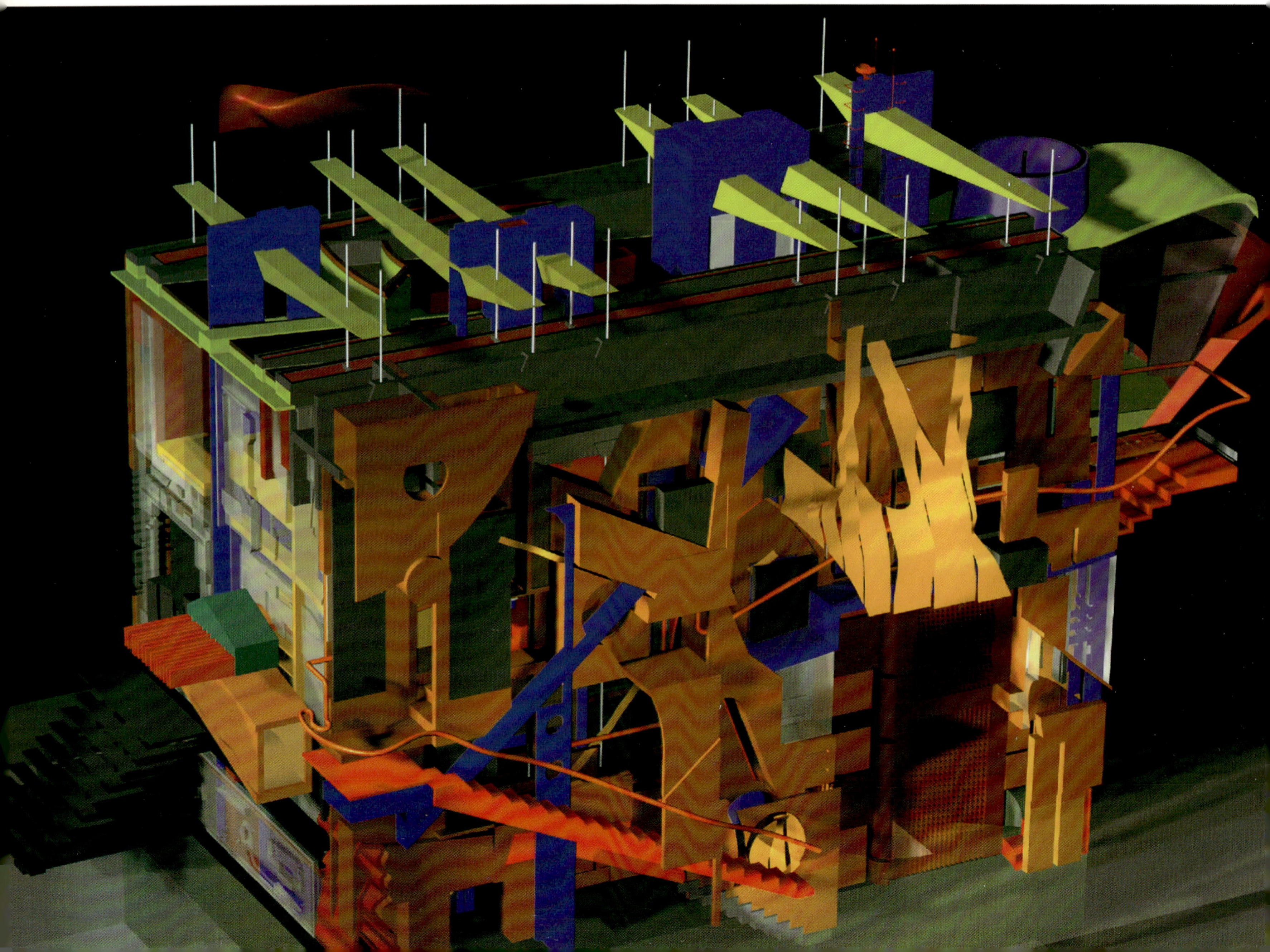

direction. It could be large as a Parthenon or as small as a garden shed, for architecture comes to any maker who is willing to go to the wall to make ideas fully blown. The great works are those that employ the emotive and fiscal reserves of a nation: the Space Shuttle might have laid claim to this definition of architecture, but it missed whole parts of the cultural spectrum – the scratchy metallic beast was just too useful to be any good for the Spirit of Mankind.

Beach Flotsam

On the beach I picked up a white rocket cone made of plastic, measuring 2 centimetres across its head. It fits perfectly on the end of my finger. It has lived in my pocket for quite a while, now being the inverted receptacle that my finger tip invariably seems to find. This morning I was walking around the kitchen, trying to throw it out, to part with it by slipping it into the recycling bin. But the object had served its apprenticeship in my pocket and became part of me; it received a stay of execution and instead entered my collection of plastic bits.

Birds

Pirates have parrots on their shoulders and scholars like to keep a perched bird nearby their desk. The antics of birds keep the workaholic sober: they bite, shit on your books and squawk at random. They prick hubris and make the only intelligible conversation when concentration is called for. When not nibbling the pirate-scholar's ear, the favourite perch of an imprisoned bird is to sit on the outside of its cage. Yet cages provide safe refuge from domesticated cats: cats turn cages from prisons into havens, they confuse what is considered inside and outside.

Breezeway

A wind catcher, made to know the shape and hardness of air. Running passages of air take away smells, moisture and excess heat or cold. Winds blow predictably and those of Chicago are subject to the Lake Effect: easterly to the lake in morning and westerly to the hinterland in the afternoon. 'Air can be funnelled into a jet or broken down and diffused' [Alberti, I.3].

Cabins

When we retire to rest, our bodies hardly move; we occupy as small a space as our species is able to. What size of room is right for our still and shared bodies? Is a bed a room within a room, much like the curtained four-poster bed used to be? See the cabins in the U-boat at Chicago's Museum of Science and Industry.

Curtains

Curtains fill the emptiness of the night window, and are spread across with a map of expectation. The morning after, they fold into the window's edge, presenting a semiliterate curvaceous blur of the night's openness, and make a perfect home for children to secret themselves.

Defeat in War and Peace

Saint-Exupéry tells how an army, close to defeat, becomes obsessed with the nurturing of simple tasks, such as the changing of a wheel, or the polishing of a gun stock. Contemporary suburbanites, at the brink of their follies, do the same; a whole afternoon is spent trolling around the malls, in search of the perfect T-shirt, and when found, the search continues to locate the same shirt, but at a lower price. This trivial human activity may well be our saviour, the hunt has become more valuable than the quarry and it indicates a weaning away from materialistic culture. If revolution is to happen in the first world, it will be characterised by consuman beings suddenly being no longer interested in shopping, and there will little anybody could do about it. (Imagine being forced to shop at gun point, in order to make the system work!)

Electrical Cords

Plugging extension cords into themselves is odd: apparently it is not good for an electric cord to be subjected to this; perhaps the residual electricity accelerates around the loop formed by the incestuous plugging.

Faults

'Faults are due either to intellect and sense, such as judgement and selection, or to the hand, such as committed to the craftsman. Errors and faults of intellect and judgement . . . are less easy to rectify than the rest' [Alberti, IX.8]. A fault is a capital moment: it makes apparent the need for change. A fault is easy to see and, even if it is an act of carelessness, it is always potent.

Flag Pole

A place to put things for public visibility: a flag pole is a vertical clothes line.

Garden

Tending plants (and animals) provides a direct link with the humility and force of the natural world. It is a form of measure that sets in context the political discombobulations of daily life. Bee keeping permits the eating of the hinterland by way of pollen from flowers set in the most abrasive landscapes in the city. (The poppy was the first flower to bloom on the nature neutered battlefield of the Somme). See Animals.

Graffiti

Nearly every day there is new graffiti on the walls and billboards of the local subway stop. Dutifully, the City Transit Authority paints it out in the morning, preparing the fresh white surfaces to be resprayed the next night. The diurnal and nocturnal cat and mouse game is reminiscent of the ways of warfare conducted in Vietnam. Now would it not be interesting to play a different game with the graffiti artists? Everyday the CTA could make a photograph of the former night's activity on a particular billboard and then glue the photograph onto the billboard. Would the graffiti writer graffiti the graffiti? Is it enough for the CTA to laminate the work/cry of the graffiti maker between the layers of CTA paint? The result is that our subways are decorated with Ply-paint, a layer of CTA paint and then a layer of graffiti – *ad infinitum.*

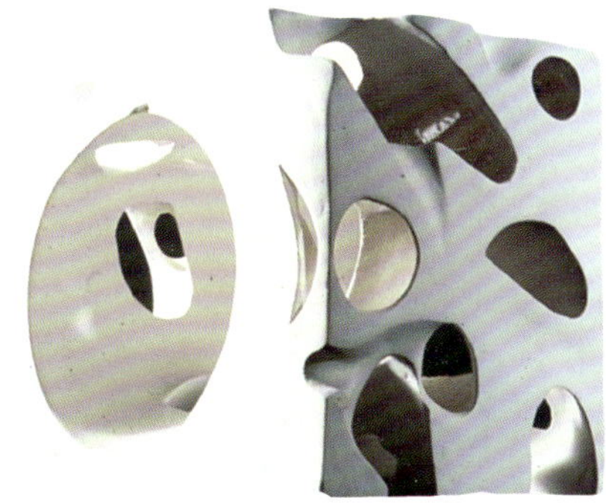

OPPOSITE FROM ABOVE: Kleptoman cell, north facade, 1989; Loaf House, view from north-east; FROM ABOVE: Fruit House, 1978; Pavement geometry #8, Laurentian Library, 1530-50s, possibly Michelangelo. Reconstruction, Minju Lee, J Kappraff, B Nicholson, B Summers 1986-96; Loaf House vacates itself, 1995

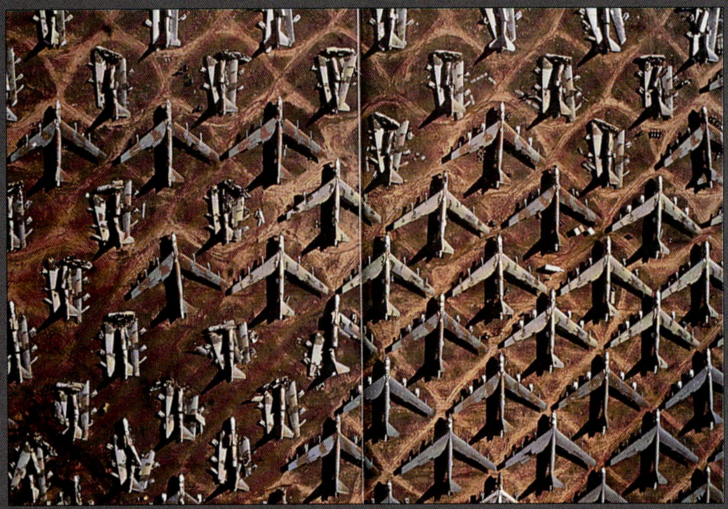
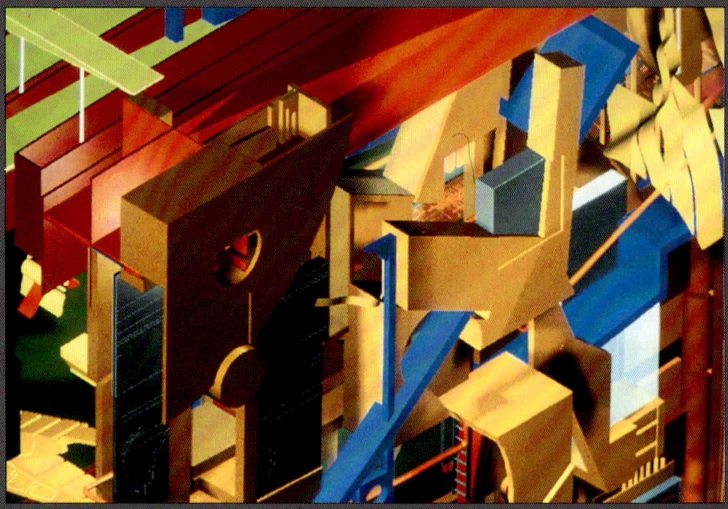

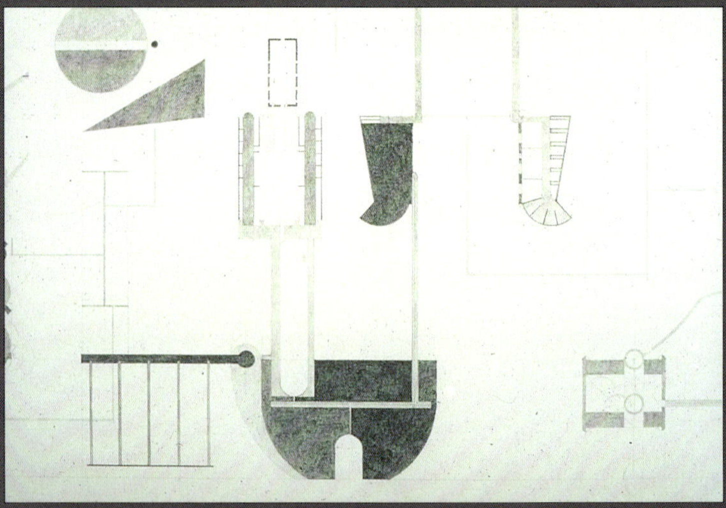

FROM ABOVE, L to R: B-52s at David Monthan AFB, Arizona; Loaf House – north wall, 1996; collage plan, 1991; Loaf House – non-specific section, 1991

Interiority
A burden of living in America, having lived in Second and Third World countries, is being condemned to use the last 5 per cent of bars of soap, tubes of toothpaste and bottles of shampoo, that regular citizens think of as finished. Packaging has a way of extending materialism, by offering up its hidden interior surface areas – to which much sticks. During the eking out of stubborn goods, the packaging can sometimes be discovered to be more useful than the packaged goods. This might induce a developed shopper to throw away the contents and get at what is useful.

Kitchen
Grind, cut, squeeze, liquefy, heat, cool, store, display.

Lost Voices
This morning I woke up, not knowing if I still had lost my voice. I did not know if I had a voice until I had spoken. What words do you utter to test if you have a voice, first thing in the morning? Surely not 'Testing, Testing, Testing'?

Magnets
Large magnets set behind sheet rock enable metal objects to adhere to walls without hooks. Set a grid of 12 magnets into a wall.

Messages
On the outside of a Hallmark Christmas card are the words 'Printed on Recycled Paper, including minimum of 10% post consumer and 40% pre consumer fibre'. On the inside of the same card are the words, 'May we always remember that Christ is the reason for Christmas'.

Model Aircraft
Building model aircraft gives one access, through three dimensionality, to the substance of the subject. The task becomes a cenotaph to three-dimensional consideration. By allowing the hands to glue for hours, there is the chance to think about the same for hours too. Craft is a word used by makers to hide the fact that they have the opportunity for hands-on thinking.

Money
Some spend their lives as if money had changed hands.

Nomads
Whose address is worth writing down in ink in America?

Notebooks
Many pages of the notebook are done against the will, a reluctant few hours each day, but it accumulates up to something. The notebook drains the head of stubborn little things that, if not reported, change themselves into leather beaded nuts the size of grains of sand and imbed themselves under the surface of consciousness.

Pit
The house stands in a pit (basement): the entire basement is a pit – a saw pit.

Possessions
Possessed by possessions.

Quilts
The Amish tuck themselves up at night beneath a quilt pieced together with shards of cloth from their own backs. The coloured fragments assemble into an eight pointed star, out-stretched across the counterpane, stitched

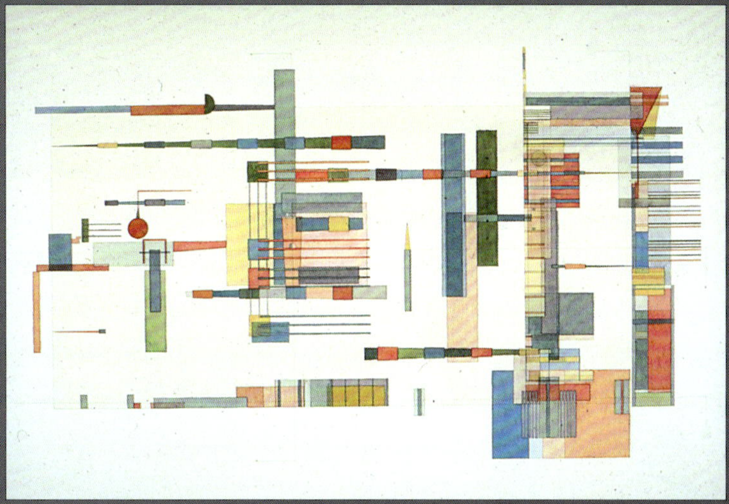

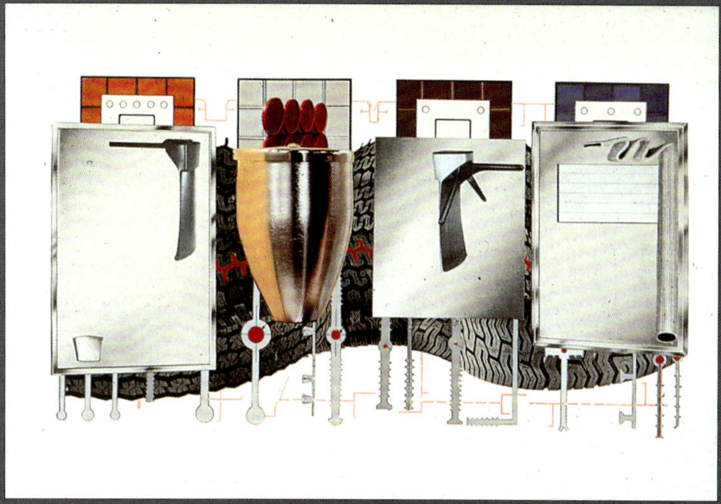

FROM ABOVE, L to R: Loaf House, south facade, 1994; B52, fragment of stabiliser, 1995; X-ray plan, 1992; Appliance House, collage, 1987

from edge to edge to form the Sign of Resurrection. As they sleep beneath the spread octagon, they restore the death of Christ and, upon waking, the quilt is folded and readied for another cycle of day and night.

Remodelling the House
Some homes are an endless site of construction. A family adjusts to the piles of intentions that block passages, and when the lumber evaporates in a frenzy of construction, it goes with a huge sigh of relief. The project of adjustment never finishes: it gets a temporary stay here and there, but then curiosity demands another alignment to life. The most stultifying houses are those that are finished – as if conditions had been found that permitted a state of perpetual satisfaction – but how we crave to be stultified.

Revolving Doors
A man and a woman come to a revolving door from opposite directions, he going into the subway and she going out to City Hall. Through the greenish wind-milled surfaces of glass, they make eye contact: they ask each other who will be the first to push the rail, to make time pass.

Sundial
A sundial can be set into a bedroom, guarding time on sunny days when there is nobody present, casting a temporal shadow that exists in a quiet vacuum.

Tape Decks and Record Players
Remember that recorded music comes from an electrical box and is not the same as music made from a hand-held instrument.

The Big Country
If you wade across the Rio Grande to Mexico, it is possible to hurl all the rocks you wish at America – and hit it every time.

Tub and Tubroom
One of the two worthwhile legacies of the Yuppie movement (the other being the awareness of good food). A tub that is in the sun: bathing should never be done in the dark during daylight hours. Tubs need access to outside air and a terrace: sunshine for the naked body to bathe in, and remember that people using hot saunas are always rolling in the snow! The combination of steaming hot water, flame light from candles and cold champagne is inimical.

Vault
A strong safe in which to keep valuable things like gold, money, papers, heirlooms etc. The vault is to be cast into the concrete foundations. The door leading to the vault is smaller than the vault itself, preventing the vault from being wholly stolen away. Pyramids.

Wrecking Ball
A house could be provided with its own means of end. A wrecking ball could be deliberately hung from the upper reaches of the building fabric, held back from its slow swing during its life, but always cocked to render the place into a blaze of poetic subsummation. The Swiss have grasped this concept for they build explosives into their mountain-pass bridges.

MARK TITMAN

STRETCH CITY

As we focus on more specific,minute and personal points, issues arise which are so broad in their impact that they can only be sited in the most universal contexts. Outside any one discipline, the most private, and non-visible scales have become part of the largest peripheral concerns – individual point and collective periphery are stretching to become one continuum.

The Context

Now that most people of the West live in cities, and with the support systems of science, we are no longer natural creatures. However, as the man-made environment becomes increasingly complex, it becomes as closely allied to a natural, chaotic, transformative order as to the Victorian linear and mechanical world. The workings of a city become less visible as they become more efficient; today, *pace* Mies van der Rohe, less is both far less and far more than before. With the capacity to create smart materials and mechanisms less than one billionth of a millimetre in size, Van der Rohe would find that honesty to materials and programmes in our cities can only be interpreted if specifically expressed. City life now requires the architect to tell stories of fantastic truth to materials, and employ theatrical exaggeration to express the changing lives that increasingly go unseen. If we make no attempt to express the complex transformations and workings of our cities and buildings, we will soon be as unaware of the influences around us as primitive man was of chaotic nature. To transform and create an environment physically is to interpret and understand its workings. A city in which individuals can externalise their changing lifestyles as they require a change of scene enables a more stimulating environment to develop over time. Constructive reinvention of self and space is rejuvenating; without renewed environmental stimulation, individuals and cities age through the destructive process of entropy. In a roundabout way, the maintenance of a life or city involves both conditions of entropy and self-reinvention: an incremental exchange between decay and construction. Seemingly simple occurrences of natural life offer us a great deal. Usually the result of an accumulative effect of transformation, they offer much by revealing hidden complexities, but also by continually converting local species or environments, they allow for involvement in a complex process.

The Inhabitants

As we have become more aware of our selves and personal space, our ethical concerns have become more universal. In *Unfinished Animal,* Rozak explains how in the Western world, with less distraction from immediate danger or material need, postwar generations have a new awareness of personality and health that coincides with environmental issues. As our awareness of self and environmental health increases, so too does our awareness of environmental ill-health. Thus, our motivation to interpret and adapt our situations and environments increases. DIY, recycling and energy efficiency are all placebo remedies for just such efforts to transform the environment. However, as most of our environments are becoming increasingly difficult to interpret and individually transform, today's popular environmental efforts count for more than simple ecological self-preservation and sustainability; they are part of an evolving lifestyle in which individuals now want to have more direct involvement with the environment.

The Buildings

As popular demand and new legislation warrant healthier and more environmentally-aware products and buildings, we are, on the whole, only equipped to have a less negative influence on the environment. However, buildings that make use of all local impacts and cumulative transformations that they themselves effect could eventually be designed to benefit inhabitants and surroundings in more positive ways. To a certain degree, buildings, like bodies, transform as they are lived in. The extent to which they do so, while also having an impact on the environment, should be augmented. A building's continued transformation relies on both durability and flexibility and, like a Chinese whisper, it requires a fabric which involves and encourages the 'player' to adopt, then adapt it. Continued adaptation is the means by which the game – and architecture – maintains itself; it is as complex, chaotic and transformative as it is linear, mechanical and constructed. Buildings designed for continuous multi-player transformations would, by the regular movements of habitation, allow the building/inhabitant relationship to have an active impact on surroundings and self. This suggests a transformative ecology of architecture where buildings are reliant on each other, their context and their inhabitants' changing lives for growth and maintenance.

The Structure

For buildings and inhabitants to transform their spaces to develop incrementally more than they consume, relies on the transformation of as many physical aspects of the surroundings as possible. A structure might create more energy than it uses by making exchanges of heat at surplus periods with, say, local species to begin a feedback loop with implications for food, insulation, materials and waste. In this case, environmental responsibility is the building's 'ability to respond' to as many of the known constituents of a locality as possible, not just sun and energy concerns, but also, for example, metals, waste, electro-magnetics, capillary pressure, moisture, air pollutants, wind, toxins, all species including micro-organisms, and visitors of any kind. This structure differs because it relies on life, and not abstract energy economics, to generate its own power, food, and extra space. It also differs from the mechanistic approach of saving devices because, as architecture, it relies on as many aspects of the inhabitants'

Vertical growth elevation of urban villa, with low zoo mass and high insect colonisation (fig 1); urban villa (fig 2)

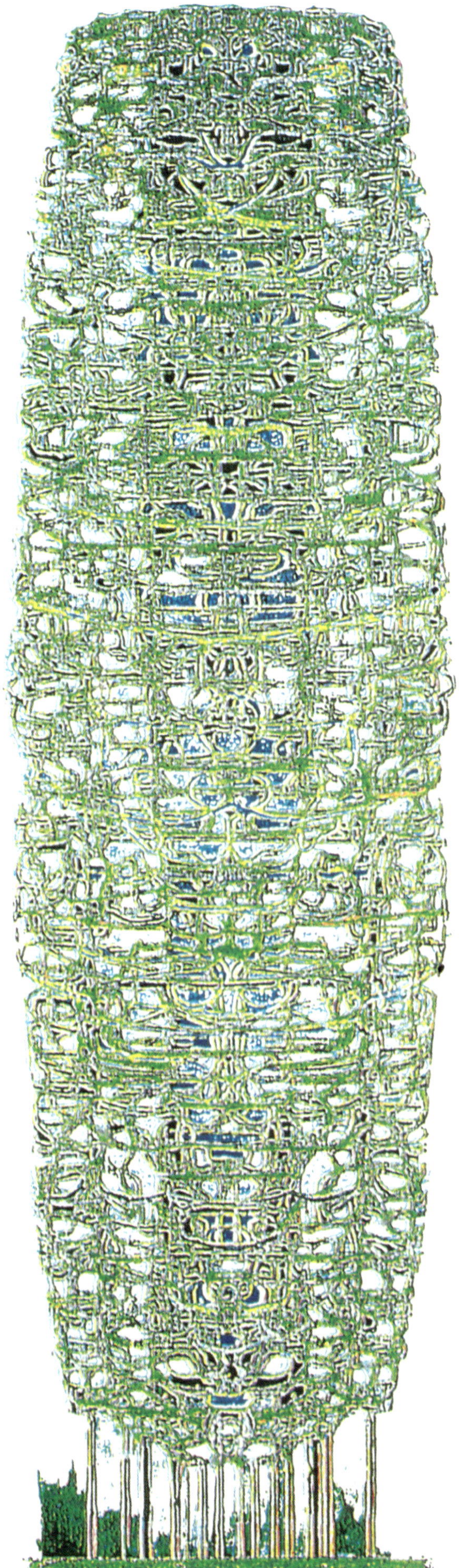

1

2

An outside room for ecologists (fig 3); cross-section through top floor studios, with 32 life forms and high zoo mass inhabitation (fig 4); horizontal growth elevation of urban villa, with high zoo mass (fig 5)

3

(including non-human) lives as possible. A growing building offers the fledgling discipline of evolutionary toxicology, a playground for alerting us to possible crossovers between ourselves, technology and nature. Humanity has been adapting the environment and transforming the path of evolution for a long time; ever since we began developing skills such as walking and tool-making. Yet, if we become too effective in our skills, we endanger our own life and that of our surroundings. Our strength now lies in our ability to create fantasy, future heritages, and to be adaptable. With growing structures, we see human and environmental evolution unfolding almost daily; thus, over time, we can adapt our behaviour and our transformations accordingly.

The Details

To grow transforming vernaculars for each plot's resources, and the multiple plays and changes being made by its inhabitants (whatever the species) requires an attractor. Details are needed to encourage the full attention and continued involvement of all inhabitants. Highly complex systems are too complex for any one individual to understand, yet possibly because of this, they fascinate and appear to be live or beautiful – consider the Chinese whisper, or a fire, or even two trillion crawling nanite machines reconfiguring in the sun. The presence of details that involve a building's players, by being meaningless enough to encourage urban appreciation and complex enough to fascinate the senses, can bring our attention into public space. Such interactions both calm and exhilarate and, unlike advertising, would not overload since there is no intellectual content. Thus, a building's detail might directly encourage environmental involvement. Details could include any of the following: cross-pollinisation; insect colonies; nanite coordination; vines; water walls; self-replicating adhesive, phosphorescent micro-organisms; toxin-converting species; soil conversion; chemically productive species; cohesive sound waves; hose cages *(fig 1)*; meniscus action *(fig 3)*; skin tissue and support trellising *(fig 1)*; water-flow static energy and gyroscopic energy *(figs 3 and 4)*, and DNA programmed formwork *(fig 2)*. In short, the various species or materials that exist in an environment do so by reason of their different, but interactive,

4

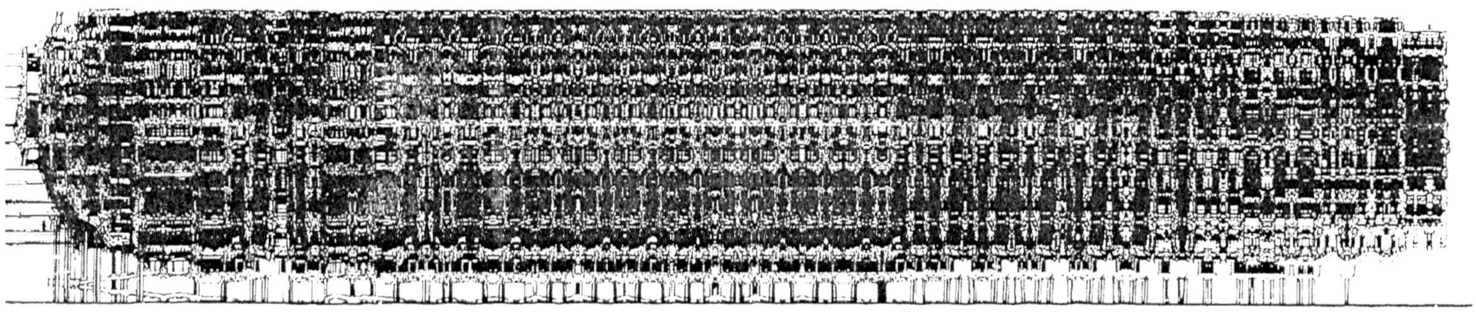

5

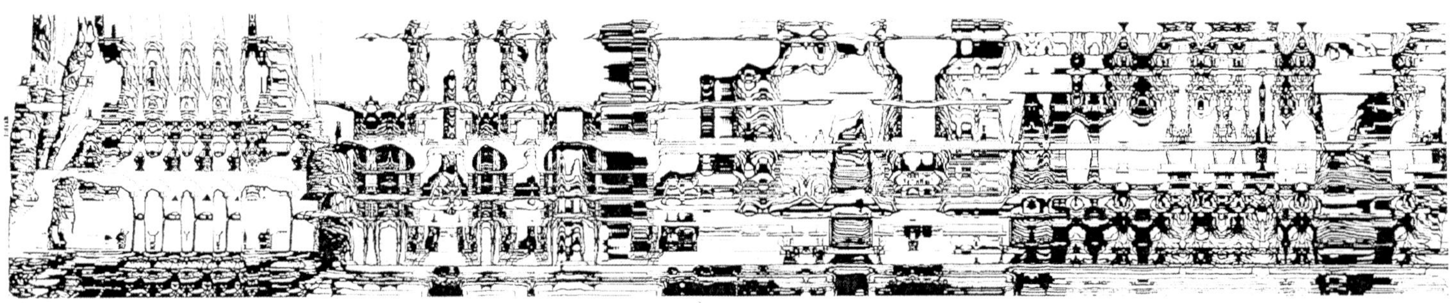

attributes: in this combination of construction and decay lies the scope for positive growth.

The Architects

Today, as people become more informed about environment and health, architects increasingly need to invest in the positive involvement of the inhabitants in their buildings. Also, the architect needs to have a more malleable concept of a building's longer-term roles in society and the environment. Building completion could become more like building birthing, followed by retainership care; the architect could offer a more extendable service whereby architecture itself becomes a service. To achieve ongoing perceived 'health' in groups of inhabitants, the architect will need broadly preventative design solutions specific to each group's changing conditions – from homeopathic bicamerality to traditional medicine, sympathetic or prosthetically transformed space. The degree to which we, the participants, are influenced is dictated by the extent to which we perceive and are able to make transformations in our space. Like the placebo effect, involvement itself is half the solution; the other half is the ability to participate actively in any transformation. It is standard practice to take out a patent on a design proposition that is not entirely feasible, making a calculated assumption that it will be in the near future. This being the case, truly innovative semi-fictional propositions can claim precedence over more feasible, practical ones. Designing with the future in mind offers much to the architect's design skills, as all design concerns a future not yet built. The architect's capacity to tell good stories can clarify public understanding of the transformations occurring now and in the future, and involve inhabitants in the process. As these transformations become less visible and more complex, the stories need to become either more complex (and then no longer stories but explanations) or more expressive and theatrical. Yet, as we discussed at the beginning of this article, the tools with which an architect works today are themselves of the order of fiction. Thus, who is to say that the most fantastical architectural solution is not, in fact, the most practical? Ultimately, it must be left open to the interpretation of the reader/player/inhabitant.

SIXTEEN* (makers)

BOARD GAMES

by Stephen Groâk

The work of Nick Callicott and Bob Sheil – Sixteen* (makers) – offers a distinctive model for architectural investigation and design in a modern environment in which the task of mastering good practice is increasingly baffling and fraught: today, architects have to draw upon an extraordinary repertory of materials and methods, often from industries outside construction 'proper', with a decreasing proportion of projects reaching fruition and practical result. The range of technologies involved is beyond the command of one person, even at the level of 'performance specification'. This expanding context creates perplexing problems, especially for the young architect: what does it now mean to 'master good practice'? Sixteen* (makers) offer a working method which accepts and relishes the maelstrom, by starting from the realities of making things.

Their work has a number of critical functions:

•each work is specific to its client and context (including the time available – invariably brief)
•focus on process, recognising that the architectural process is more unique than the product
•the process springs from the fundamental properties of the site, which it then seeks to reveal
•construction involves a form of *bricolage*, combining selections discovered – as it were – while combining the real site and its imaginary beach
•exploit craft (drawing, fabrication, connection etc) as an investigatory method – not simply as representation
•they combine and contrast materials from a spectrum of states of conversion, from their natural origins to refined man-made forms (is that the same as 'the raw and cooked'?)
•exhibits a machine-like aesthetic, displaying the real process of manufacture and implying components which move – a sense of accidental time
•spatial organisation is not treated in a informal, inexplicit manner – it emerges from the exploration of site, context and use.

Sixteen* (makers) have worked with various craftsmen and sculpture technicians, to develop their own manual skills, but more importantly to use this route to understanding material properties and their respective problems of connection. However, the work is not sculpture, although – as with any good architecture – it displays sculptural qualities. The emphasis remains on design for use and social exchange:

•kitchen/bathroom (basin stand and worktop)
•dining room (furniture, overhead lighting)
•urban street (craft display building)
•computer services bureau (furniture)
•machine workshop (workbench)
•shop front (sign and window box)
•exhibition spaces (display systems)
•suburban allotment (burying a metal 'tuning fork', archaeology in reverse?)
•Dartmoor – but at an existing concrete emplacement (cradle to support plant life)

Some years ago, there was a great interest in game theory and gaming simulation. In many respects, it drew upon a tradition of war games. Harvard Management School developed simulations to enable their students to rehearse complex situations in which there was no necessary winner or loser, simply the need to develop certain skills and recognitions of dynamic complexity. The board game *Diplomacy* is probably the most familiar version. The chess version (*Kriegspiel*) of war games is also known to a wide public: one of its features is that each player only knows their own moves, and whether their proposed move is legal, and when they have captured an (unknown) piece. Many such games display a quality which is fascinating in the context of the design process: some moves are made to discover what reaction they induce, not for their direct application.

The external works of Sixteen* (makers) enjoy this quality. The interventions in the site exist sometimes simply to change the site, not to change it into something specifically. An the consequential changes in the ways that people move around the site – ie redefine the relationship between people and environment – reveal choices, and needs (is this a useful term?) that might not otherwise be apparent.

It is this concern with people doing something on a site – and the exploration of how that can be magnified, intensified, modified by the patterns of assembly nearby, made more enjoyable or useful by providing some manufactured object(s) – which identifies their work unmistakeably as an architectural investigation. The artefacts themselves have an astonishing presence. Quirky, shifting slightly as if from one foot to another (but structurally stable, I hasten to add . . .), relishing the materials and the very different techniques required for their respective problems of cutting, shaping, joining, finishing, fixing in place, touching, viewing. Somehow, comfortably and quickly, they seem to have been lived in.

Sixteen* (makers) also demonstrate rather helpfully that design and construction can – but not inevitably – be research tools and methods, that they are not simply the means of recording the results of research already conducted in some other way. In this way I find the work very refreshing.

the creative act is manifest not solely within the author or work and is rarely the result of individual action alone.

The city is a palimpsest
Charles Abrams

intervention takes place in a way which seeks to test the relevance of working methods on a specific social site supporting an identifiable audience. In each of these experiments, they may be distinguishable as occupants engaged in routines of habit as well as contemplation.

In modern architecture, where the rationality of the structural frame and the building masses threaten to dominate, there is often an architectural vacuum in the left-over portions of the site. It would be good if instead of filling this vacuum with decorative gardens, the organic movement of people could be incorporated in the shaping of the site in order to create an intimate relationship between Man and Architecture.
Alvar Aalto

interaction, as a creative strategy, is a means by which even the most powerful of formal gestures is of little value unless it recognises some characteristic of the audience's need.

The spoken word, the tool held in the hand: regardless of why and how they developed, language and technology emerge as the two indispensable, learned sills that must have preceded any attempts by our ancestors to deliberately and wilfully keep track of the flow of events in the human environment, to reckon time, to set it all down in a logical order – to make a calendar.
Anthony Aveni

an invitation is formed by the presence of the unexplained intervention. This and the subsequent audience exploration offers the possibility of redefining public sites, setting a precident for actions contrary to existing patterns of use.

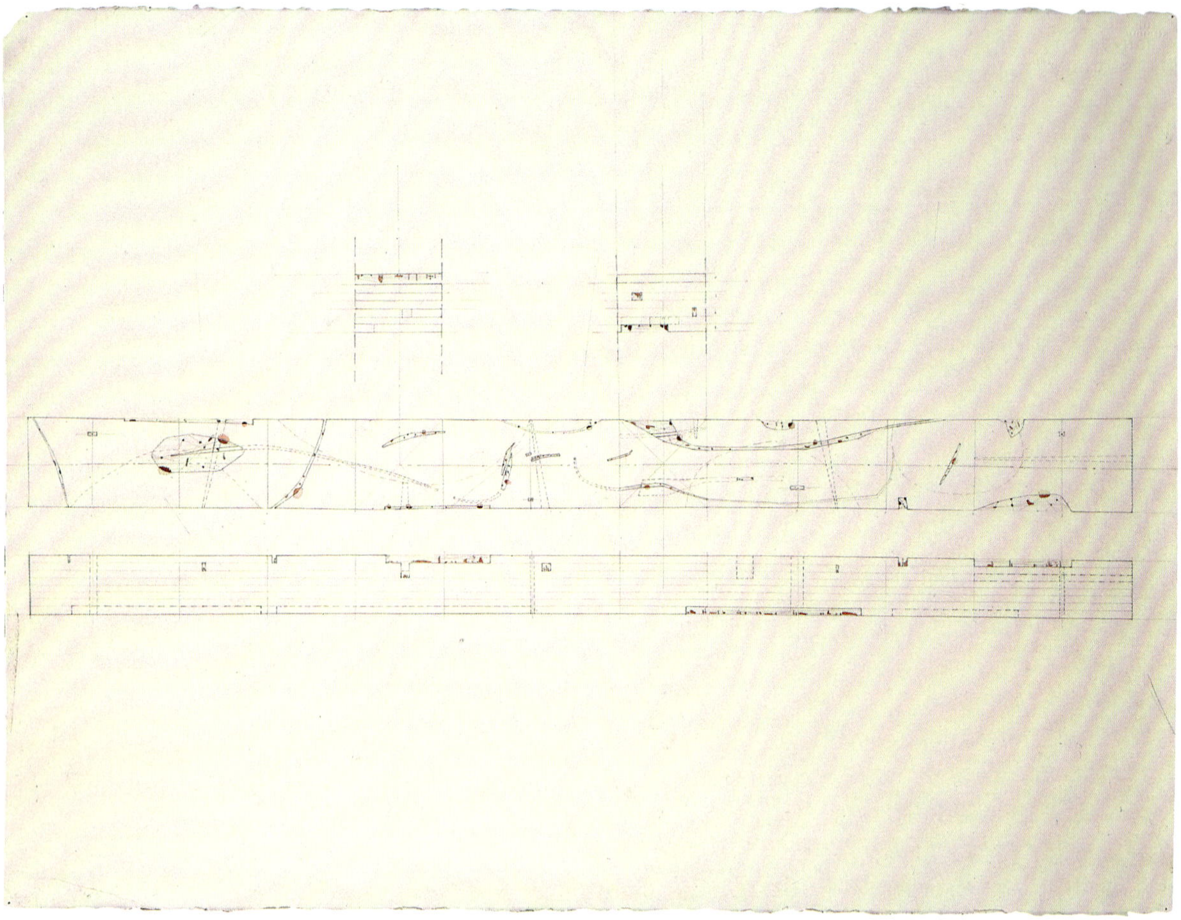

FROM ABOVE: Plan and elevation of 20-metre slab (to be built in gallery), pencil and watercolour, 1995; The City of Earth, *overhead view of installation, pencil and watercolour wash, 1996*

JOHN ANDREWS

NOVA MAPPAMUNDI, DRAWINGS AND DESIGNS

by Peter King

It would require imagination to appreciate, say, the poetry of the Meghaduta (the Cloud Messenger), by the fourth-century Sanskrit poet Kalidasa, in which a lover living in exile asks a cloud to carry his message of desperate longing to his beloved, and tells the cloud which route to take and what it will see on the way. A great part of Hindu religious practice consists of an appeal to the imagination, and in the Isa Upanishad *(verse 8) even God is described as a kavi, ie, a seer, a term that later came to mean a poet.*

KM Sen

These pen and ink drawings by John Andrews are types, prophetic similitudes (what else are architectural plans, sections, elevations and perspectives?) for an installation to be exhibited at the Meridian Gallery in Melbourne later this year. They perform an intermediary, 'intravisual',[1] glimpse or contemplation of a work on its way from what is commonly and lazily regarded as its idealised pre-embodied 'form-as-desiring' to its satiated embodied 'desire-as-form' or 'form-to-be-desired'. This essay is not a review of the installation as it will be, but a provisional set of takes and speculations on the impulses, imagery (both pictorial and constructed) and ethics presently concatenating into a discovering of Andrews' architectural and, in Denis Hollier's sense, 'anti-architectural' project.[2]

As it is usually configured (ie, unconfigured and undesigned), the Meridian Gallery exhibition area is a gabled, large, almost folksy barn (one could easily imagine Thomas Hardy's Wessex choruses gambolling in it). For the installation, Andrews will lower the height of the space by occluding the sturdy gabled area with a low ceiling plane. Lengthwise, up the central space, will be erected a cyclopean wall or building, or urban or landscape or 'world-idea' section (20 x 8 x 9 metres). On the three framing walls will be hung drawings.

This bald list of operations would imply that Andrews is constructing, in large miniature, a model of a Ludwig Hilberseimer crepuscular *Wolkenkratzer* (as proposed and illustrated in Hilberseimer's *Großstadt Architektur,* 1927)[3] in its arid 'urban-idea', flattened environment. Instead, Andrews' clouds (*Wolken*) scrape and scratch (*kratzen*) their formings (thinnings and bulkings) into the wall and float over it: they are caught and released as in a dimensioned weather map; their declensions and ascensions are accorded a Ruskinian *telos*, a Turneresque indwelling and irradiating 'Truth in Clouds.'

It is in this ever-forming body of work that Andrews introjects the *painterly* truth of Ruskin into the constructed *architectonic Treusein* (being true/loyal) valued by Loos; in the prose of his *Ins Leere gesprochen* 1897-1900 (Spoken into the void) and in the furniture-making praxis of his old friend Josef Veillich (where the ephemeral is lost yet lives 'in that which lasts').[4]

Similarly, ephemeral, necessarily true events and loci (for idiosyncratic Christian belief-structures – the Tower of Babel/Babylon, the Granaries of Joseph/the Pyramids, the Pillars of Hercules – are inscribed, again introjected and represented as ever-present living spaces in contiguity with living spaces that are represented then-present, true, constructed, or, as they were necessarily believed to have been constructed (to make the world cohere): Rome, Paris, London – as represented in the medieval world-maps, such as *The Hereford Map* (*c*1240). *Kavi* Andrews indites and spreads a new, critical, idiosyncratically true, comprehensive, cohesive, if not, immediately coherent, *mappamundi*. He orders his clouds.

The time of Andrews' drawings and installation is a Bergsonian *temps espace*, not a *temps durée*; it is, in a sense, a time in which personal and social events and epiphanies are captured and mobilised within an abiding metonymy that is constructed according to their powers of cathection and their motile, *moteur*-like aura. It is not only the time of a *mappamundi,* but it is also cognate with the slippages and swellings of events in Thomas Mann's *Der Zauberberg* (The Magic Mountain). In the novel, the convalescent cannot will recovery, and the time of convalescence dilates. Historical time is accordingly devalued, and any historical moment or project can be made operant, not so much recalled as it is presented, validated by others arguing about it, participating in it, in a methexis.

Cathexis (occupation as in a military operation) and methexis (Plato's 'participation') compose the primary behaviours and modes of Andrews' work; and both simultaneously discover and occlude the work's primal scene of itself as, in Lacanian terms, a morcellated body, for the parts of which there is no vicissitude of Lacanian 'fading', *aphanasis*. The drawings and installation offer a dialectic 'going the wrong way', towards the dilation of the *inform* of potentiality, rather than towards its reduction and dissolution.

Another German writer, Robert Musil, helps us grasp the concept of the motile 'world-idea' of the work. Ulrich, Musil's *Man Without Qualities*, reflects in his diary:

> [The Eternal Artist] loves creation as long as he is creating it, but his love turns away from the finished portions. For the artist must also love what is most hateful in order to shape it, but what he has already shaped, even if it is good, cools him off; it becomes so bereft of love that he hardly still understands himself in it, and the moments when his love returns to delight in what it has done are rare and unpredictable. And so one could also think: What lords over us loves what it creates; but this love approaches and withdraws from the finished part of creation in a long ebbing flow and a short returning swell. This idea fits the fact that souls and things of the world are like dead people who are sometimes reawakened for seconds.[5]

Device to turn the black dust of diamonds into gold, gold dust and gold leaf, pencil and ink, 1996

Andrews' achievement is an abiding awakening of architectural impulses; more importantly, pulses synaesthetically stretched and indited (the inditing scrivener is a lover or a concentration and trope of his desire) into constructing space. He produces a paradigm from the work's preconditions paralleling the ethical spaces of the world maps (his style,[6] an experience of two spaces in Mexico – a museum stocked with medical instruments abutting onto a square full of scriveners inditing in their timber booths). In this paradigm, there is no 'finished part of creation' but a monstrance of forms eructating in different scales and sites.

Unlike *The Hereford Map*, Andrews' corpus does not have a trapezium heaven for a frame (another trapezium, although rounded off somewhat, recurs within the map itself at a smaller scale as the island of Crete holding its labyrinth). However, the corpus holds its heaven (and limbo and hell and world) as immanent to itself: they, in some forms, inform themselves, inform it. Its registrations are metaphysical; a baroque corporeality not only slices through the abstracted modernist box, but also enacts, and provokes reveries on an architectural practice of affects, mobilised by that corporeality, its intricacies and plenitude. Andrews constructs a trope of Western architectural,unconscious inflecting and underscoring; inflected and underscored by, the conscious; architecture's Lacanian (fictional) Real – inchoate and invested; intense.

Intensity cannot be called high or low without re-establishing the scale of values and principles characteristic of moderation's mediocre reality. Be it exertion or inertia, intensity is the extreme of difference, in excess of the being that ontology takes for granted. Intensity is an excess, an absolute disruption which admits no regimen, region, regulation, direction, erection, insurrection, nor does it admit their simple contraries. Thus it wrecks what it makes known, burning the thought which thinks it and yet requiring this thought in the conflagration where transcendence and immanence are no longer anything but flamboyant, extinguished figures – reference points of writing which writing has always lost in advance. For writing excludes the limitless, continuous process just as much as it seems to include a nonmanifest fragmentation – which in its turn, however, presupposes a continuous surface upon which it would be inscribed, just as it presupposes the experience with which it breaks. Thus, writing continues by discontinuity; it is the lure of silence which, by its very absence, has already delivered us to the disastrous return:

> Intensity: the attractiveness in this name lies not only in its generally escaping conceptualisation, but also its way of coming apart in a plurality of names, denominations which dismiss the power that can be exerted as well as the intentionality that orients, and also sign and sense, and the space that unfolds and the time that expatiates. But along with all of this comes some confusion, for intensity's name seems to restore a sort of corporeal interiority – vital vibrancy – whereby the faded teachings of consciousness-unconsciousness are imprinted anew. Whence the necessity to say that only exteriority, in its absolute separation, its infinite disintensification, returns to intensity the disastrous attractiveness that keeps it from letting itself be translated into revelation – a surplus of knowledge, of belief – and turns it back into thought, but thought which exceeds itself and is no longer anything but the torment – the tortuousness – of this return.[7]

The drawings and design figure forth a surplus of invention and contiguity in which the flamboyant excess is prolonged in the perversely 'vitally vibrant' moment of its extinguishing. The closure into form (tropes, motifs and traits) enacted by the corpus is an hallucination, a fit. Andrews' *mappamundi* is a convulsion of the bases, the tectonic plates, of architectural representation into the presentation through a kind of surgical operation – the sharpness of those spears and the arcing of those cuts! – of an 'extra-existent'[8] (just as the unconscious is 'extra-existent') impossible object, a perilous quest, a hunt, a nomad architecture. As Deleuze and Guattari remark on the plateau 'Treatise on Nomadology – The War Machine':

> The relation between [the traits] is not that of form-matter but of motif-support, where the earth is no longer anything more than ground (*sol*), where there is no longer even any ground at all because the support is as mobile as the motif.[9]

The Hereford Map is organised around an optically emphatic descending line of spaces – Paradise, Babylon, Jerusalem, Rome, the Pillars of Hercules – all entrenched on their sites; Andrews' installation is mobilised around what he names 'cities' and 'shells' that are foci for haptic viewing, flashes and meanders spaced and spacing like the nomad's crafted jewels and weapons and their trajectories.[10]

It is no wonder that Bernard Palissy, author of a text on a shell-like fortress, cited by Bachelard as a great dreamer of shells, was a craftsman-nomad, potter, and enamellist.[11] Palissy also privileged the haptic – touching with the eye, and, in a sense, he sets some of the programme for Andrews' project: '[His] daydream expresses the function of inhabiting in terms of touch'.[12] Bachelard's naming of Palissy as a 'hero of subterranean life'[13] points to, or touches, another drive of the project; to penetrate below the body and canon of architecture, and to perturb it. In Andrews' work, the canon is treated in much the same way (note the synaesthesia) as Thomas Mann's Herr Ferge's pleura.

> But the local doesn't reach very far down, it only benumbs the surface flesh; you feel it when they lay you open, like a pinching and a squeezing. I lie there with my face covered, so I can't see anything: the assistant holds me on one side and the directress on the other. I feel myself being pinched and squeezed, that is the flesh they are laying back and pegging down. Then I hear the Hofrat say: 'Very good'; and then he begins, with a blunt instrument – it must be blunt, not to pierce through too soon – to go over the pleura and find the place where he can make an incision and let the gas in; and when he begins moving about over my pleura with his instrument – oh, Lord, oh, Lord! I felt like – I felt it was all up with me – it was something perfectly indescribable. The pleura, my friends, is not anything that should be felt of; it does not want to be felt of and it ought not to be. It is taboo. It is covered up with flesh and put away once and for all; nobody and nothing ought to come near it. [...] I fainted; I had three fainting-fits one after the other, a green, a brown, and a violet. And there was a stink – the shock went to my sense of smell and I got an awful stench of hydrogen sulphide,

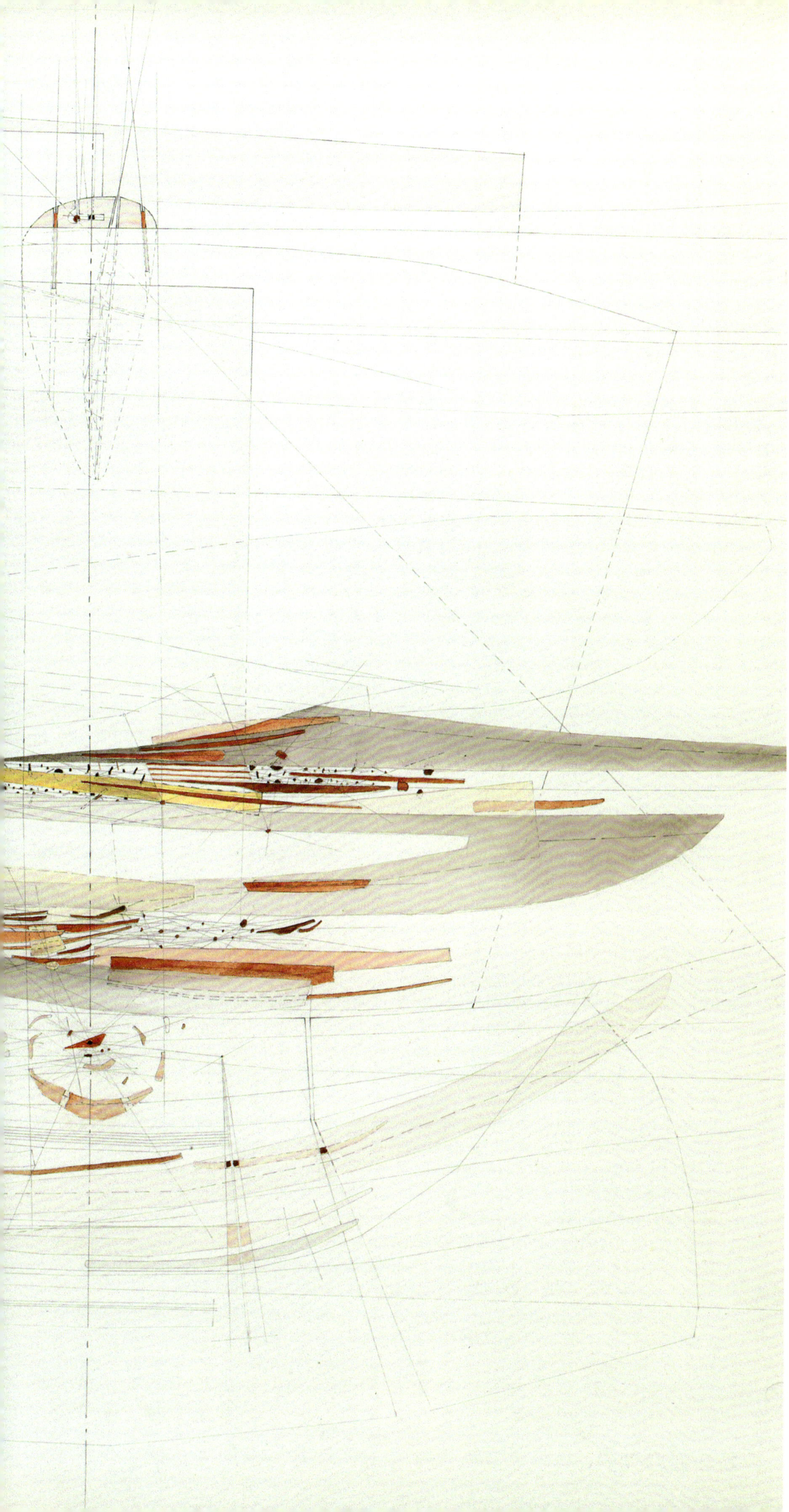

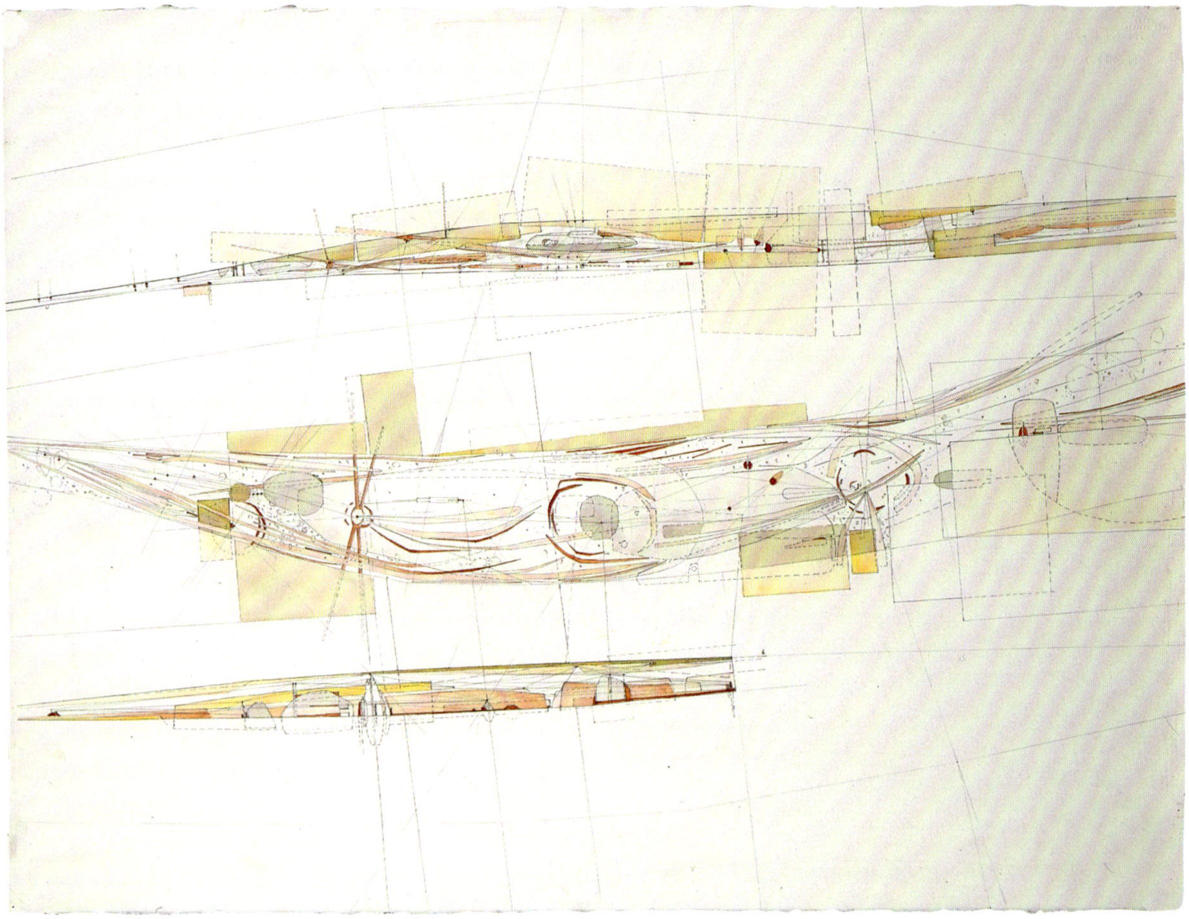

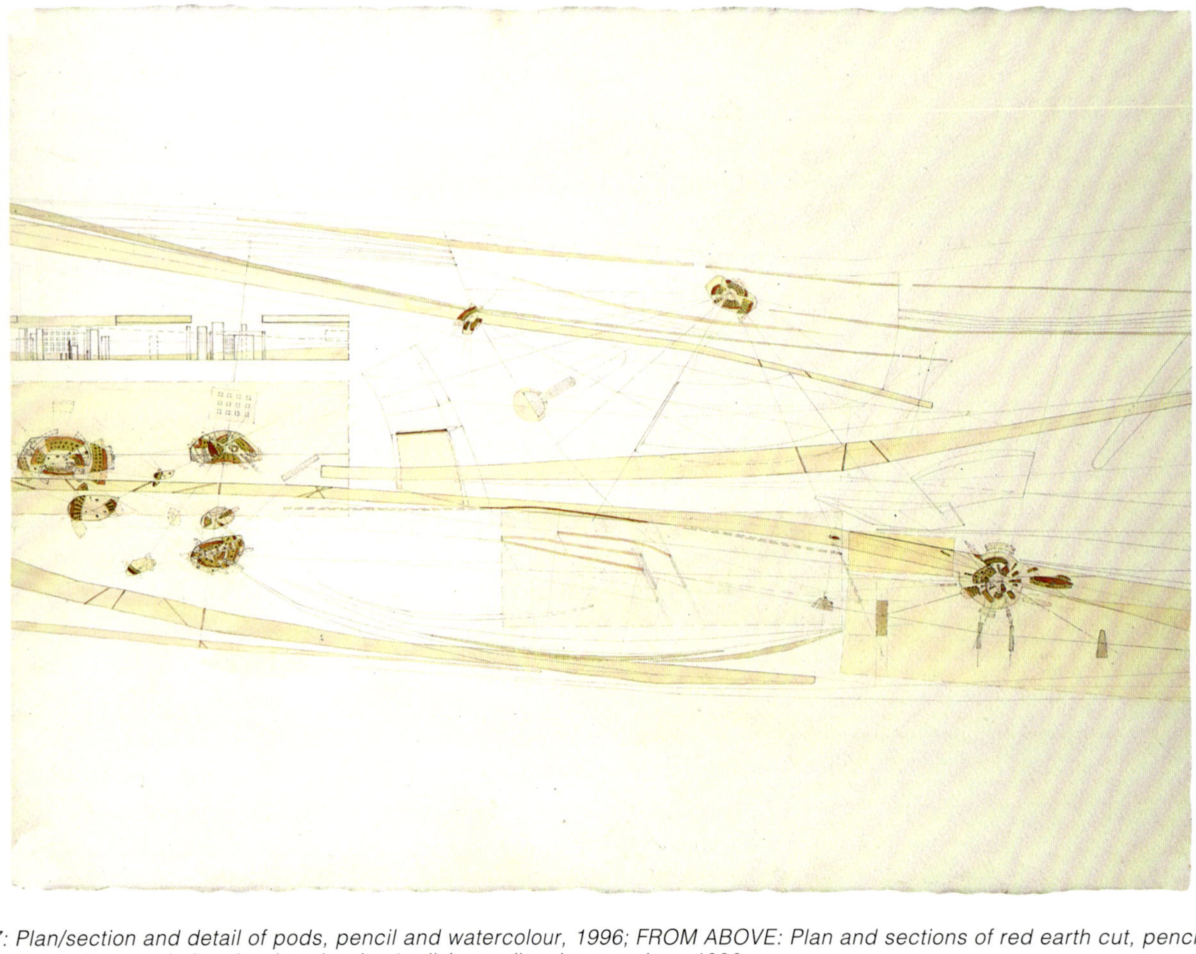

PAGES 56-57: Plan/section and detail of pods, pencil and watercolour, 1996; FROM ABOVE: Plan and sections of red earth cut, pencil and watercolour, 1996; submerged city, drawing showing 'wells', pencil and watercolour, 1996

> the way it must smell in the bad place; with all that I heard myself laughing as I went off – not the way a human being laughs – it was the most indecent, ghastly kind of laughing I ever heard.[14]

The tickling, shock and laughter are cognate with that which is critical and tragic in Andrews' project: the exposure, perturbation, and unhousing of architecture, leaving humans, in King Lear's sense, unaccommodated. The map that Andrews spreads is of the flaring moment and momentum of Ground Zero. But it is at this stark time, as Musil's Ulrich points out, that the imagination is torn into homing itself.

And yet, remarkably, in such an apparently incontrovertible condition of the present, there is something that leads into a desert; something like an unsuccessful proposal of love, or some similar exposure, the moment one does not unreservedly participate in it.

> Along our way we find ourselves walking through the narrow violet-blue streets of the city, which above, where they open to the light, burn like fire. Or we step out of this tactile blue into a square over which the sun freely pours its light; then the houses around the square stand there looking taken back and, as it were, placed against the wall, but no less expressively, and as if someone had scratched them with the fine lines of an engraving tool, lines that make everything too distinct. And at such a moment we do not know whether all this self-fulfilled beauty excites us profoundly or has nothing at all to do with us. Both are the case. This beauty stands on a razor's edge between desire and grief.[15]

Andrews' map hugs the ground it shakes. Its frame is abandoned. The scrivener no longer indites but stamps someone else's love on the paper sheet.

> For what if it were God Himself who was devaluing the world? Would it not then again suddenly acquire meaning and desire? And would He not be forced to devalue it, if He were to come closer to it by the tiniest step?[16]

Notes

1 On 'intravision,' see Omar Calabrese, *Neo-Baroque: A Sign of the Times*, (trans) Charles Lambert, Princeton University Press (Princeton), 1992, p161. 'Our perception of the inexpressible [. . .] presupposes a specific sensorial state, defined by Jankélévitch as intravision, a kind of vision 'between' things and 'within' the subject.'

2 *See* Denis Hollier, *Against Architecture: The Writings of Georges Bataille,* (trans) Betsy Wing, The MIT Press (Cambridge, Mass and London), 1989.

3 For an illustration of a *cortège* of these, *see* Hanno-Walter Kruft, *A History of Architectural Theory: From Vitruvius to the Present*, (trans) Ronald Taylor, Elsie Callander and Antony Wood, Princeton Architectural Press (London, Zwemmer and New York), 1994, plate 179.

4 Massimo Cacciari, *Architecture and Nihilism: On the Philosophy of Modern Architecture,* (trans) Stephen Sartarelli, Yale University Press, (New Haven and London), 1993, p154.

5 Robert Musil, *The Man Without Qualities*, (trans) Sophie Williams and Burton Pike, Alfred A Knopf (New York), 1995, p1224.

6 'Indeed, in medieval jurisprudence, "style" had drifted farther away from its older rhetorical associations and had become a pragmatic means of identifying or authenticating legal documents: the maintenance of a formal or procedural standard protected the document against forgery. It provided the document with a provenance. The historical link to a place and time of execution, in other words, was forged on the mechanical level of legal procedure, or even of penmanship. This was also the function of the clerk's paraph or flourish, an abstract and unrepeatable signature meant to link the document with a particular hand and to foil counterfeiters. This recalls the old sense of style as "title or appellation". Falstaff, for example, exclaimed, "Ford's a knave, and I will aggravate his style". The usage is ancient in English, but survives today only in the phrase "self-styled".' (Christopher S Wood, *Albrecht Altdorfer and the Origins of German Landscape,* Reaktion Books (London), 1993, p62.

7 Maurice Blanchot, *The Writing of the Disaster*, (trans) Ann Smock, University of Nebraska Press (Lincoln and London), third paperback edition, 1992, pp56-57.

8 Gilles Deleuze, *The Logic of Sense*, (trans) Mark Lester and Charles Stivale, Columbia University Press (New York), 1990, p35.

9 Gilles Deleuze and Félix Guattari, *A Thousand Plateaus: Capitalism and Schizophrenia*, (trans) Brian Massumi, University of Minnesota Press (Minneapolis) 1987, p401.

10 Ibid.

11 Gaston Bachelard, *The Poetics of Space*, (trans) Maria Jolas, Beacon Press (Boston), 1969, pp127-32.

12 Ibid, p131.

13 Ibid, p132.

14 Thomas Mann, *The Magic Mountain*, (trans) HT Lowe-Porter, Secker & Warburg (London), 1954, p310.

15 Musil, op cit, p1225.

16 Ibid, p1189.

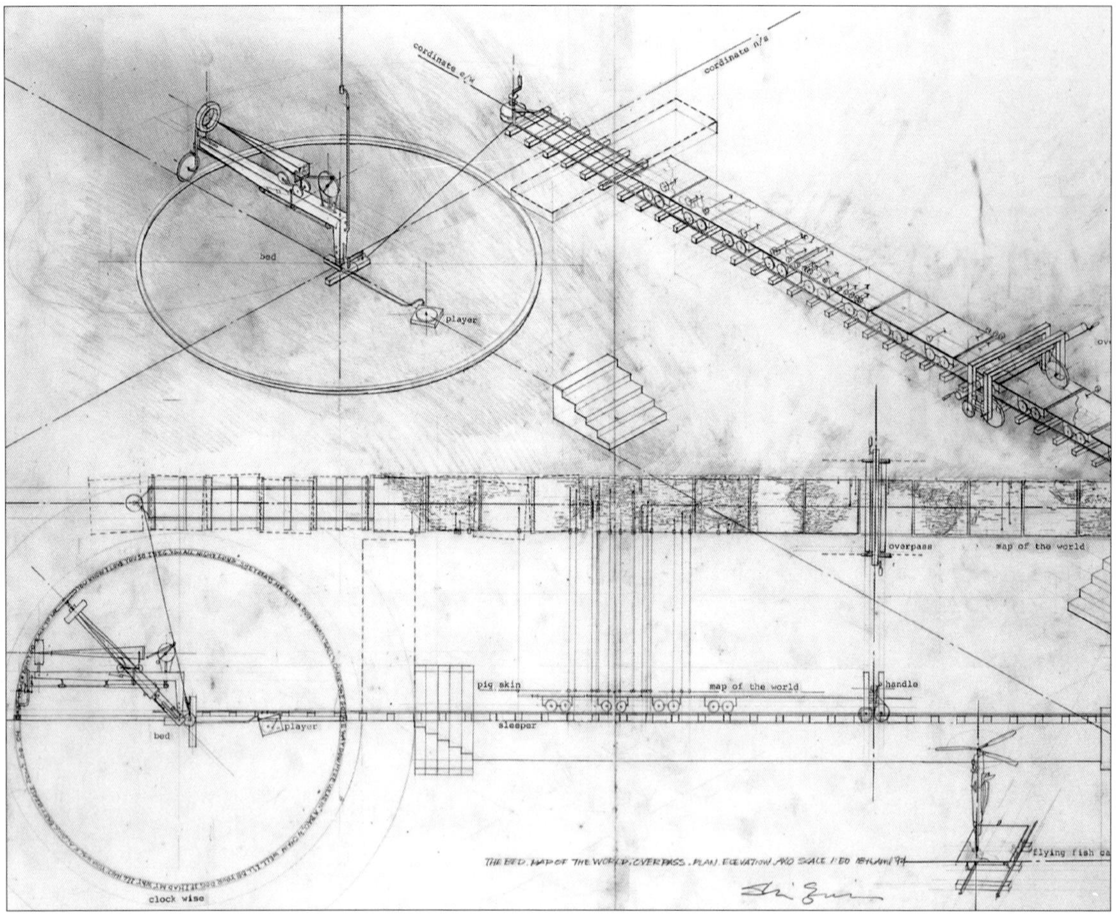

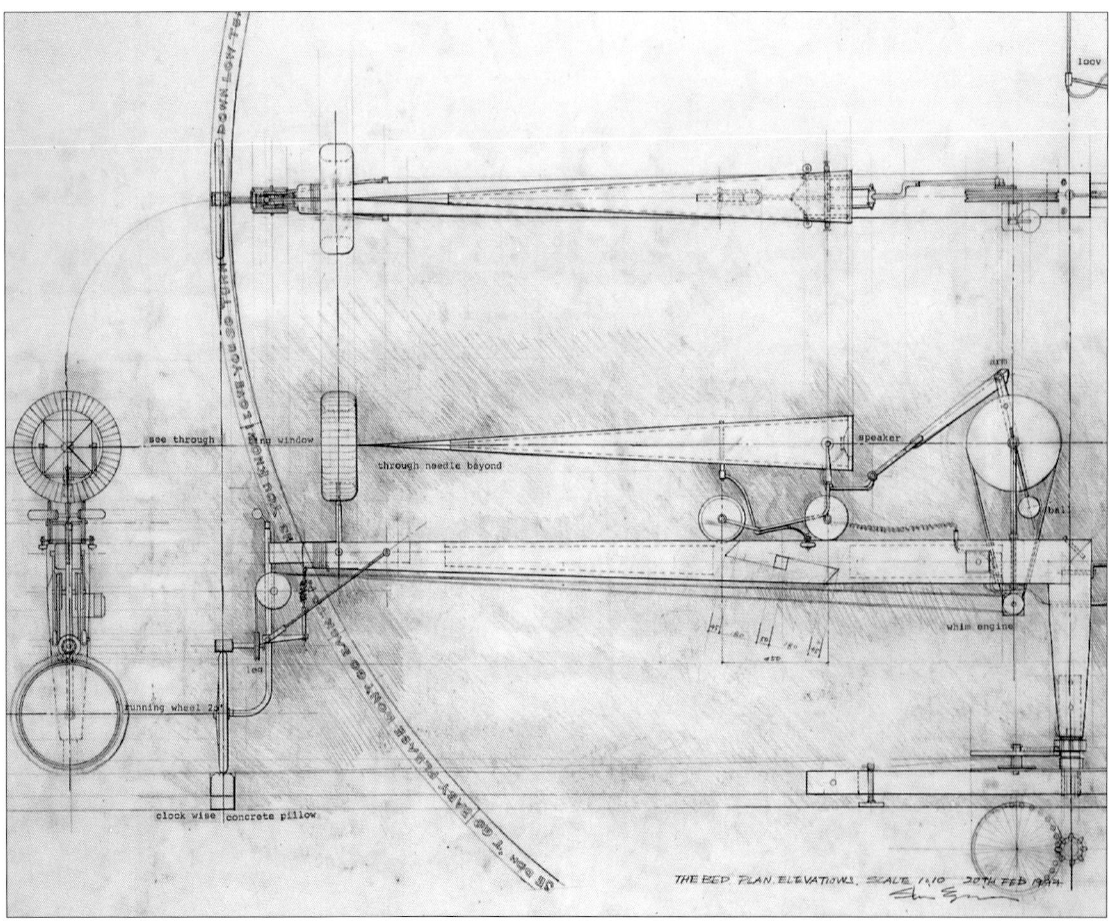

FROM ABOVE: Turning Things – *'Bed', 1994; 'Map of the World', 1994*

SHIN EGASHIRA

FORMING ENCLOSURES

Constructing something solid and tangible that speaks about something transparent and fragile is the nature of these machines; from them, the relationships between the body, material things and landscape flow, altering into a poetic enclosure.

Turning Things

'Eupkecha', a fictional insect in a novel by Kobo Abe, is described as a legless beetle who lives within a completely enclosed eco-system, slowly rotating the body, while simultaneously eating, digesting, and discharging its own shit. The home of this insect is somewhere in the African desert, in a village where people use the eupkecha like a clock. The whole town's consumption cycle is determined by this tiny animal's diet. Every year, just before the spring rains, the 'clocks' fly around the village searching for a partner and time disappears for a week.

Impossible Vehicle is the title of the work placed within the Spiral Garden in Aoyama, Tokyo, in spring 1994. It is like an over-scaled clock that turns this public arena into a space which, by conducting speed and movement of flow and sound, is imbued with a sense of anticipation. Waste from the city's consumption – such as scrap metals, bricks, floor boards, timber beams, railway sleepers, and pig skin – was mapped and collected, using construction methods that are about to disappear from the world of contemporary architecture.

Sixty-nine parts were put together to form three types of objects essential for vehicular travel: *Bed* is an engine for making love; *World Map* is a musical score for navigation and *Overpass* allows for each object to be passed independently of the another, yet to function as a whole. Each element is distinct, like scattered pieces of puzzles waiting to be put together.

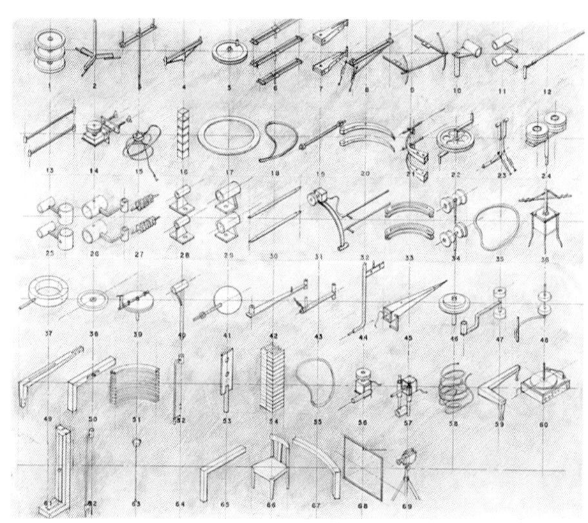

FROM ABOVE: Spiral Garden, Aoyama, Tokyo, 1994 – Impossible Vehicle, *axonometric, plan; construction drawing of the 'Bed'; sixty-nine parts collected from the city*

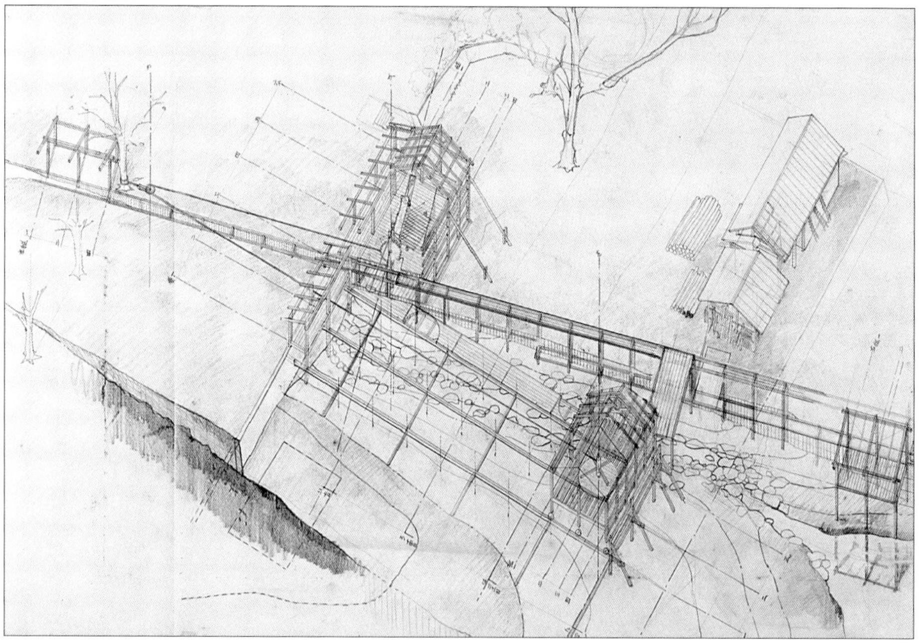

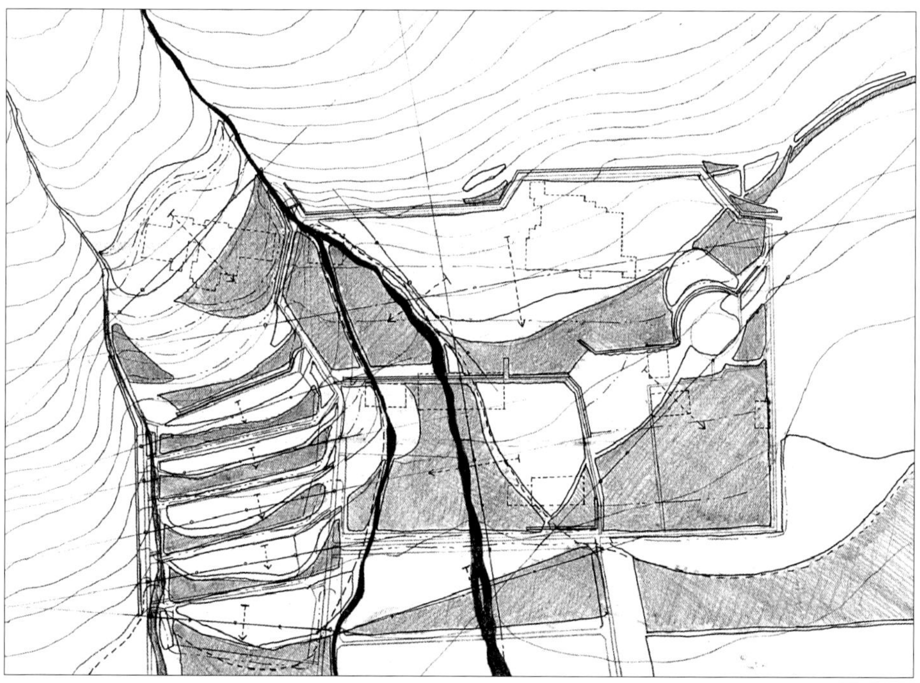

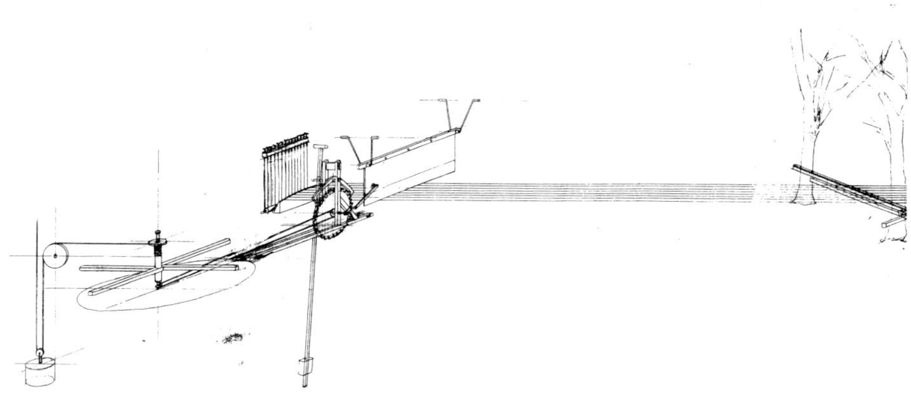

Turning the Earth
Yamagata Farm Estate in Tochigi prefecture was established a hundred years ago and now lies in neglected ruins. The aim of the project is to rearrange the existing texture of landscape by cultivating artworks to form a new ground for the public. This first stage of the long-term development plan will create a new entrance from which land will start to unfold. Reversing the process of preoccupied land, and manipulating a formula which has been associated with farming, forms the strategy for the proposal.

• Cutting and shifting: a river runs along the valley and has been diverted for the water system; the valley is 'cut and pasted' into a series of terraced fields and levelled ground. There is a barn in the middle of estate – one half of the structure stands on the surface of the infilled area, under which is the hidden topography of old river bed. Unstable foundations have affected the timber structure of the barn and it is now on the point of collapse. The proposal has been put forward to cut the barn in half, remove it from the unstable foundations, and move it 30 metres across the hidden river to the other side of original ground.

• Reforming artefact: in order to move one half of the structure, some sort of mechanical procedure will be necessary. The idea is to gather redundant agricultural machine parts and tools and transform this barn into a hybrid structure – a cross between a winding musical box and a plough. It will become a new appliance for turning the earth. It will play music as it moves, slowly reading the texture of the earth.

• New entrance: as it moves apart, removal of the soil between the two halves of the barn will expose the old river bed and create a space between the new ground and the old. This gap will become the new entrance to the old landscape.

OPPOSITE: Yamagata Farm Project, concept sketch; FROM ABOVE: New entrance, axonometric; shifting diagram of earthworks; musical structure

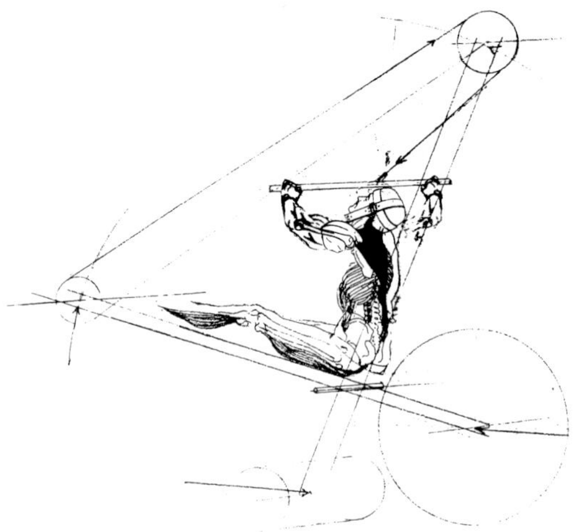

1

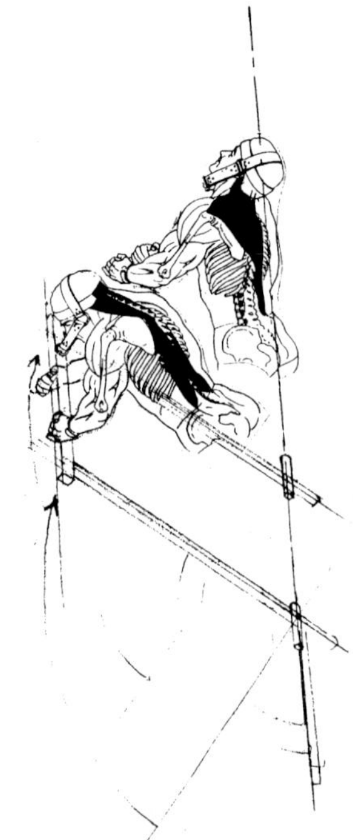

2

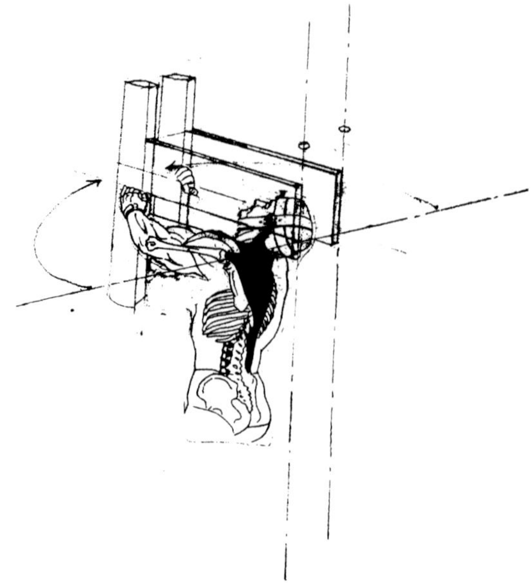

3

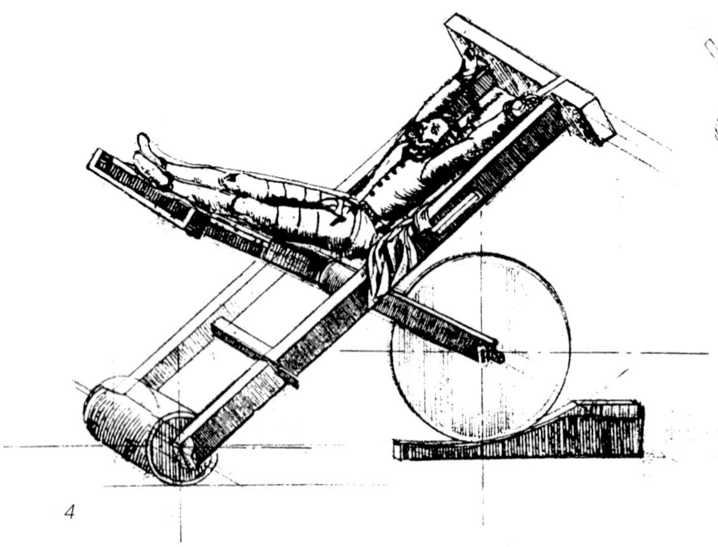

4

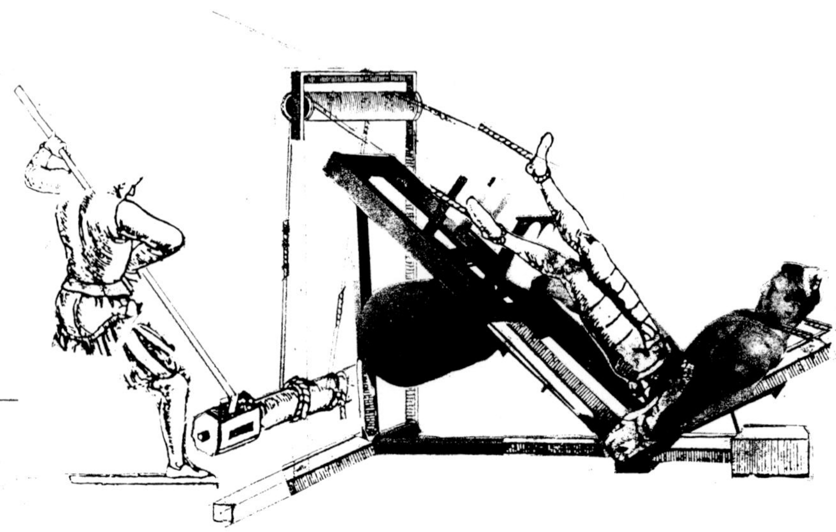

5

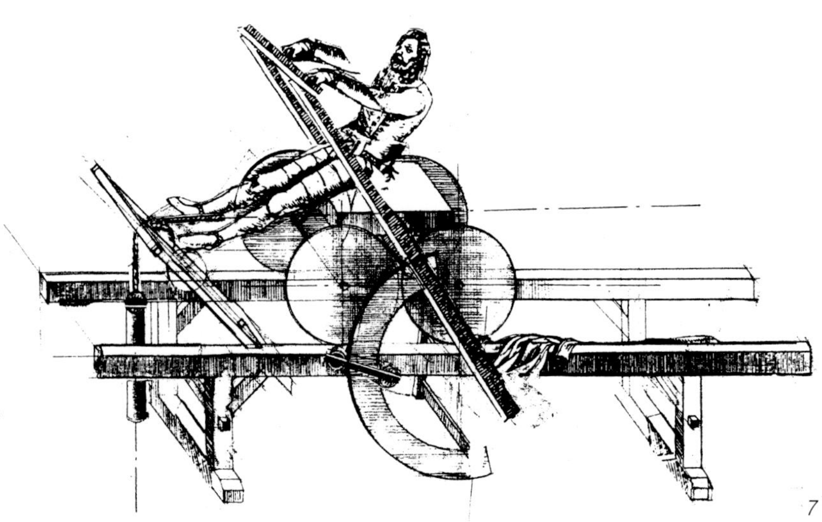

6

7

Turning the Body
An excess of novelty associated with our body seems to be creating an interior environment for our living sphere.

In the basement of the Tower of London, glass cases display beautiful instruments from the Middle Ages used for turning and stretching the body (they were used more widely in a later period of political stability but one of religious turmoil). For a long time, torture and punishment have been closely related to the politics of architecture and have been reflected in the art of architecture. These disciplines can be seen as kinds of machines which explore forms of physical reform, often producing mental and physical stress as well as concealed curiosity.

Tsu-kai, a Japanese word, conveys such meanings as 'that which gives me the greatest thrill', 'intense pleasure'. The first character *tsu* signifies pain and sickness, and the second *kai* refers to the feeling of pleasure and delight. Inside the great sense of pleasure is often noticeable the seed of pain; likewise, great pain can often bring us pleasure beyond our imagination. By contorting our bodies in opposite directions, are we turning a fantasy into a nightmare, or are we stretching the body of our pain into a sense of heightened pleasure?

Beyond the Tower of London lies the world of the 20th century as it draws to an end. Walking down a West End street, there is often a modern building in which some form of torture is underway, though obscured by the large glass facade. This building is The Gym. Within its walls, bodies are bound by all kinds of contraptions, not so far removed from the machines of medieval torture. Here, the process of enclosure is complete: structures are built around the body and the body is moulded to fit the structure.

Beauty of Our Pains is the title of an installation composed of reconstructed fitness machines which would not have looked out of place in the Middle Ages. They represent fitness and the act of confession: the extraction of beauty through pain.

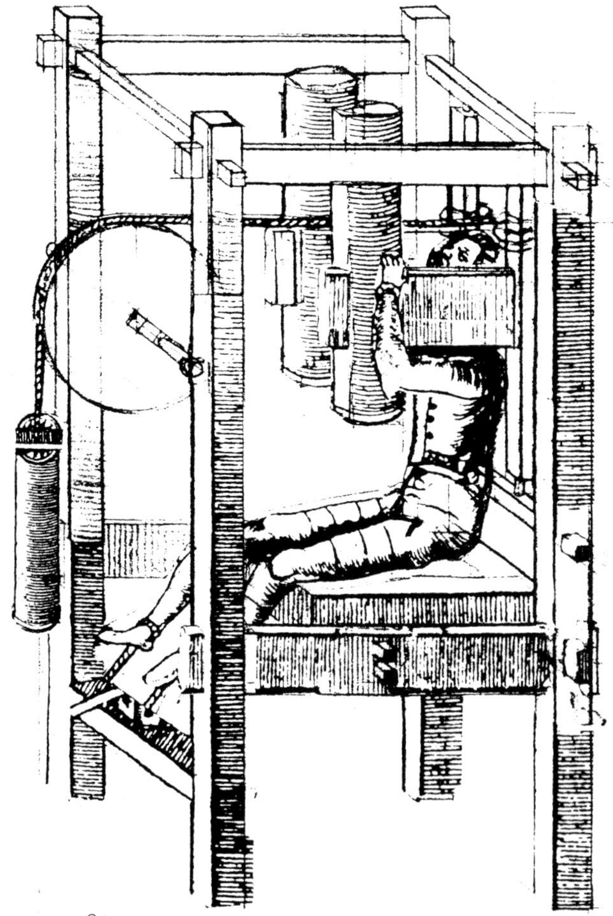

8

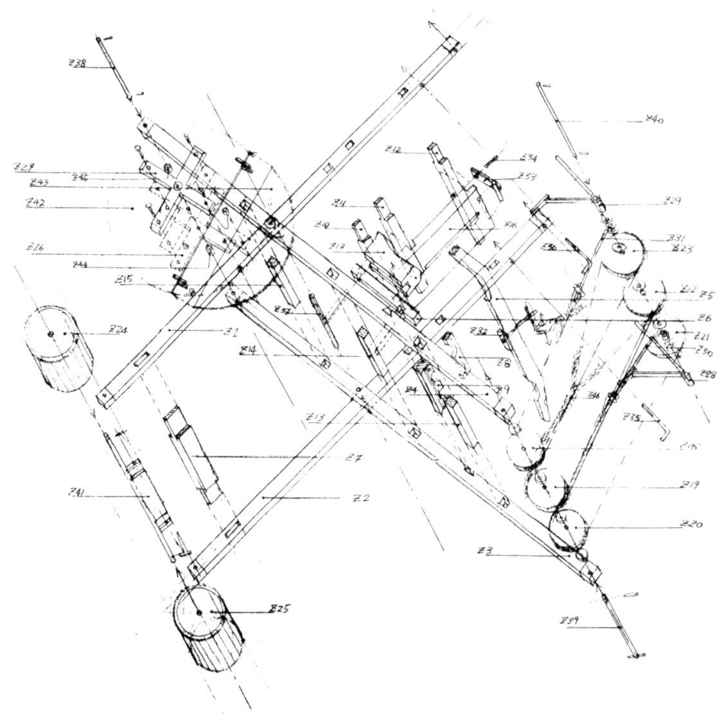

9

Beauty of Our Pains – *fitness body diagrams (figs 1-3); collages (figs 4-8); axonometric (fig 9)*

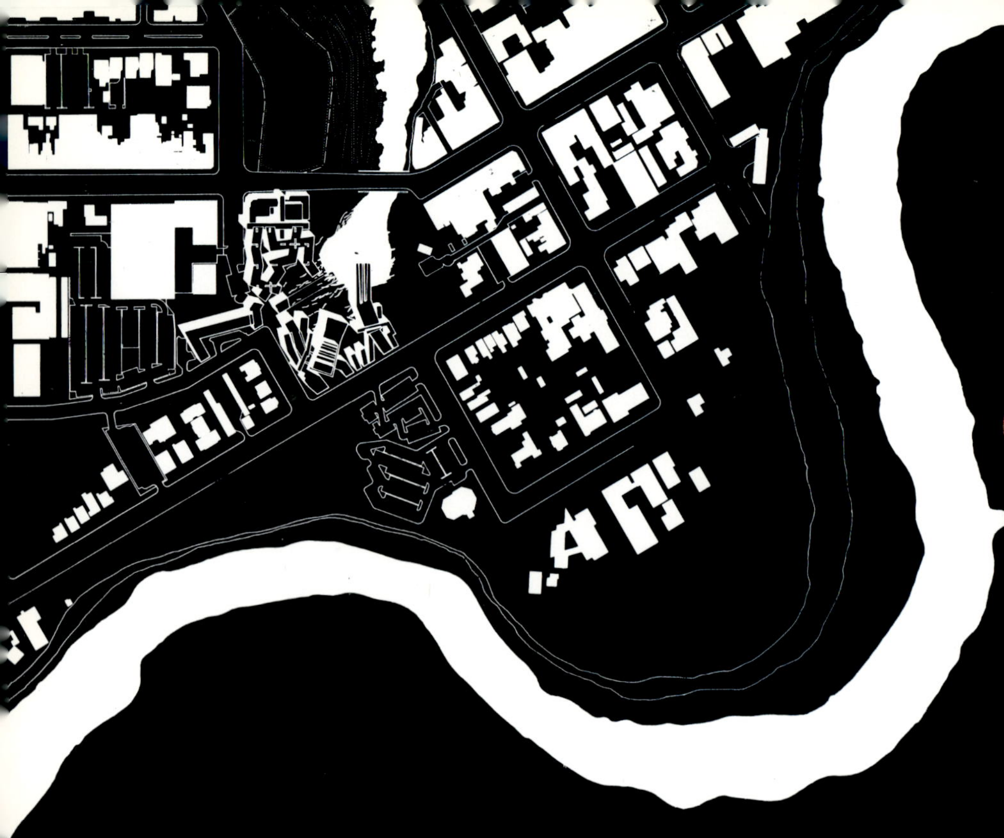

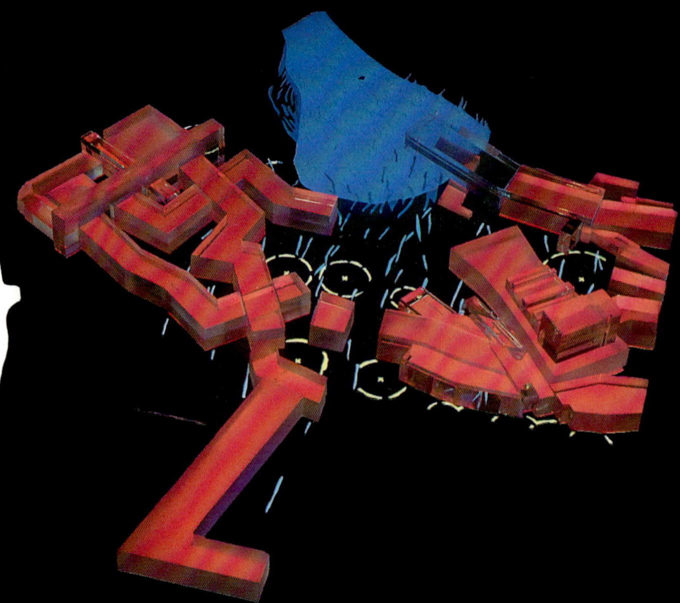

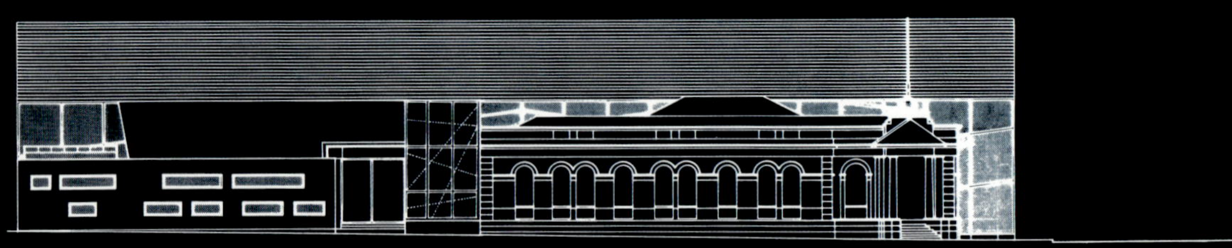

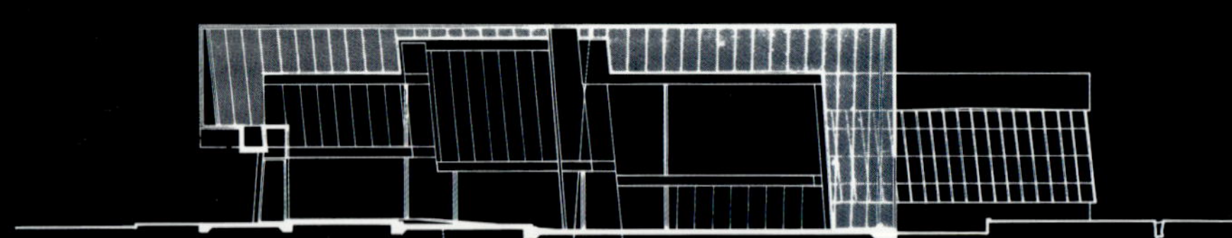

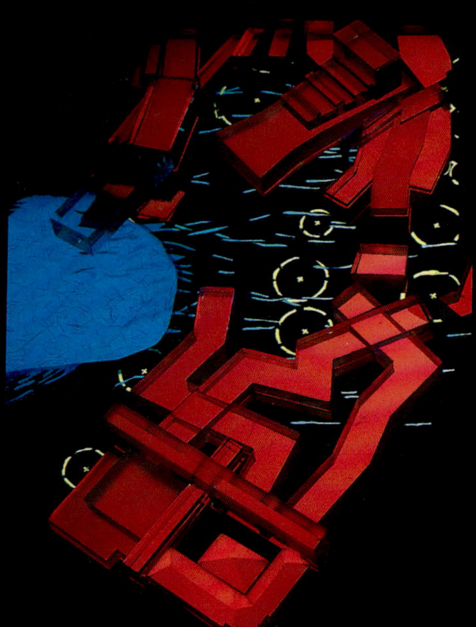

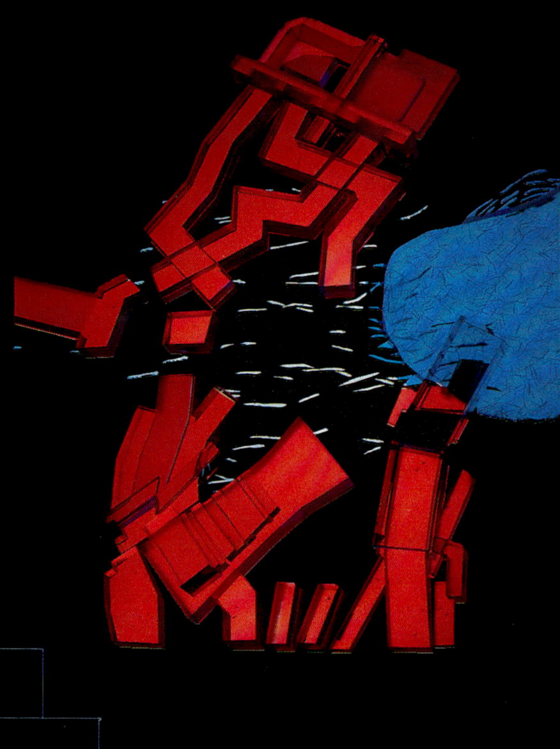

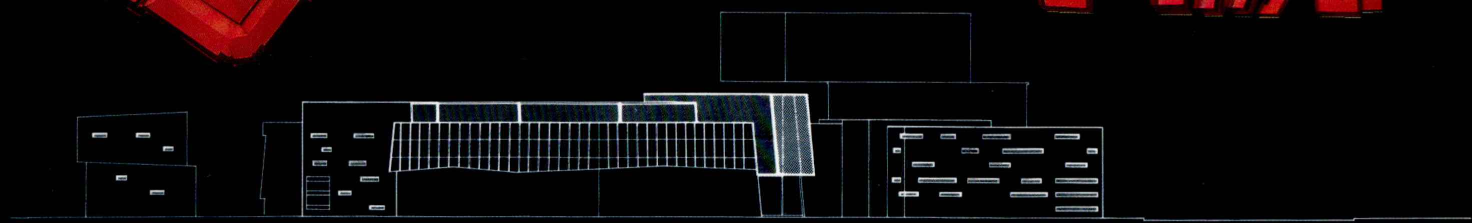

Lab – BATES + DAVIDSON

ARCHITECTURE AFTER GEOMETRY

These two projects (both building proposals for design competitions) are the outcome of an exploration of architectural organisation and order produced by texture rather than geometry. In each project, the line (a fundamental geometrical element and condition) is transfigured to operate not as an arbiter of geometric ordering (ie, as orders of symmetry, axiality, the grid, radiality or replicating figures), but rather to emerge as a generator of textured fields and zones. Previously in architecture, the line has operated as an enforcer of geometric ordering – and consequently of exclusion – by *delineating* difference. With these projects, we have sought to implicate the architectural line with another role, another utility.

As an indexing of differences, or as a spatialisation of categorical identities, the instrumentality of architecture has often been fixed as a typological assumption. This fixity assumes both a material and a psychological dimension. As materiality, it is the phenomenon of the boundary (again, the line). Psychologically, it is the domain of certainty, of resolute description. Our critique is in the exploration of the instances whereby architecture is neither bound by the materiality of a boundary, nor certified by a proper and therefore complete description.

In the projects, the employment of architectural lines is increasingly multitudinous and excessive.[1] Within this excess, the line loses its function as a clear designator of difference and property (and by implication, propriety), such that differences, while not being eliminated, at least become more paradoxical. Geometrically speaking, lines 'work' by instituting orders of exclusion, of demarcation, delineation and delimitation. In shifting from the employment of lines as geometrical constructs to the use of textures and fields of lines produced out of redundancy, superfluity and excess, we have struggled to redraw the description of a line. The attempt in all cases is to maintain a degree of readability, a legibility of differences (whether these be programmatic, thematic, or merely a function of site versus object), while at the same time constructing an organisational permeability that violates the role of the edge, boundary, surface, or wall.

The aggregation of lines, the excessive over-lap and intertwining verges towards becoming a 'texture field'. As a field, the functioning of any singular element, of any particularised moment of demarcation is transfigured by the effects of multiplicity. Quantity does in fact have a profound quality. This manoeuvre confronts one of the primary achievements of architecture – singularity. The confrontation is by no means resolved by a simple inversion of the singular being replaced by the plural, but rather, it is the transformation of singular moments, with their clear, unambiguous materialisations into moments of multiple, self-denying affiliations and affinities.

Within the field, singularity is not so much lost or abrogated as it is compounded to such a degree that it becomes something other. In a recent essay, Stan Allen described the characteristic of what he called 'field conditions':

> we might suggest that a field condition would be any formal or spatial matrix capable of unifying diverse elements while respecting the identity of each. Field configurations are loosely bounded aggregates characterised by porosity and local interconnectivity. The internal regulations of the parts are decisive; overall shape and extent are highly fluid.[2]

We are interested in the dissolution of the boundary and the maintenance of the form, of the subject.

In order to extend the speculation involved in these projects, we have hypothesised the architectural consequences of a Giacometti portrait. In Giacometti's paintings and drawings, the line (as a paint stroke or as pencil mark) is the primary, if not the sole, graphic inscription. In each work, the subject image (be it a portrait, still life or interior) is imminently readable. Yet at no point does a singular line form the edge of a shoulder, or define the outline of a vase. Rather, these announceable, describable elements emerge out of an excess of lines, an excess which operates to form a conspiracy of description. This conspiracy is the network of heterogeneous affiliations which contrive to insinuate a wholeness out of disparate, disordered elements. The image, the object, attains visibility as an emergent difference.

Giacometti's materiality is distinct from the materiality of architecture. To produce fluxion within the line of a wall or as the edge of a building requires another domain of techniques. In Giuseppe Terragni's *Casa del Fascio (1932-36)* or the *Casa Giuliani-Frigerio (1939-40)*, there is an apparently resolute edge or border to both buildings. The quadratic surface of each is undeniable, but close analysis (such as that made in the extensive published and unpublished critiques of Peter Eisenman) suggests that a determination of the categorical role of any one surface is in fact problematic. Surfaces are multiple; duplicitous, in fact. A retreat or collapse to any one surface, acting as a base line for all other surfaces, is clearly impossible. Within this context, all surfaces are provisional and their inter-relationships, disputable. A space of simultaneity accumulates out of these shifts.

The Terragnian space is not merely volumetrically complex, as one might expect, but in addition, it revises the relationship of the architectural object to its context. The context is not one which is received, but is one which is constructed. In such instances, the status of the object itself alters, the architecture moving to assume a new inception, acting now as mediation. This is not a facile conjoining of object with context, a 'building as part of the site'. It is the production of a dynamic fluidity that renders oppositional, bipolar terminologies irrelevant.

Concurrent with this assault on the line, our investigations have included an extended analysis of the textures evident in thin-rock sections. In these studies, we have looked for examples of organisational arrangements that could provide the provocation necessary to rethink architectural orderings. Issues of embayment, interstitiality, lamellar orientation, flow and fluxion, texture, matrix and blebs, and the emergence of multiple visual logics, all offer architectural effects which contribute to the ordering of an area, field or surface, of differentiation without absolute exclusion.

> In thin section the junction between two crystals may appear as a straight line, a simple curve, or a complex curve; in the third case the crystals interdigitate or interlock, possibly so intimately that they appear to be embedded in one another.[3]

Within both fields of investigation, the *line* and *texture fields*, we have concentrated on attaining a degree of permeability and spatial (as well as programmatic) inversion in the pursuit of new social and political arrangements. At both the Wagga Wagga Civic Centre and the Scottish Architecture and Design Centre a central concern has been the introduction of a more heterogeneous description to the categories of administration (offices), public space, landscaping, and circulation. Essentially, this has been an interrogation of the architectonics of the 'category', a questioning of the spatial confirmation of discrete objects, programmes, functions, and events. It is our belief that the political dimension of space lies in its ability to be materialised and conceptualised by means of new, and evermore speculative orders.

WAGGA WAGGA CIVIC CENTRE (1995)

The Wagga Wagga Civic Centre Competition (1995) was a two-stage competition.[4] The brief comprised accommodation for city administration offices and council chambers, a public library, a regional art gallery and the renovation and enlargement of the existing civic theatre. With 50,000 inhabitants, Wagga Wagga is the fourth largest 'city' in New South Wales, Australia and is located approximately 150 miles north-west of Canberra.

The Centre of Town is Also its Edge

Wagga Wagga evidences a unique instance of urban form, with the civic centre site being both the very centre of the city and, simultaneously, the edge of the city. The original development of the town was tangential to the river, using it as an organising or set-out device for the grid. Operating as the link between the old, historic section of Wagga Wagga, aligned to Fitzmaurice Street and the newer, expanded axis of Baylis Street, the civic centre site sits at the shift which identifies the primary geometrical ordering patterns of the city. This territory of intersection and conjunction is the locus of this project. The project does not attempt a resolution to this condition.

The city is marked by the tendency of all buildings facing the street to form a line, while the surfaces of the buildings away from the street are diverse in their form and figuration, creating a variegated edge. The back spaces in the commercial streets are residual, providing predominantly for parking and service access.

Textural Zones

The site has been organised by a system of textural zones which, through orientation, alignment and direction, seek to develop an overall site coherence through a specific graphic interpretation and response to all the diverse site and siting conditions. Emanating from the existing historic council chambers, these zones have been developed eastwards in a continuous sequence, specifically to engage and negotiate the discontinuous qualities of the whole site. These textures set out the parameters of spatial ordering or zoning for the different sectors of the site, providing the developmental framework for the building elements of the civic centre programme.

A separate series of textures has been utilised for the subsequent development of the site landscaping. In the first instance, this tactic has endeavoured to create an alternative orientation to the original site and to the predominant circulation movement which operates west to east (or from Baylis Street to Tarcutta Street). This new site texture consists of rivulets and islets, forming a residual and inverted archipelago. In striving to break down the absolute water edge of the Wollundry Lagoon as it meets the land edge, a textural field of elongated blebs is superimposed on the site, suggesting a zone of excess, with too much water on the land, and too much

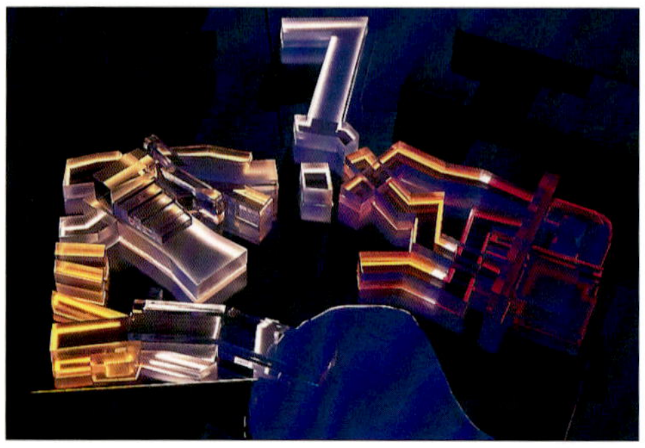

land in the water.

At night, the rivulets provide ambient illumination, with light emerging from the water to define and articulate pathways and circulation in the field between the administration building and the library/theatre/gallery complex. Operating almost as one of the islets, the civic centre restaurant is a partial island, floating beneath the overhang of the regional art gallery.

The texture zones overlap, with graphic transparency translating into a compound event map. The overlaps (the transparencies) provide a new figuration which is distinct from either its origins or from a direct superimposition. The textures have been used in this instance as insinuations within the field of the landscape. The emergent differences are condensations out of this graphic matrix.

Administration Offices

Following, but integral to the zoning strategy for the site, a specific policy of treating buildings as lines has been adopted. The tabular cross (cardinal datum) of the administration building public foyer, simultaneously describes the domain and the orientation of the existing historic council chambers as a shadow of the city's founding grid. The three filaments which lodge in the cross' north-south axis form an open weave which spreads across the site, traversing the space of the hinge between the major and minor grid systems of the city. The filaments describe an undifferentiated, though comprehensible pattern over the site, denying a primary orientation or alignment.

The three bent or redirected filaments contain the administration departments and offices of Wagga Wagga City Council. By virtue of their distinct operational responsibilities, these departments conform to a variety of public, inter-departmental, and autonomous engagements. By allocating the administration offices into these three filaments, we are able to project a programmatic segmentation which allows for the containment of each department or sub-department into a specific location and siting. Each zig or zag, or combination thereof, in the filament allows for a tuning of the space allocations. Additionally, the filaments provide a spatial structuring to form extended sequences of segment to segment, amalgamating into the three large identifiable filaments, or into partial filaments, terminated at the common intersections. Finally, as they spread across the site, the interlocking, interweaving lines of the filaments act as a recombinant grouping to form a compound whole, with internal courtyards in counterpoint to the single block extending into the landscape. The grouping counters any monolithic designation for the office accommodation. The multiple gradients between public accessibility and non-accessibility, departmental autonomy or interdepartmental co-dependence, between current dispositions and future reconfigurations, all are forecast by this new ordering.

Structural Louvers

The council offices have two distinct surfaces which correspond to specific structural and environmental exigencies. The north, east and west facades are continuously glazed, protected by a structural louver/screen wall. The south-facing segments are masonry, with infill and operable strip windows.

The structural louver/screen has precast ferro cement and concrete-encased steel components. The screen system has been conceived so that there is a specific variable relationship established between the environmental role of the screen and its structural characteristics. As the orientation of the building segments move away from the north, there is an environmental requirement for additional vertical screening elements and fewer horizontal louvers. This has a direct structural correspondence, for, as the columns become more closely spaced, the relative load carried by each is reduced, thus reducing the requirements for a horizontal support against vertical buckling. The four variable sections for the structural louver/screen also show that as the wall is articulated there is also a variation in the faceting by an adjustment to the column angle below the crank point.

The structural louver/screen facades show a continuity of horizontal banding which modulates in response to the angles of the sun. This modulation is 'tuned' to the numerous orientations, allowing for visual contraction and expansion of the surface.

Commercial Offices/Library/Theatre/Gallery

A transverse line (the supplementary commercial spaces and auditorium) is drawn across the site as a single crystal, projecting and connecting the Quinn property across to the main site area. This line closes Morrow Street and operates as a building without a back, with each surface operating as a front facade in relation to a specific programmatic event. The building thus forms affiliations with numerous corresponding features of the site context.

The 'almost' parallel lamellae of the public library are lodged in the host areas surrounding the autonomously oriented civic theatre. As agglomerated crystalline masses, they incorporate the imprint and potentially the form of the theatre, whilst providing for refraction and reorientation. The extensions of the lamellae re-emerge as discrete forms and buildings to create a pseudo-urbanism to the edge of the site at Tarcutta Street. This 'urban edge' recomposes itself as an array of prismatic forms which recombine and extend back across the site in the form of the regional art gallery.

Within the interior of the public library, the intersection and overlap of the lamellae act to zone the library into constituent aspects of the programme. Sectionally, by illumination at these overlaps, the building alternates in volume, with the resultant gaps at first-floor level bridged by short ramps and walkways.

The newly-formed urban edge, which is a figural continuance of the public library, serves to densify the site along Tarcutta Street. We expanded the given brief in order to introduce additional activities and services (tourist bureau, ticket office, office for a community theatre group) to this part of the civic centre. The buildings at this edge form small, autonomous integers, or they are fragments and segments which extend out of the larger mass of the civic theatre or the regional art gallery.

The regional art gallery is itself a massing of three or four systems of directionality and volumetric interpenetration. The large form of the main gallery space inflects outwards in order to open up the vista from the civic theatre across the Wollundry Lagoon. This volume extends out over the lagoon, anchored on columns which also support the restaurant island. Movement through the numerous gallery spaces is by means of a series of ramps, which are themselves the junctions between the volumes of the gallery spaces and are sources of illumination into these same spaces.

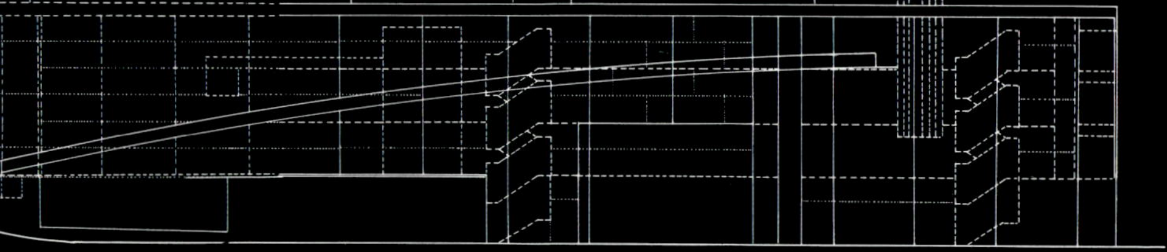

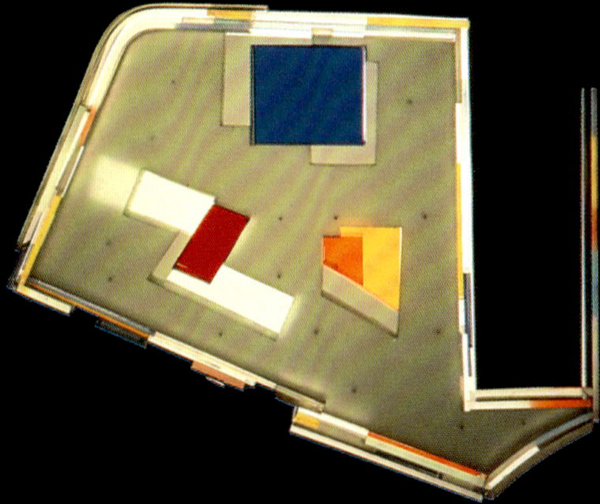

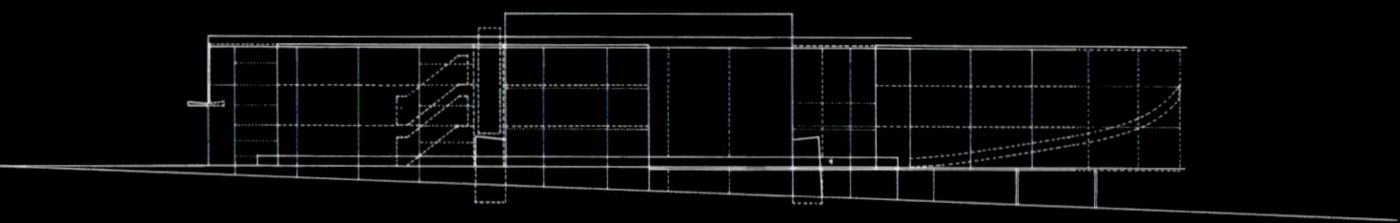

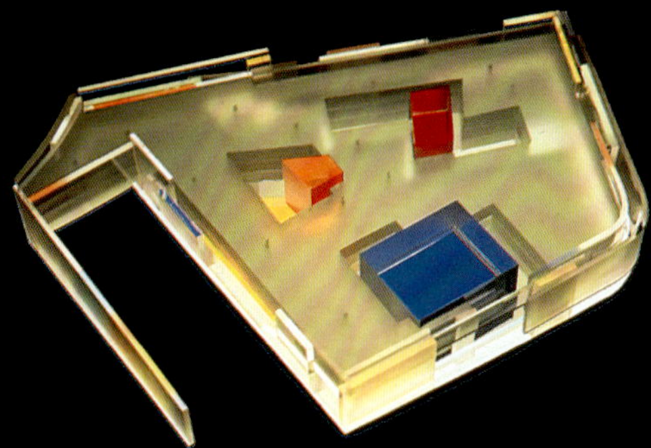

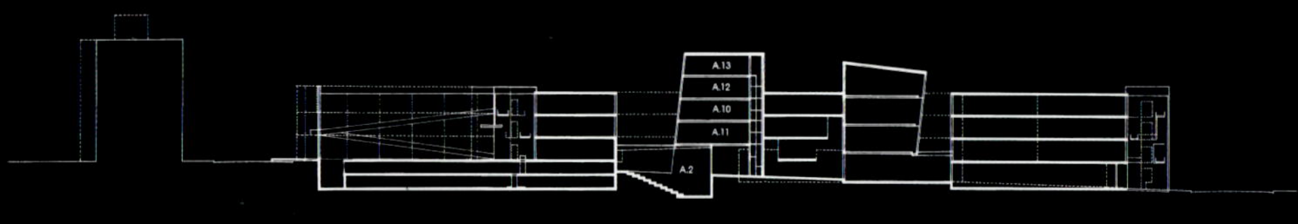
A.13
A.12
A.10
A.11
A.2

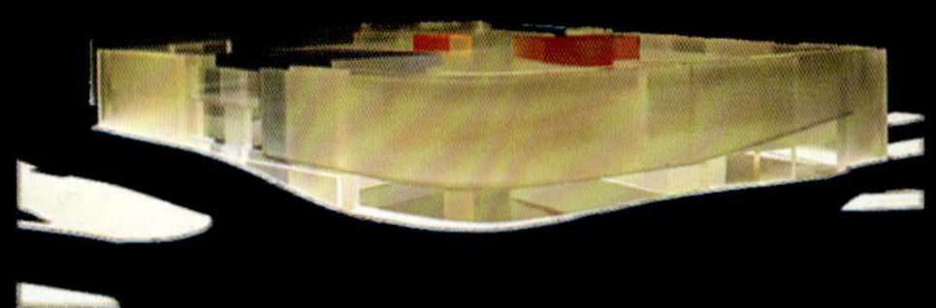

SCOTTISH ARCHITECTURE & DESIGN CENTRE, EDINBURGH (1995)[5]

The project incorporates the primary urban figure-ground patterns which constitute the historic development of Edinburgh, and synthesises them into a dense and coherent, formal arrangement consisting of three interposed elements: a ribbon wall which bands the project's edge and contains circulation/services/ lobbies; prismatic crystals to delineate major Scottish Architecture and Design Centre/IMAX public spaces, and a volumetric matrix, essentially containing the programmed commercial space.

These primary elements provide for separate and distinct spatial orderings which nonetheless have a permeable relationship to one another through their spatial interpenetrations and geometrical texture.

The ribbon wall is a densely layered zone of structure, stairs, elevators, ramps, balconies, walkways, service spaces, amenities, sun shading, screens and ventilation. Conceived as a flexible provider for all the programmatic elements and an instrument of environmental control, the wall's spatially layered configuration allows an intense blending of public and private spaces along the edge of the site. While primarily serving the office spaces' utilitarian functions, the layered band also incorporates other programmed elements, such as the bus stop, and mediates between these and the site's topography and surrounding context.

The SADC and the IMAX are configured as three prismatic crystals; each combined with a figural void atrium, emerging independently from and penetrating the three floors of office space. The categorical distinction between the commercial office space and the SADC/IMAX facilities is thus made spatially and functionally permeable at locations where these entities share synonymous programmes.

The SADC and IMAX have adjoining, merged foyers on the ground floor and, at higher level, administrative functions assimilated within the central volumetric mass. Where the various SADC constituent elements maintain clearly characteristic programmes, they are specifically arranged within the prismatic crystals. Each of these three elements would, in addition, be materially differentiated from the enswathing office space.

The commercial space has been developed as a volumetric matrix which provides the ground and envelope for the entire proposal. The spatial ordering of the three floors provides a capability of division into a variety of distinct zones or areas which, in conjunction with the atriums, provides all office spaces with high quality natural light and varying internal and external outlooks. The offices' conception (with the organisation of the perimeter banding and atriums) provides the basis of a natural ventilation system, supplemented with heat or humidity as required, employing a central plant room with unit plant to each area.

The project utilises and reconfigures the existing gradual sectional change across the site, establishing two referential levels. The lower level at the Haymarket Plaza is the low point of a sloping ground plane which permeates the entire building through to the upper site at the Link Road and, in turn, provides a horizontal datum for the volumetric matrix. The ribbon wall mediates these two datums, responding specifically to the changing perimeter site levels, conditions and programmes.

The volumetric and sectional particularities of the major SADC and IMAX programmed spaces, together with the prismatic crystals, are geometrically ordered to create a visually permeated, programmatically complex and spatially interleaved section which opens up under, through and across the entire building area.

Notes

1 *See also* LAB; *Application et Implication*; exhibition at the Magasin Centre Nationale d'Art Contemporain, Grenoble, 1993 and Europan II competition entry for Grand Synthe, Dunkerque, 1994.

2 Stan Allen, *Field Conditions in Architecture and Urbanism*; the Berlage Papers, #17 (Amsterdam), 1996.

3 MacKenzie, Donaldson, Guilford, *Atlas of Igneous Rocks and Their Textures*, Longman Scientific and Technical (New York) 1982, p45.

4 The competition for the Wagga Wagga Civic Centre was a two-stage competition for which LAB was one of five architects selected for the second stage. *See Wagga Wagga Civic Centre Competition Catalogue*, Wagga Wagga City Council, Australia, 1996.

5 The two-stage competition for the Scottish Architecture and Design Centre prescribed three major elements: Scottish Architecture and Design Centre, IMAX cinema and 18,000m^2 office space, with a bus stop on the site.

PAUL URSELL

THE EVOLUTION OF PROSTHETIC INTRAOCULAR LENS DESIGN

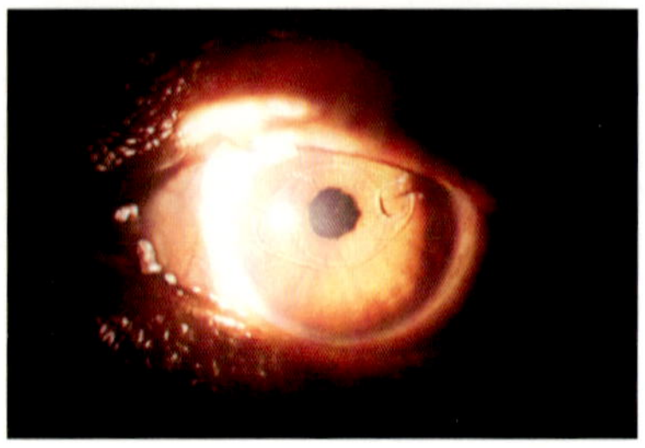

The horrors of the Battle of Britain claimed many lives, but one of the more obscure benefits of this aerial carnage was the genesis of the evolution of cataract surgery. This is now one of the most successful surgical procedures ever designed by mankind. Harold Ridley was an ophthalmic surgeon at St Thomas' Hospital in London during the Second World War. He treated many of the pilots who had sustained injuries when the canopies of their aircraft exploded into their faces. They had sustained penetrating injuries to the globe of the eye when shards of Perspex from the canopy had lacerated their eyes. Ridley noticed that, when left *in situ*, these Perspex shards were particularly inert and did no further damage to the eye apart from the initial trauma. Ferrous metals by contrast, leached and destroyed any epithelial structures, and any organic matter caused catastrophic infections. The Perspex, however, caused little or no inflammatory response. Ridley made the leap of imagination and deduced that the transparent Perspex could be made into a lens and inserted into the eye as a replacement for the natural lens which had to be removed during cataract surgery.

Ridley and the First Intraocular Lens

The human eye contains a crystalline lens which acts in conjunction with the cornea to focus light onto the retina in the emmetropic state. It is composed of transparent crystallins which refract light. This lens becomes progressively less transparent with age and brunescent changes develop. The normal form of cataractogenesis leads to an increase in volume as the crystalline nucleus of the lens becomes sclerotic. The lens itself is suspended by a fine scaffold of zonular fibres from the ciliary body and is enclosed in a capsular bag, the anterior capsule being thicker than the posterior capsule which is 0.5 millimetres thick.

Cataractogenesis causes a loss of transparency of the crystalline lens and leads to visual symptoms; some degree of change is universal over the age of 50 years and pathological changes are found in 80 per cent of eyes over 80 years of age. These changes cause a gradual dimming of visual acuity and a loss of fine contrast sensitivity. Also, bright lights produce glare symptoms similar to dazzling during night driving. The brunescent changes also lead to altered perception of colours, and it is interesting to note that Leonardo da Vinci is reported to have had cataracts; his work in later life is less detailed and has a yellow hue. Clinically, the nucleus of the lens becomes less transparent and yellow to the observer.

The challenge of cataract surgery is that removal of the cataract involves removing the lens, which subsequently leads to serious refractive changes. The refractive error can be corrected in the normal manner with contact lenses or spectacles. These are both associated with significant loss of visual field and spherical aberrations, and, at best, are sub-optimal. The ideal situation would be to replace the cataract with an intraocular lens (IOL) prosthesis as close to the nodal point of the eye as possible. Ridley placed the first intraocular lens on 19 November 1949 at St Thomas' Hospital, London. The cornea was opened superiorly along half its circumference, and the anterior capsule amputated. The cataract was expressed out of the eye using positive pressure and the remnants washed out with irrigation. The posterior capsule was left intact and an intraocular lens (IOL) placed into the posterior chamber of the eye, behind the iris and in front of the posterior capsule. The original Ridley IOL was a simple lens disc and the operation was performed by the surgeon, using loupes. The operation was traumatic and led to significant post-operative inflammation inside the eye with subsequent vision loss. This was because the Ridley IOL required the posterior capsule to remain intact to provide support in the correct position, and the presence of the IOL, with the increase in inflammation, led to a great deal of scarring of the posterior capsule This then opacified and obscured the patient's vision. The Ridley lens was a simple round disc and was positioned inside the remains of the capsular bag; eccentric contraction of the bag during the scarring process led to decentration of the lens from the optical axis.

Anterior Chamber Lenses

Although revolutionary, the Ridley lens proved to be associated with many post-operative complications, the majority of which were associated with scarring and contraction of the posterior capsule as well as postoperative inflammation. The logical step was to remove the posterior capsule during the operation and place the IOL resting on the iris in the anterior chamber, the AC IOL. This required the lens to have a number of stabilisers to hold it in position. The round central lens portion of the IOL was called the optic and the stabilising arms were called haptics. These haptics rested in the angle of the anterior chamber between the iris and the periphery of the cornea; they were more successful than the original Ridley lens. The problems associated with the posterior capsule were eradicated and, although the optic was located anterior to the nodal point of the eye, they achieved good optical results.

The haptics of the AC IOL were initially made from PMMA (a more modern and refined form of Perspex) in a single piece design, and then from other substances such as nylon or platinum. These haptics gave the IOL an overall diameter which was a fixed value for each make of IOL, however, biological variation ensured that the diameter of the anterior chamber varied between 10 and 14 millimetres. If the IOL was too small, it moved around and caused optical aberrations as light from the edge of the optic impinged on the retina. It could also cause damage to the iris behind and the cornea in front. If the lens was too large, it caused considerable pain and in some cases eventually eroded through the wall of the eye. Attempts were made to alleviate this: first, by manufacturing lenses with a variety of haptic shapes; second, by manufacturing lenses with different diameters to fit the individual's anterior chamber. However,

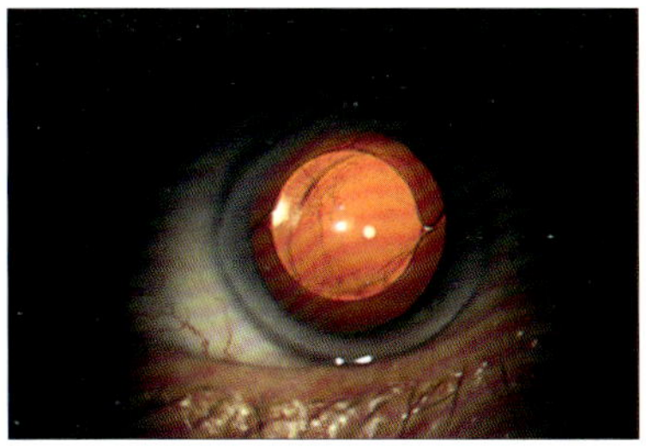

FROM L to R: 'Lobster Claw IOL' in human eye, placed into the anterior chamber and secured in place using a special haptic which grips the iris from both sides; modern PCIOL placed into the capsular bag behind the iris. The pupil has been dilated and the picture is taken using retroillumination

the diameter of the anterior chamber is notoriously difficult to measure accurately.

The position of the AC IOL left it perilously close to the posterior surface of the cornea, which is covered by endothelial cells, the purpose of which was then unknown. It was later discovered that these cells maintained the deturgescence of the corneal stroma and thus its regular structure and optical clarity. The AC IOLs disturbed the normal flow of nutrients across the anterior chamber and, if at all loose, physically abraded the endothelial cells which in turn died. The cornea in many patients with AC IOLs eventually opacified permanently and became painful over the following few years, requiring corneal allografting. Despite these disadvantages, AC IOLs were the chosen implant from the 50s through to the mid-70s, but due to the associated corneal decompensation most were replaced thereafter.

The original observation by Ridley – that PMMA was safe in the eye – had a caveat stating that this was so only if there were no sharp edges irritating intraocular structures. The manufacturing methods of early IOLs left the surface of the lens rough and with many surface irregularities, which were in themselves capable of causing irritation. Modern IOL manufacture has ensured that edges and junctions are smooth and polished.

Iris Clip IOLs

Endothelial decompensation and pressure necrosis of the iridocorneal angle were the main complications of AC IOLs, due to the positioning of the lens too close to the back of the cornea and the placement of the haptics in the anterior chamber angle. The iris clip IOL was developed to place the optic of the IOL further away from to the corneal endothelium and to secure the IOL using haptics which grip the edge of the iris through the pupil. Two main classes were produced where the optic was either in the anterior or posterior chamber. The anterior chamber lenses were the first as the optic was supported by the iris. The haptics prevented the IOL from irritating the anterior chamber angle and kept the lens centred. The iris is a mobile structure both vertically and horizontally and the iris clip lens required the pupil to be permanently pharmacologically 'miosed'. This meant that the patient had to indefinitely use drops four times a day. The iris and IOL could also prolapse forwards and impinge on the corneal endothelium; to prevent this, the second generation iris clip IOL had the optic in the posterior chamber. These lenses did not cause as much corneal decompensation as those with the optic in the anterior chamber. The clips, however, remained in the anterior chamber and still caused considerable damage to the iris.

The Modern Era and Posterior Chamber Lenses

The natural progression from the iris clip IOL was to place the clips around the iris and suspend the optic of the lens in the posterior chamber behind the iris. Support of the iris was required as the posterior capsule of the normal lens was removed at the time of surgery by intracapsular cataract extraction (ICCE). This was because the operation to do so was easy to perform and simple to learn. The advent of operating microscopes and fine instruments and sutures enabled surgeons to dispense with operating loupes and perform more complex surgery. Extracapsular cataract extraction, ECCE, similar in concept to the original surgery performed by Ridley, was introduced in the mid to late 80s. This involved removing the substance of the lens but leaving the posterior capsule intact, and this provided an ideal place to position an IOL. These posterior chamber IOLs were placed into the remaining capsular bag; the ideal physiological place to replace the original crystalline lens. Soft J-shaped haptics stented the IOL in position and were originally made of polypropylene, however, they had a poor physical memory and disfigured in time, leading to lens decentration. Modern IOLs are usually made of one piece of PMMA for both the optics and haptics. Holes are placed in the optic and haptics to enable the trailing haptic to be manoeuvred into the capsular bag, in a similar way to using a telephone dial, and are thus called dialling holes.

ECCE surgery has become a worldwide standard operation enabling patients to have sufficient vision, only one week after surgery, to drive. This operation is still used today and provides a remarkable level of visual rehabilitation. The major disadvantage of this operation is that a wound sufficiently large enough to express the cataractous lens has to be made This is usually 10-11 millimetres in length and the larger the wound, the longer the patient's vision takes to recover. The length of the wound is related to the incidence of adverse post-operative complications. Phakoemulsification probes have been developed to emulsify the cataract inside the eye using a tip which vibrates at 50Mhz. This requires a wound of 3.2 millimetres to be enlarged to implant the IOL, which has a diameter of 6 millimetres. This procedure enables patients to drive the day after surgery and is taking over from ECCE as the standard operation in the mid-90s.

The Future

The current aim of cataract surgery is to minimise the trauma of the operation on the eye. The design of the IOL has been refined to such an extent that the majority of IOLs implanted today are posterior chamber IOLs with a 6-millimetre optic diameter and PMMA, J-shaped haptics. PMMA is an inflexible solid requiring enlargement of the wound after the lens has been removed by phakoemulsification. New materials are being used for optics which are foldable and can be placed into the eye folded through a smaller incision, and unfolded in the capsular bag. These materials, silicone, acrylic and hydrogel, are made into IOLs of similar design, however, they all have different subtle complications. IOLs have come full circle: the design has become standardised, but the material of which the IOL is made becomes the variable, and the compatibility of these materials governs the relative outcomes.

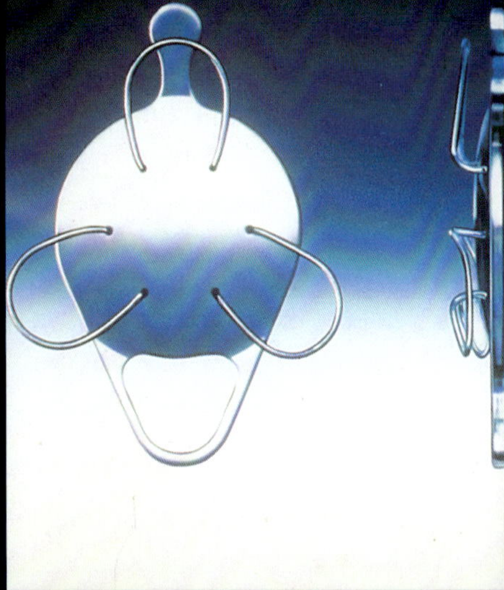

1

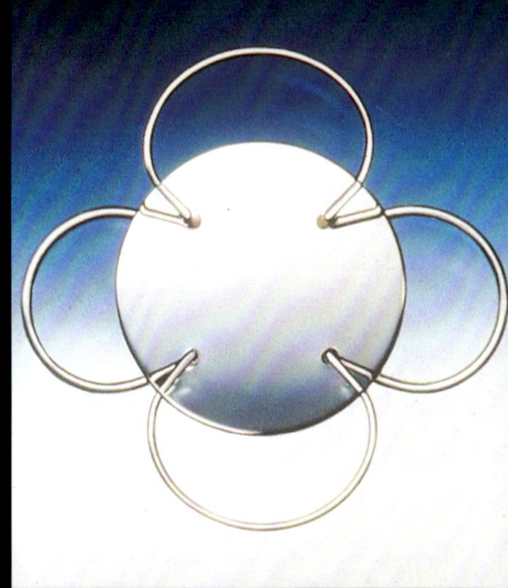

2

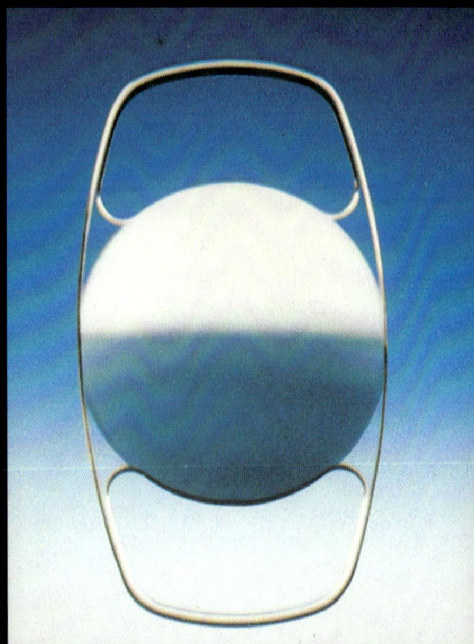

3

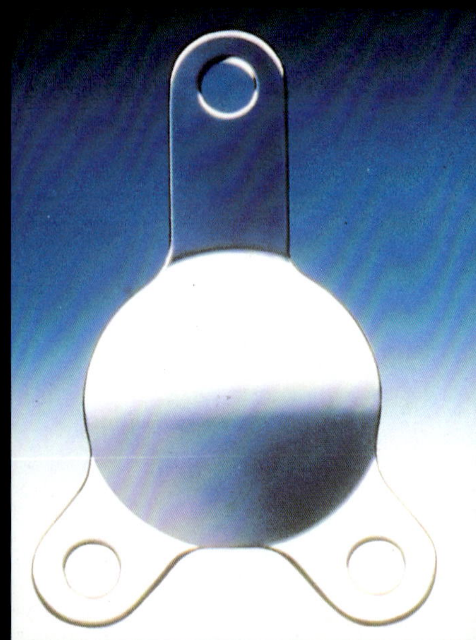

4

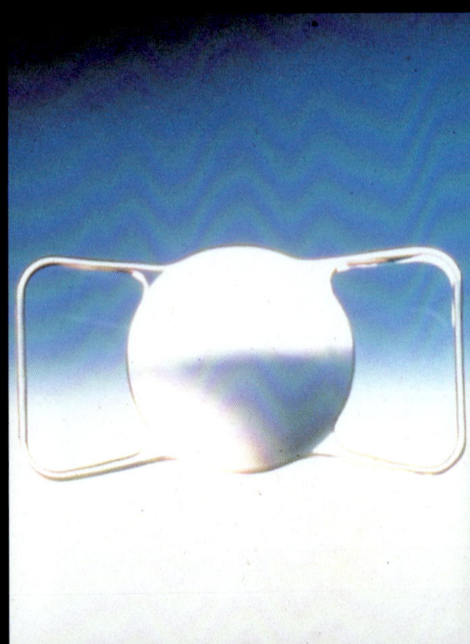

5

6

Lenses supported by haptics which pass throughout the pupil to support the optic (figs 1, 2); early posterior chamber IOLs (PCIOL) (figs 3, 4); early anterior chamber IOLs (AC IOL) (figs 5, 6)

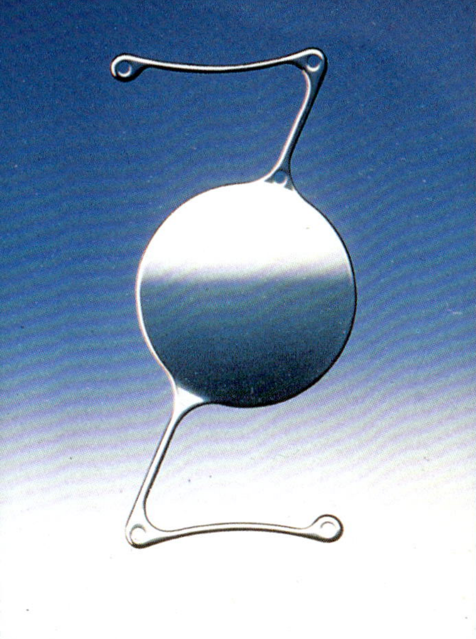

7

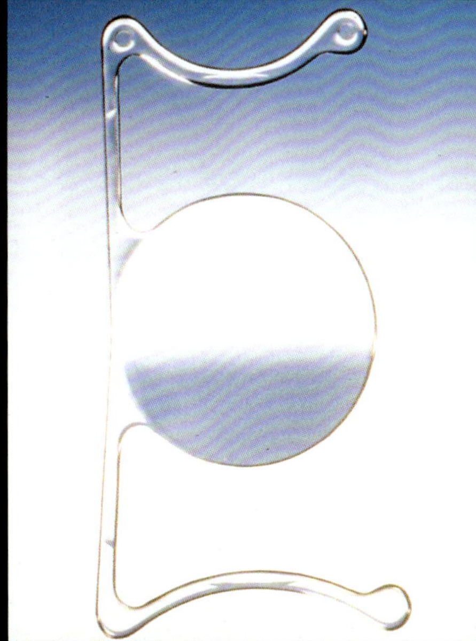

8

9

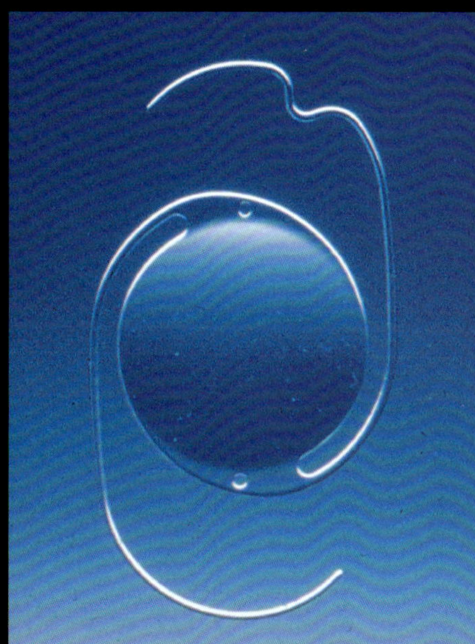

10

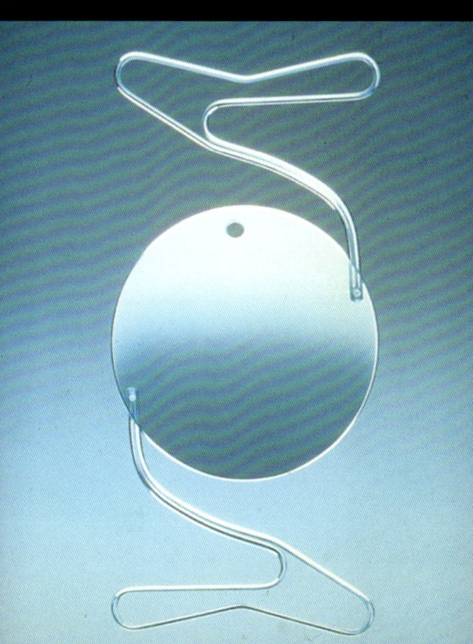

11

12

Later AC IOLs, with open, 'springy' haptics to alleviate pressure in the anterior chamber angle. The holes in the haptics are used by surgeons to position the IOL (figs 7, 8); modern PCIOLs, with optic positioned inside the thin capsular bag which remains after the cataract has been removed (FIGS 9, 10); a later AC IOL (fig 11); lense supported by haptics (fig 12)

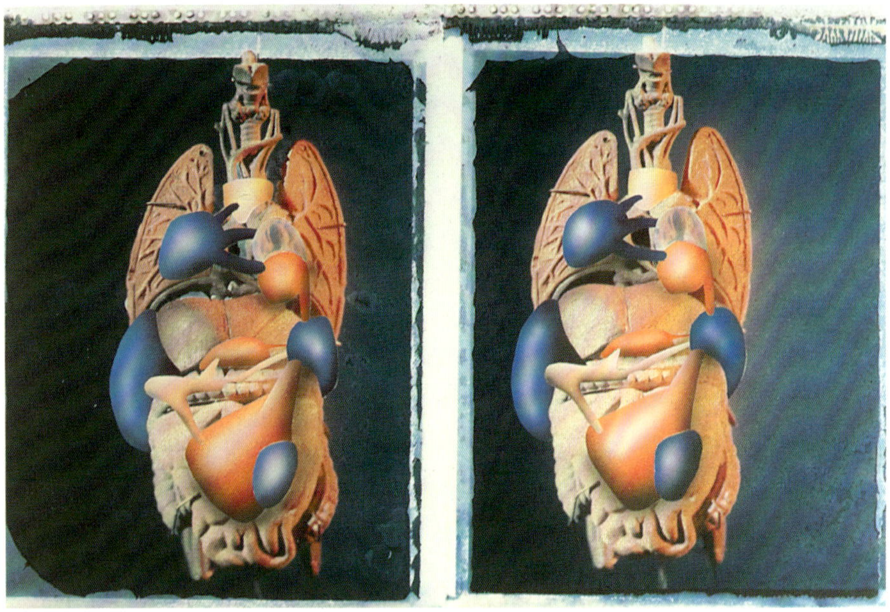

1

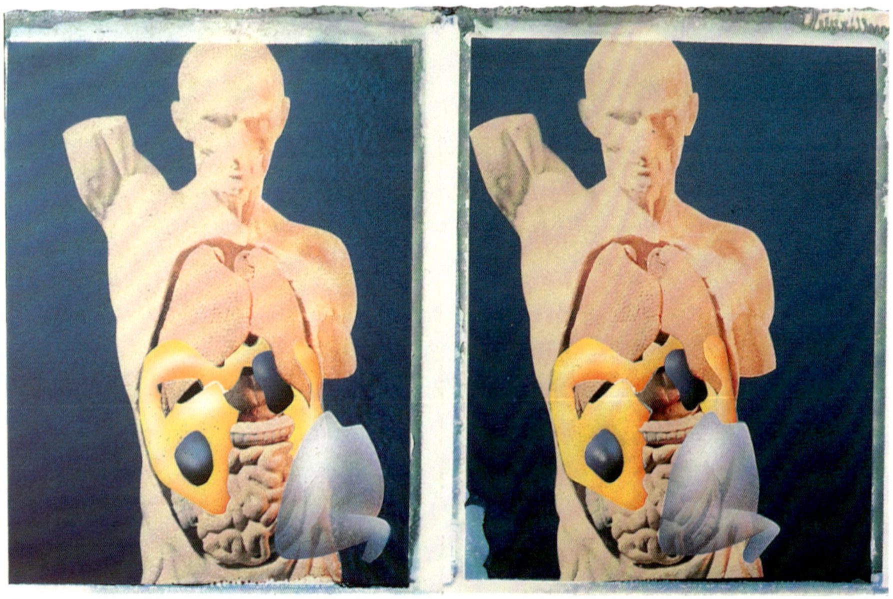

2

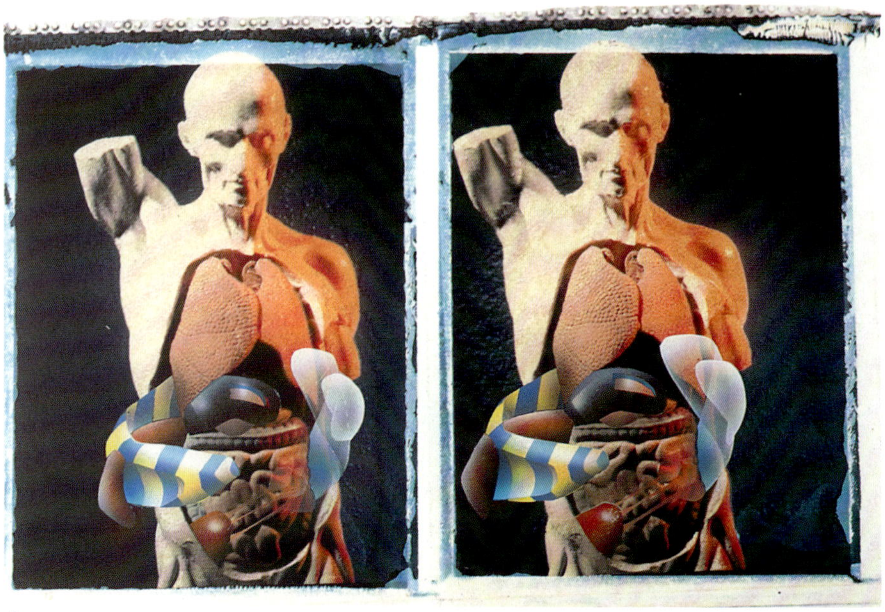

4

NAT CHARD

ARCHITECTURE OF OUR INTERIOR

This work originated through an interest in anatomical models which seem much more sophisticated than their architectural equivalent. Their level of abstraction becomes apparent when compared with plastercasts of dissected bodies or superelastic 19th-century wax versions. They are, however, primarily representational and adhere to the disciplines of scale and dimensional accuracy with which we are familiar. Like many architectural models, they have removable parts that allow us to understand interior relationships which would otherwise remain invisible.

What sets them apart is the way in which they play on our understanding of the body to establish their transparency within our imagination. In architectural models, sections are usually taken as they would be in drawings, a vertical or horizontal slice. The anatomical version takes layered sections, as if peeling a leaf from a cabbage. We already know that the body is largely symmetrical; different sections are taken either side of the axis of symmetry.

We know that above the middle of our forehead, the condition does not change drastically so two more layers (divided by the same axis) are cut, one side revealing the skull, the other, the brain. A further series of detailed layered sections is taken through the back of the skull side to explain the typical condition. On the side with the deeper (less familiar) section, a normal ear is placed to locate us.

From these sections we can construct the transparent layering of the body in our imagination. Where things become asymmetrical amongst the major organs, the elements can be removed piece by piece, many of them having their own cross-sections (consistent with the economy of means that these models exhibit and their concern for context, these are mostly partial sections). Only in asymmetrical conditions are both sides described. The deluxe models have interchangeable genitalia (and chests): only what is critically different between sexes is changed. Where a condition becomes typical at a certain layer, there is a change of section. The models engage us by requiring our intellectual complicity to complete them.

While I was trying to unravel the techniques displayed in these models, it was hard not to consider their content. Our primary points of contact with architecture are where we use it as a tool – where it is highly programmatic. Preparing food and drink, getting rid of our waste, sleeping and reproduction (the staircase boasts a large percentage of the population) have their own dedicated spaces. The organs which they relate to were clearly portrayed in front of me. If we could modify them, surely this would alter the programme of architecture and re- or deprogramme existing examples. However, as much as we try to reduce the importance of programme we are haunted by these simple practicalities. For us, a building without a lavatory is clearly meant to be occupied for short durations.

Ethically, we are comfortable with pacemakers or artificial hearts, the prosthetic implants which lengthen our lives. The project of the city has consistently been to deny nature. We build roofs to refuse the rain, make light to avoid night, heat to escape winter and cool to deny summer. But this project has extended beyond basic necessity, or comfort, and ranges from the unashamed decadence of synthetic pleasures at Las Vegas, Orlando or Tokyo to almost any artistic production. We already modify our bodies in this separation of desire and survival (with enormous spatial consequence) by using contraceptives, for example.

The speculation in this work is that architecture might be possible within as well as outside us. Fresh from a visit to New York, I was also searching for tactics to subvert malevolent programmes of thrilling spaces, however intertwined they might seem. Although it was to be a rhetorical project, I set out to find out how

3

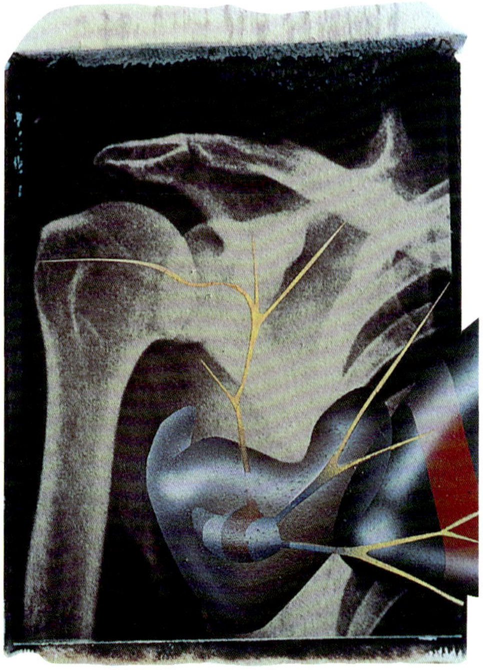

The infrastructure of the digestive system: 'plumbing' diagram (fig 1); exploded location of digestive elements (fig 2); detailed modification (fig 3); advanced version, exploded for clarity – the ultimate version would be compact enough to fit within the existing canals (fig 4); ABOVE: Imagined Organs, *1994-95*

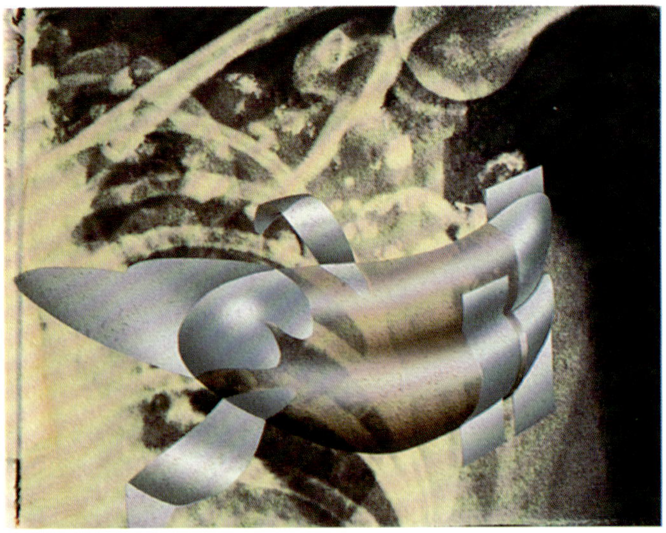

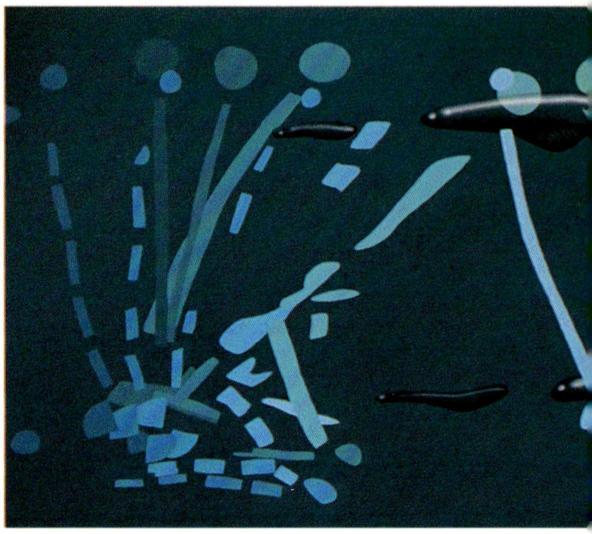

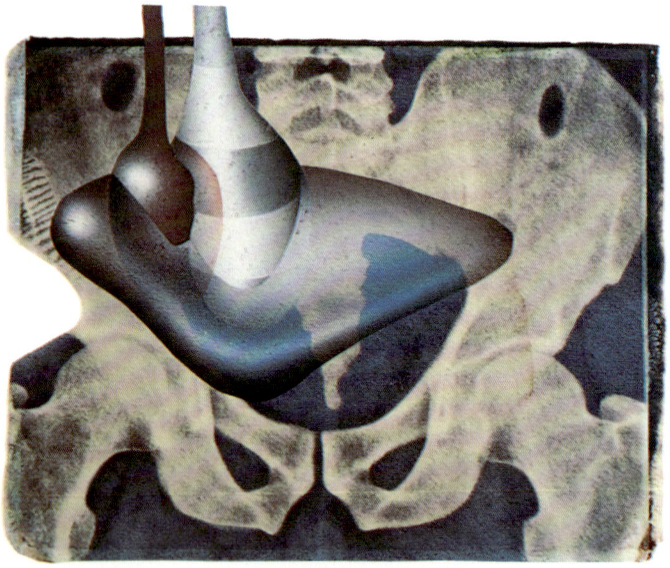

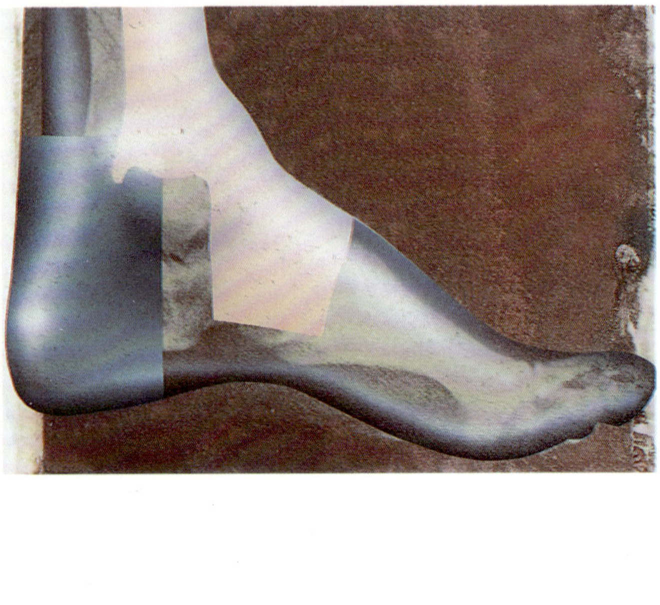

ABOVE, CENTRE: Imagined Organs, *1994-95*; BELOW: Immediate and Recollection Perceptions of the Foot, *1994-95; OPPOSITE:* The Space Between Two Pairs of Walking Legs, *1994-95*

it might be achieved. In the course of my research, the disciplines of nano and biotechnology were beginning to be popularised and seemed ideal for my purposes. This turned out to be the case, as in fact they were ideal for almost any purpose. This ability to do just about anything, coupled with a lack of specific characteristics, took the edge off the project and caused the drawings to be much more diagrammatic than hoped for.

Digestion seemed to be the most appropriate place to start. There is an enormous infrastructure to support our eating habits and dispose of our waste. If we could turn more of our food into fuel and store it for short term retrieval, there would be a number of implications: it would further separate the enjoyment of eating from the practicalities of survival and make it possible to maintain a preferred bodyweight independent of our eating habits. The more important spatial implications would be on the disposition of infrastructure. Our points of contact with the outside world, in these respects, could be further apart in both time and distance. Apart from the direct effects this would have on the food and waste industries, it would have repercussions on the structure of our working day and the way in which we lead our lives in general. A few judicious modifications to our bodies could fold the city inside out.

Figure one is primarily a plumbing diagram, figure two an (exploded) attempt to size and locate the elements, and figure three, a detailed modification. They all describe developments of the same system, which can take surplus food out of the digestive system and process it for short-term, fast-retrieval storage and subsequent digestion. A

feedback loop either scavenges undigested nutrients which have been through the system or allows surplus storage to be deposited, bypassing the digestive system. Figure four shows the most advanced version, exploded for clarity in the stereoscopic drawings and, in its intended position, as a single image. The ultimate version would be compact enough to fit within the existing canals.

I built my own anatomical model out of an *écorché* figure, and the organs from a plastic kit. The stereoscopic pairs were constructed photographically using Polaroid transfers. The less than perfect resolution of this technique allowed me draw on the synthetic organs to create an equivalence with the photographic image. The stereoscopic drawings can be seen as intended using stereo launettes[1], of which the mark two version is easier to use and gives better results.

Improvising Space

Architecture is compromised by paralysis, its most potent moments existing before completion or during ruination, when our imagination is engaged by what might be or what has already taken place. While it is inhabited, we exaggerate the delights of decay to cover the frustration that our work is the passive victim of physical and chemical abuse. Our spatial effects might be thrilling on first acquaintance, but how many survive a revisit or repeated occupation? Attempts to avoid stagnation have tended towards flexibility, usually meaning, at best, a choice of alignment rather than a variation in condition; the adaptation over time responding only to ideas of utility.

Even when we have the tools to vary the spatial performance of architecture, we use them to deny time. Hot or cold, wet or dry, dark or light, we forbid the cycles of nature to interfere with the internal programme. The technology of building is so primitive that we allow a wide tolerance when we establish a space to support an activity. This therefore tends towards excluding distractions rather than initiating support. In doing this, we acknowledge that we cannot sustain a precise relationship over time and that we have no right to determine the nature of that relationship.

The architecture which this work starts to propose involves an active and reciprocal relationship between the space and the participant. Separated from a generic idea of programme, the architecture responds to the intuitive, the improvised and the accidental. The role of the architect is to propose the flavour of the space – not its choreography. The spaces are driven by the desires and anxieties of the participants as well as practical programmatic requirements, such as supporting the body. As they learn the space, they can reveal and conceal these conditions, and even make forms and spaces of deceit.

Four sequential sections and a perspective of a hall and staircase propose the idea. At first, the hall is occupied by one person. The skin rises up to meet her feet and the space opens up towards her destination. The Taurus-like section reveals her indifference to the middleground. She is distracted by noises off to her left and involuntarily constructs two probing, anxious spaces to seek its source. Simultaneously, similar spaces appear behind and beyond her as possible boltholes should the noises prove a threat. In stage two, the staircase space appears bulging into her space. She does not recognise its signature and prepares to meet the stranger, losing interest in the boltholes. The second person emerges in the third frame, making some impression on the hall. In the final section, the inexperience of both participants is revealed by the conflicts of desire embodied in the space.

For the space to work well would require the commands to be as intuitive as possible. We carry electronic signals on our skin all the time. If we lose a hand, the prosthetic replacement can usually be driven by sensors on the skin which pick up signals to the same digit in the phantom hand. It would be tedious to have to wire up to use the space so it would sense the signals remotely. The ideal skin material does not yet exist though the new technologies of intelligent gels[2] (soft aggregations of long chain molecules which can shrink or swell in response to stimuli) and elastic biomolecular machines[3] (synthetic chains of amino acids which can transform heat and chemical energy into motion) look promising. The space would carry a memory of its existence, both through the materiality of the skin, stretchmarks, wrinkles, bruises etc, and in the computer monitoring its behaviour.

There are obvious problems with the drawings. As time is such an important component of the space it needs to exist in the drawing. The participants' experience is a composite of their immediate perception with what Bergson describes as 'recollection perceptions' and 'perception recollections'.[4] The section describes an accurate moment, but this is never perceived. The space has changed

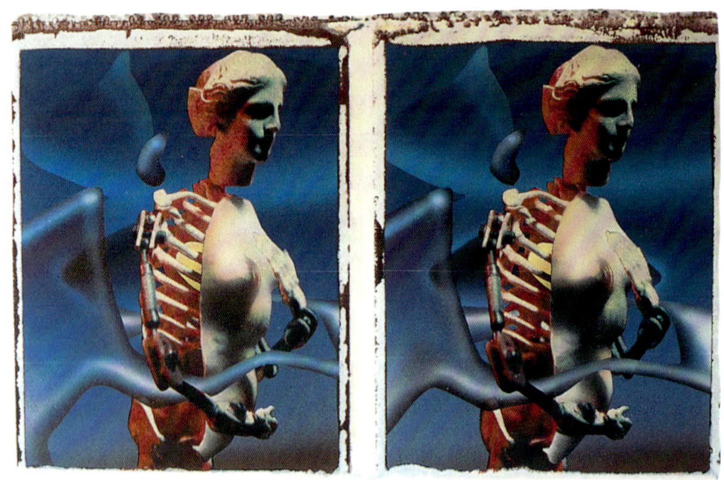
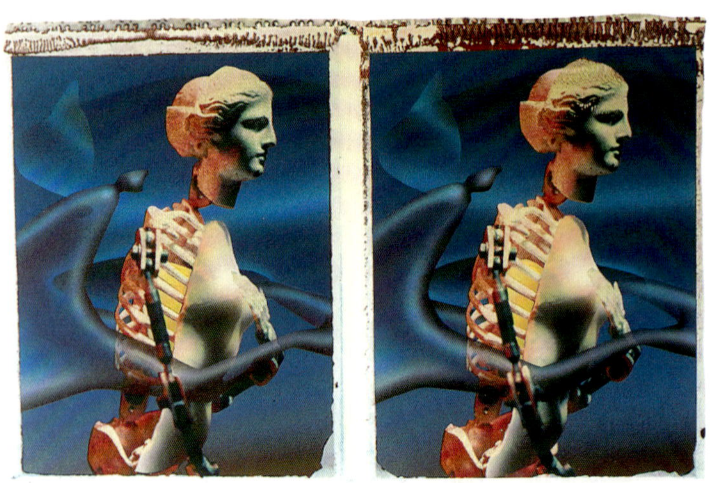
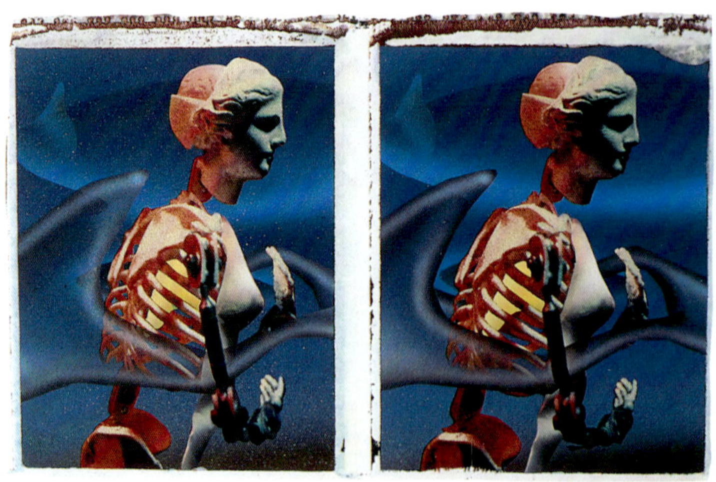

FROM ABOVE, L to R: Interstitial Shadows, *1994-95;* Aware of Someone Behind Her, *1994-95;* Context Interference, *1994-95;* Frame 7, Stereoscopic Film, *1994-95;* Frame 9, Stereoscopic Film, *1994-95;* Frame 10, Stereoscopic Film, *1994-95*

behind the participants, and although they are aware of this, unless they look round repeatedly (which would have its own effect on the space) there is likely to be a difference between that which exists physically and their imagination. This is complicated by feedback loops as the participants consciously adjust their subconscious commands as they see the effects. A set of studies examines this composite, as well as speculating on how the participants might imagine their modes of projecting the space. They show imagined organs conducting this work, bringing out the separation between what exists and our powers of perception. Other studies check that the space they construct is not the same as the perceived personal space they habitually carry with them.

These and other drawings explore how we are conscious of our bodies and the spaces we could construct around them. Although the behaviour of these spaces accentuates issues of duration, they have many recognisable physical attributes and are experienced through familiar modes of perception. None of the drawings, however, shows any windows. In the second part of this work I was interested in exploring other forms of transparency, especially those involving extended media. Of course, the nature of the skin in the drawings would provide a formal transparency for those outside – although they could not see the inhabitant, they would know when it was inhabited and would maybe recognise the occupant through the space's mannerisms. What really interests me is the context of the project. If the space is time dependent, then the context has to be 'now' rather than 'here'.

My experience of virtual reality has been limited to a couple of arcade games and I have to confess that I have found it a particularly hostile environment. Apart from the tedious ordeal of being shot at wherever you go, the surroundings are impoverished by the requirement that they are constructed of as little information as possible. Although this might single the medium out as the ideal habitat for psychopathic minimalists (quite a fashion in London recently), it clearly fails as a representational means. You do not need to don the sweaty headgear to know this. The Gulf War stood at the threshold of the virtual age. In the comfort of our living rooms we watched the same images as the bombardiers through the same medium. The immediacy of the image emphasised the separation between their experience and ours. More than ever before, the information was despatialised by the interface.

Nam June Paik's *One Candle* is of great interest to me. A video camera surveys the flame of a candle, the magnified image of which is then projected onto the surrounding walls. Using old video projectors with three colour tubes, the colours remain separated on the wall. As we enter the room, we disturb the air which enlivens the candle and, in turn, the multiple projections on the wall. These huge dissected flames initially attract our attention. In this piece, the secondary experience has an equivalence with its origin

The most elegant way I could find to establish an equivalence between the immediate space and its context was for them to exist through the same medium. If the form of the skin which makes the space is driven by electronic signals from our body, then it would make sense for the electronic signals in the ether to determine its texture. Navigational signals might inscribe a monotonous frown, while broadcasts and telecommunications might register their nature and level of activity. Certain climatic conditions would cause interference with these signals, electronic storms would manifest their own display. The painted walls and stained glass windows of churches have an analogous role of providing their space with a context beyond its immediate surroundings (usually in both time and space). The registration of these signals as texture would be much more engaging as interference rather than coded figures. The architect's only role in this would be to establish the range of amplitude.

An opaque skin could therefore provide the transparency which could gather events of the moment well beyond our normal range of perception. This would establish time rather than place as our locator while we inhabit this space. But what of our role as participant? I would suggest it is a privileged one, for there cannot be many creative acts which are as immediate in both time and space. As architects, we are distanced in both respects from what we propose. It is the same for filmmakers, composers and painters even if you accept the studio as an analogue for the gallery (or vice versa).[5] Only in improvised work is such immediacy possible. This project is about improvising space.

This sets up an overlap in the relationship between what the architect provides and what the participant brings with them. The overlap exists in the physical manifestation of the space and its construction in the imagination. A colleague asked me, 'Where is the clock on the hall mantelpiece, where is the picture on the wall?'. The answer is that as the skin holds time, it does not need representation through the clock and as for the painting, the hall embodies the spaces of our memory and imagination.

Learning from the chronophotographic techniques of Marey, Pierce Jones and others, I made some drawings to describe duration within the space. These and subsequent drawings were external to the body. Although there is a view that the perspective is an accurate representation of human perception and location, for reasons I mentioned earlier, it was not suitable here. To embody the time relationships more clearly I made a short, animated stereoscopic film. The perception of depth through stereopsis is so closely linked with perspective that this might seem a strange decision, but it provides a level of engagement which might overcome the problems of a displaced viewpoint. The film shows simultaneity of events that were not possible in drawings. I also worked on photographs which hold duration apart from Marey-derived chronophotographs. The photo finish camera records a cut in space rather than the normal camera's cut in time. Using an improvised version, the separation over time of the figure from its shadow indicated that this technique promises the potential for developing the work further.

Notes

1 Launettes available from Agar Scientific, tel: 01279 813519

2 Yoshihito Osada & Simon B Ross-Murphy, 'Intelligent Gels', *Scientific American*, May, 1993.

3 Dan W Urry, Elastic Biomolecular Machines, *Scientific American*, January, 1995.

4 Giles Deleuze, *Bergsonism*, (trans) H Tomlinson & B Habberjam, Zone Books (New York), 1991, p22. *Matter and Memory*, (trans) Henry Bergson, NM Paul & WS Palmer, Zone Books (New York), 1991.

5 Daniel Buren, *The Function of the Studio*, (trans) Thomas Repensek, MIT (Mass), 1988, pp201-08.

ALISON SAMPSON

INSIDE OUT: CLINICAL PROCEDURE RELATING TO CAESAREAN SECTION AS PRACTISED ON BODIES, OBJECTS AND BUILDINGS

The monumental 'male-ness' of the public vision contrasts, traditionally, with the corporeality and intimacy of the female space. In recent decades, this clear demarcation has undergone a shift. The monument has become the body itself: fetishised, exposed, mutilated. Graphic, invasive, even sinister, the ten pieces that make up the body of work question the public–private opposition by exposing 'private' material, the Caesarean section, to public vision.

Inside Out is an allegory for the development of an architectural practice (allegory: giving a narrative description of a subject under the guise of another having similarities to it; cushioning the blows to the body). Sources from surgery and embroidery are employed to introduce an alternative method of working with sites, especially those where the fabric/purpose needs to be altered, updated, or mended. Currently, turning buildings/sites inside out is practised more by engineers than architects and will remain on the periphery of architectural practice as long as visual design is seen as being marginal to 'conservation' work.

The *Inside Out* manifesto has two steps: applying clinical practice in the design/making of models (Turning The Body Inside out) and then following everyday architectural procedure to apply the design, as modelled, on the *living* building/site (Turning The Building Inside Out). The altered and/or repaired site is a likeness (not an identity), formal and conceptual, of the cut/fabric/flesh. In comparing the respective operations on bodies and buildings, more possibilities are raised than merely questions of form. The position of the architect/surgeon; the position of the building/woman who is being operated on; and the position of the public/theatre audience are also called to issue. *Inside Out* does not provide a definitive answer to the broad questions it raises. Emphasising deeds over words, whilst granting the latter the attention they deserve, the project is an exploration which will be used to formulate new possibilities for specific sites and contexts in future practice – corporeal, material, and geographical.

The Operating Theatre (Turning the Body *Inside Out*)

The usual way of revealing the interior of the body in medicine, by word of mouth, is inadequate when trying to overcome dilemmas during childbirth as it is considered too slow and gives only a dim view of what is happening. The cheapest and quickest way of facilitating delivery is by getting down to work on the body, sectioning it, and introducing access to the interior by artificial means. As textbooks of surgery have established, the skin is marked, pierced *(fig 1)*, and stretched back with hooks, then the perineum is retracted to make an opening *(fig 2)*. The obstetrician uses large scissors to section the thick wall of the uterus, forceps to remove the baby, and a variety of implements and stitches to mend the body.

Inside Out shows the true site of operations. Honing in with a surgeon's eye, we see the parts, but nothing of the whole. The absence, or inertia, of the body is what strikes the viewer and the site is perhaps not abdominal, but genital. In the piece 'Unfolded' *(fig 3)*, the labial folds clearly suggest the vaginal opening; its accoutrements (outsize scalpel and pins) implicit violation. The grotesque spectacle of these moments is frozen in time, an (operating) theatre performance. Despite the pain, the obstetrician is redeemed by the fact his hack-and-sew surgery is working to a positive end: to deliver a new baby, and hopefully maintain the mother's life too.

Architectural obstetricians deliver a new building/form during the operation and must carefully heal the site to the best of their ability. Obsessively precise, their cuts make interstitial spaces between tissues, connecting, supporting, dividing. Here, in the act of violation, the obstetrician leaves his own traces: stitches of light and space, solids and voids, between the private refuge and the onlooker. Reading the allegory leads to questions being raised on material/professional performance; the woman's body itself and the status of the casual spectator. In the following paragraphs these positions are examined in turn, before the possible consequence of the operation is considered.

The Professional Performance

The work is not carried out without some necessary gallows humour. In a clinical striptease, the procedure of everyday surgery is reordered by some external constraint. Here, the interior is revealed before it is dressed and, perhaps ironically, 'stitched up'. The latter, complete with loose ends of fabric/flesh, is the work of some medical madman. Rather than minimising pain on the operating table, the sensation of the woman is maximised, indulged – and detailed. In such a space, structure must be secondary to the requirements of the eye (but the viewer would be forgiven for speaking out if scissors and spatulas were accidentally left in the wound in a moment of forgetfulness). This distinction between bodily sense and sight gives a distance to the performance, affording the woman's body on the table some dignity: she is an actor on a stage, not a piece of meat.

The obstetrician uses medical technology to disempower the woman on the table, changing her body, in his opinion, for the better. Stitches and pins, retractors and forceps hold the wound open, enlarging the life of the body. The function of the instruments, once intended to be there only temporarily, is extended to new purposes, like the space that holds them. The obstetrician's audience and patient trust him; he is, after all, professional. When compared to another profession, that of architects, the question is raised: 'If all this seems strange in medicine, how different is it when an architect seeks to impose his own idea of expert knowledge on a site?'

The Theatre of the Body

The split between inside and outside, and between senses and

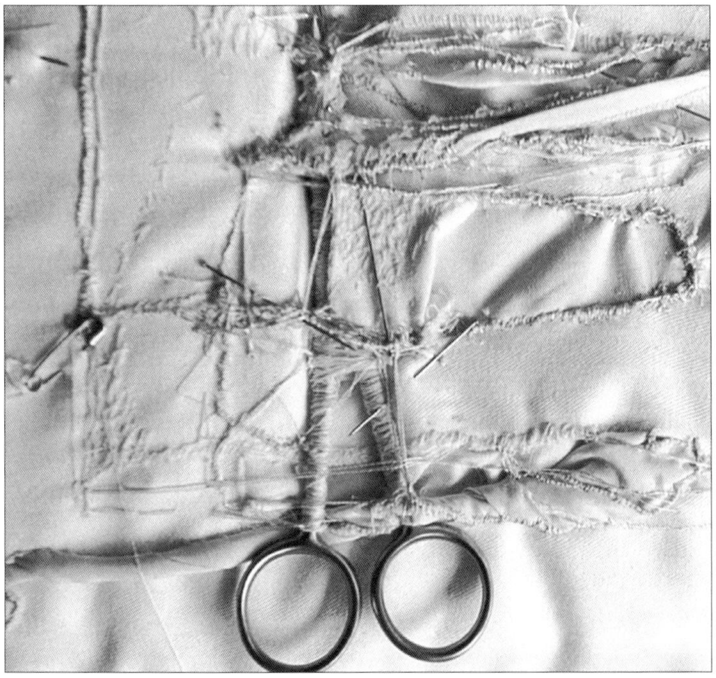

1

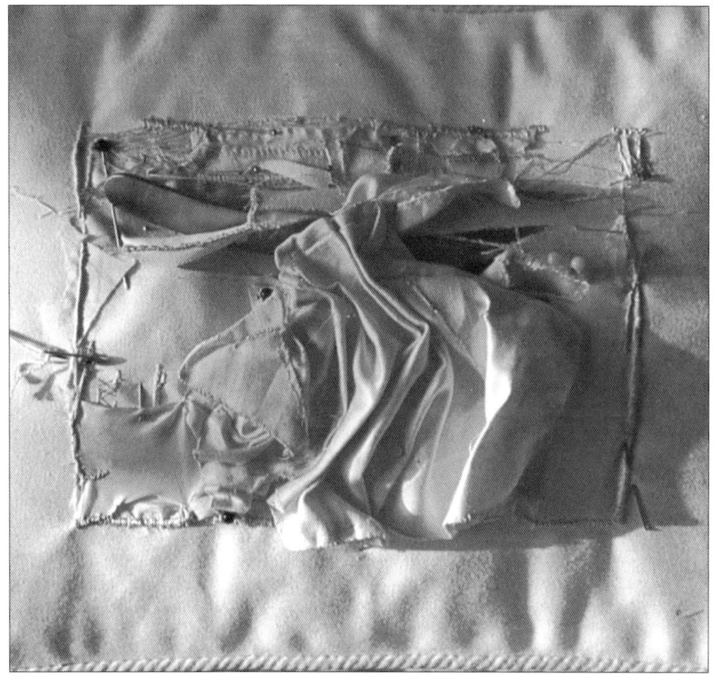

2

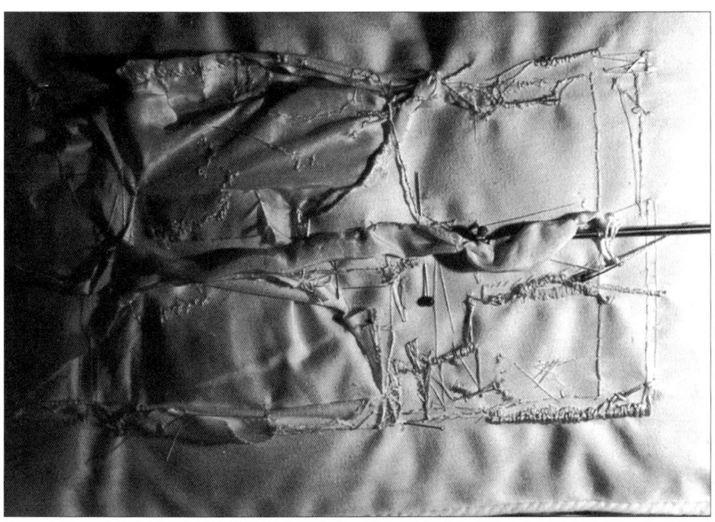

3

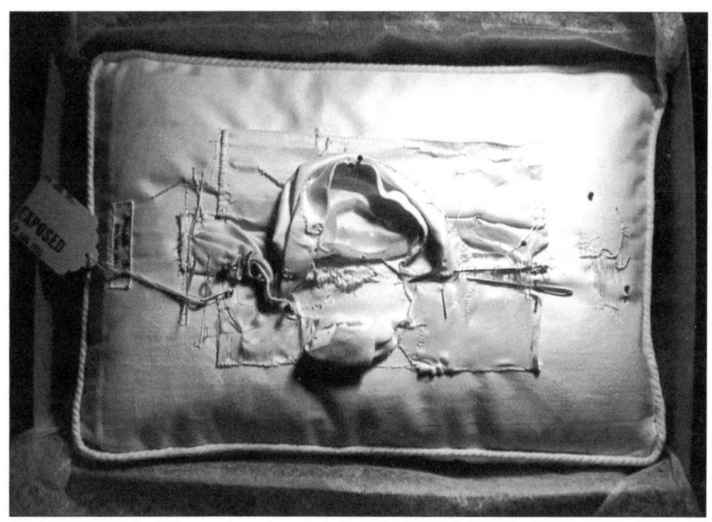

4

Pierced, *1995, second of series of ten sewn objects, downproof cambric, silk, viscose thread, down, unbleached calico, lens tissue, utility board and surgical scissors, boxed and labelled, 24 x 36 x 9cm (fig 1);* Retracted, *1995, third of series of ten sewn objects, materials and dimensions as* Pierced, *interventions made with small spatula and dissection pins (fig 2);* Unfolded, *1995, sixth of series of ten sewn objects, materials and dimensions as Pierced, intervention made with scoop spatula (fig 3);* Exposed, *1995, eighth of series of ten sewn objects, materials and dimensions as* Pierced, *interventions made with darning and suturing needles and metal stiches (fig 4)*

sight is gender loaded. The exterior of the building, showing no feeling, is masculine. The soft interior, scene of sexuality and reproduction, is feminine. Spaces within the wound are also marked out as male, or female. The cut made by, and containing, the obstetrician, interrupts the normal social relationships and spatial hierarchies of the body, not fitting with the polite sequence for moving through the 'female' space. Yet, the boundary is not so clearly drawn. In order to modify the interior, the surgeon must mark and pierce the exterior. In his choice of cut, he lays himself open to the scrutiny of his students, peers and patients.

During Caesarean section, the woman lies passive and vulnerable on the table, yet in many cases is conscious. At the point of the knife, she looks back out at the world, as from behind a curtain. Not just the object of a dispassionate scrutiny, but an object of mystery, she is empowered by her roles of both actor and spectator in the unfolding performance. Her refuge is not only normally restricted from view, but is also beyond the threshold of privacy. Inside, but outside, like her, the obstetrician is vulnerable in his moment of control, open to scrutiny.

The body cannot be seen as an object when the relation between the inside and the outside becomes so convoluted. The revealed flesh is a surface that neither conceals or reveals, but it is itself fetishised. Like the body as fetish, the operated upon building is all surface, with no interior, a *mise-en-scene* for mystery. By cutting into the body, the obstetrician works on the form where function has ceased, or is disrupted, modifying some of the old ways, and facilitating a number of new ones. The body during surgery continues to live, at once serving prosaic and conceptual functions, the latter being all conditions of sight: refuge, theatre, museum, clinic. In operating, the obstetrician does not have it in his power to dictate the specific way in which the space will be utilised (the body must be left to its own devices in this respect), but can only use his knowledge to allow for long-term possibilities. After the operation is completed, the obstetrician continues to watch his patient and the conditions he has established. Positions of authority have shifted and now the operator himself is vulnerable, the one under the knife.

The Role of the Spectator

Inside Out sewing is not intended to be subordinate to the eventual end product of the architect, but equal (and different). Like big architecture, this installation is not primarily targeted at architects, but at the public, who (as shown by their comments) should not be underestimated in their willingness, or ability, to take up their place as operators. Materials used on this site are those of needlework: the stereotypical occupation of genteel elderly ladies belying the bloody mess of hack and sew surgery. The public is drawn into this scenario, the immediate appeal proving to be largely sensual. Reactions have ranged from identification to something more visceral: shock, entrancement, recognition, covetousness, anxiety. Such an approach has been welcomed by the many viewers who have taken time away from their shopping to comment. The changed morphology of the site is mainly defined by the material qualities of the body/fabric and the working method (for example, it is virtually impossible to get a clean edge on the cambric because of the looseness of the weave, so alternative stitching methods must be applied). Like any body, the cushion has a life of its own: any reaction has to be anticipated and allowed for (the down-stuffed interior is liable to bleed when pierced, so invasive action has to be carefully controlled and any breaks managed and patched immediately to prevent leakage).

Inside Out asks little more of the viewer than a capacity to enjoy, but makes the spectator feel uncomfortable, having been drawn in. This incongruity leads them to ask further questions about the 'meaning' of the words/works. The transfer of the operation to a material double allows the stages of the procedure; the operated-on body and the resulting spatial relationships to be individually observed, scrutinised, dissected, discussed. For the spectator to move into the space of the work, a name is given by the author (for example, *Exposed*), which precipitates further readings. In being read by a casual viewer, the work extends beyond the frame within which it was created to enclose the body of the reader. In this particular piece *(fig 4)*, the body parts have become so far detached from the body that their space invades the public territory, operating on the sight of the onlooker. Views are allowed, not only from outside to inside through the cut, but from within the wound, looking at the encircling soft tissues at close range, and back out to the exterior. This raises the question, 'Where is the boundary of this work: is it the cloth, the wrapping, the box, the shop window, the street, the city?'

The Theatre of Operations

The work's ability to be read, enables it to be translated into a new site, a body, or a building. The obstetrician's lessons extend beyond the architect applying alternative methods of construction/repair to a site, instead cutting across the entire field of operations. Architects should not be afraid to question, or tamper with the limits of their work. Perhaps surprisingly, a good example of how the operator can reconstruct working methods in line with the *Inside Out* manifesto, is found in traditional conservation work. This is illustrated by the everyday surgical procedures orchestrated by an architect during a programme of repairs recently completed on the roof of a fourteenth-century church.

From engagement, the architect placed emphasis on commencement on site so that scaffolding could be established and exploratory opening-up could occur in order to minimise abortive work. When opening-up took place, not only was the damage worse than predicted, it was worse than anticipated. The architect instituted a radical programme of surgery which was carried out with full consent of the appropriate statutory authorities. He also operated in the client's interest (to procure funds for the work from various sources) and then worked closely with the contractors and expert craftsmen (finalising much of the detail design on site). The schedule of services followed the same programme of work as carried out during Caesarean section: scrutiny; marking the site; selective opening-up; 'temporary' works; reassessment of the scope of work; major opening-up and stripping back of the materials of the roof to reveal the structure; cutting out, repair and prosthesis using modern techniques and materials; stitching of various types, covering, and so on. The work culminated in a new lead roof being dressed over timbers that had been substantially operated on.

Here, and in turning the body *Inside Out* the architect is positioned inside and outside his own work. The site demands that construction on site commences before the programme of working drawings is finished. The body/building therefore begins to manipulate the operator. The architect/obstetrician is not simply the author, but the building/site has more authority over him than he has over it. His performance shows more similarities to that of the midwife than the surgeon: operating in the clients interest; marshalling resources, but allowing the site and materials to influence decision-making.

The Theatre of the Everyday (Turning the Building *Inside Out*)

When called on to operate on a body, the midwife would not impose limits on the body, but work within constraints beyond her control. Her practice combines technical knowledge, a working method, an identification with both the form/content of the female body, and a certain frankness about mortality. *Inside Out* highlights the fragility and durability of the body – and its ability to be healed. An admission of pain (through the inversion of the body) and mortality are both acknowledged as part of the healing process. Following the *Inside Out* manifesto from beginning to end, the midwife-architect can make a new kind of value judgement: determing the way in which visual pleasure is maximised. She must operate on the building, cutting with all possible skill and care (having considered if (a) the site is up to the operation in material terms; (b) there is something worth revealing; (c) she works with, not on, the body, and (d) she guards both the mother and child's lives without judgement). This does not mean, at any time, that the body is sacred.

Transferred to architecture, clinical procedure may create spaces which have consequences for how the body is viewed within its environment. Exposure as (operating) theatre; the spectator is distanced from the viscera, but intimacy is maintained. In making these spatial moves, questions are raised about what is, or should be, 'temporary' *(fig 5)*. Given all this, and despite all the talk of subjugation, pain and mortality, *Inside Out* has positive ends. The midwife-architect may leave a morcellated body at the end of her work, but the midwife, by operating, has also brought a new organism into the world, different from the mother, with a life of its own and, in turn, capable of making new generations.

5

Dressed, *1995-96, Church of the Holy Rood, Sparsholt, Oxon, interventionary materials used on this Grade 2 listed building: oak, epoxy resin, mortar, steel, lead, lime mortar and others. Project undertaken by the author included replacement of existing lead roofs with new and extensive timber repairs for the client, the Parochial Church Council, Sparholt (fig 5)*

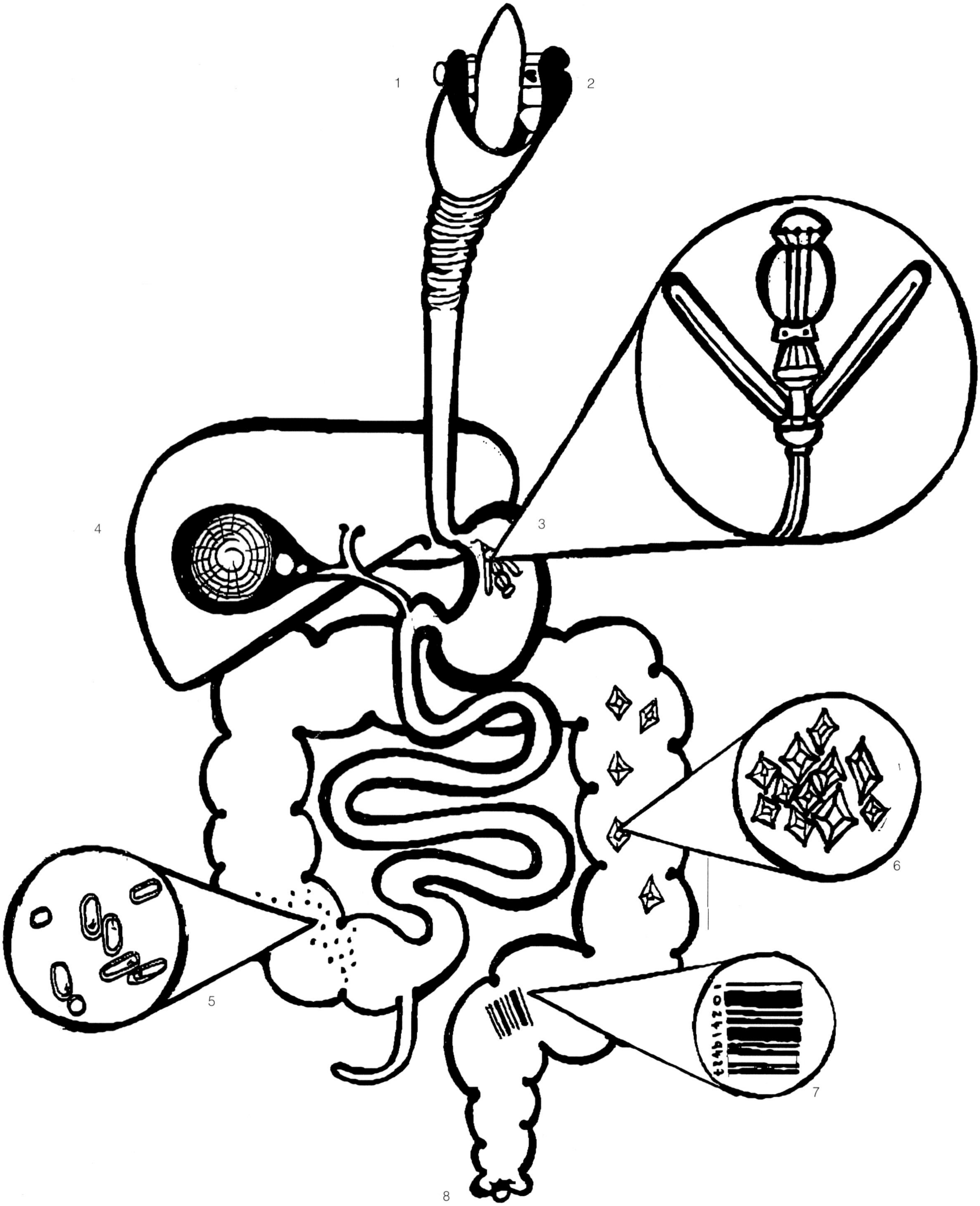

Key: (1) labrette or oral piercing, (2) decorative fillings on teeth, (3) stomach sculpture, (4) gallstone cultures (5) genetically engineered cultures (6) crystal gardens (7) rectal barcode or tattoo (8) anal piercing

RACHEL ARMSTRONG

THE BODY AS AN ARCHITECTURAL SPACE – FROM LIPS TO ANUS

(The Gastrointestinal Tract as a Site for Redesigning and Development)

'Man is sick because he is badly designed . . . ' Antoin Artaud, 1947

Antoin Artaud dreamed of a body without organs. He considered the famous poets of his time, listed them and evaluated the relative time spent defecating, urinating, sleeping, eating and washing in comparison to the 'creative' act. His conclusion was that the body organs of the artists required an energy investment in their base functions out of all proportion to the amount of energy invested in the higher, creative acts. Organs were therefore distracting and even impeding the body from carrying out its aesthetic activities.

Decline of the Symbolic Power of the Organs

The interior body housing the organs is alien territory, considered to be a redundant space. These neglected and despised organs were once associated with magical powers and healing, and were embalmed in preparation for their vital role in the afterlife. In the Old Testament, Jonah was redeemed by the grace of God in the intestine of a whale after having taken to the seas to escape.

Since the scientific enlightenment, these mystical organs have been trivialised, and are now considered to perform a supportive role to the exterior creative body. Lacking detailed analysis and artistic evaluation, our internal anatomy is granted no intrinsic value or aesthetic appeal; it is badly mapped-out, scantily documented and deeply misunderstood:

> I bring my intestine up out of my mouth and let it fall at my feet . . . I bring out into the open all the things I have taken in that they are not mine and thereby make room for something new. I make and external order out of an internal tangle . . . [1]

Organs as Contaminants

Organs have gradually been associated with the symbolisation of noxious spaces, with the deterioration of the body and the loss of personal identity. Enlightenment scientists, in the absence of methods of preservation and with rudimentary medical interventions, attributed the processes of senescence and pathology to disease-ridden organs. With increasing age, the gradual dissolution of flesh, and its replacement with shapeless organs, appeared to become more pronounced, and the emerging elderly body seemed to be caricatured as a precipitation of soft innards in a skin bag. These vengeful organs continued to insult the failing flesh, filling up with effluvial secretions; shitting and drooling, in anticipation of the total dissolution of the external body. This inversion of organ visibility over the body flesh was understood to signify the onset of death-related processes:

> at ninety they lose their teeth and hair; they have at that age, no distinction of taste but eat and drink whatever they can get, without relish or appetite. The diseases they were subject to still continue without increasing or diminishing . . . They are despised and hated . . . '[2]

Artists and philosophers theorised methods of escape from these anti-aesthetic organs. Having located the mind in the brain, which held a special anatomical relationship separate from the common organs, they speculated on identity without formulating a common language, either literal or metaphoric, to communicate with or about our internal organs.

Even biologically, the brain is continuously seeking a relationship with the external body flesh in preference to the organ systems, and informs us of organ distress through 'referred pain', a sensation in a sick organ which is felt in part of the skin rather than at its true site of origin.

The organs, ignored by the brain, continue to function autonomously, periodically filling up with slime, consuming creative energy and emptying the effluvia of their irritant discourse into the most filthy of all our organs, the cavernous sewer we call our gut.

Building the Body Sewer

The gut is such an inherently uninhabitable place that, even developmentally, it is sealed off from contact with the outer membrane of the body by the cloacal and buccal membranes. These seals perforate at around one month during embryological development and the embryonic gut starts to reel in its herniated folds and bud off the digestive organs. The intestinal loops are then sealed out of sight, inside the abdomen. As the child grows, the intestines occupy less volume in the decreasingly protuberant abdomen and settle under gravity, suspended by blood vessels and ligaments, to fill up the spaces in the bony pelvis in the form of the adult bowel.

Assessing the Terrain

The adult gastrointestinal tract is composed of a variety of differently shaped, muscular tubes which add up to around 7-10 metres in total length. These individual sections have different characteristics and, according to medical classification, are the: oesophagus (25 centimetres); duodenum (24 centimetres); small intestine (3-10 metres); ascending colon (12-20 centimetres); transverse colon (45 centimetres); descending colon (22-38 centimetres); sigmoid colon (12-75 centimetres); rectum (12 centimetres), and the anal canal (4 centimetres). These components are primarily occupied with the processing of food, which is masticated in the buccal cavity (mouth/teeth) and sequentially propelled, stored, secreted on and slowly absorbed before waste products are expelled as faeces.

This process is slow, inefficient and messy, and essentially employs the same techniques as the housefly who spits its digestive juices on to its food before sucking the paste back up for absorption. The main difference between the processing of human foodstuff and that of the insect, is that the messy procedure is hidden from our gaze. Inside the creative flesh, the intestine is filtering the partially digested food-paste through microvilli and transporting it into the bloodstream.

The gut's membrane is thin and delicate and suited to the processes of digestion. However, it is also surprisingly robust, mobile and sufficiently plastic to warrant reassessment of its assumed anatomical, physiological and aesthetic capabilities to be a potential site for redesign and/or augmentation. The gastrointestinal tract may be reconsidered in preparation for the demands which will affect our bodies in the coming millennium.

It is possible that with the advent of intravenous nutrition – simulating idealised quantities of foodstuffs, and vitamins and minerals to maintain a healthy body – the future regulation of our calorific intake and supplementation may take place intravenously or directly into the body cavity (peritoneum). When this occurs, the gut's primary task of processing food and excreting waste products will be lost, and may be replaced by other pursuits. The shrivelling-up of redundant parts of the intestine has already been demonstrated by the case of the appendix, which is a small segment of gut budding out from the start of the colon. The function of the appendix in herbivores is to break down vegetation with the assistance of bacteria. Human beings have evolved with an omnivorous diet and the appendix has become smaller and redundant in response to this dietary preference. The gastrointestinal tract of the future may be of different dimensions or, only being capable of supporting aesthetic activity, may even disappear totally as a functional structure.

Reinventing the Role of the Gastrointestinal Tract

Once freed from the obligation to reserve space and energy for nutrition, the gastrointestinal tract could be adapted to encompass new functions. What these future concerns might be remains speculative, but there are a number of artists and performers who have investigated creative possibilities in this area. The main obstacle to this re-evaluation, is gaining access to the gastrointestinal terrain and finding the appropriate equipment to document or transmit the images.

Access to the Gastrointestinal Space

In order to directly see the interior of the body, the traditional techniques normally employed are medical interventions such as surgery or dissection. This process is inherently problematic to the live artist/explorer, as the method of inquiry directly fragments the continuity of the gastrointestinal tract and is synonymous with disease processes and/or death.

The artists who have investigated the gastrointestinal system have reconsidered its relationship to the body. Like Artaud, many consider the 'natural' human body to be badly designed for the environment in which it exists, and in particular in its efficient use and relationship to its interior spaces.

> Never being born, escaping the wheel of continual birth and rebirth, no mouth to suck with, no anus to shit through . . . No mouth. No teeth. No tongue. No larynx. No oesophagus. No belly. No anus . . . The body it is the body/it is all by itself and has no need of organs since the body is never an organism . . . organisms are the enemies of the body . . . '[3]

Some artists who have gained access to specimens from medical laboratories, or anatomy books have used the images of organ systems as symbols rather than experimental documentary self portraits. The recontextualisation of the extruded gut in *Loop my Loop* (1991) from the exhibition 'Effluvia' by Helen Chadwick, presented an impossible relationship between the bowel and hair entwined in a love knot, suggesting a new aesthetic harmony between the interior and exterior body space.

Challenging the Pathological Gaze

Recent advances in medical imaging techniques have opened up the gastrointestinal space by providing access to even its deepest recesses without the need for death, or a major surgical procedure. The possibility of experimentation in a living body provokes a different contextualisation of these live images, in reference to the role and aesthetic qualities of the gut. The literal, rather than metaphorical, space of this site has been especially facilitated by ultrasound imaging and flexible endoscopy. Other imaging techniques such as CAT-scans (Computer Aided Tomography, an X-ray technique looking at tissue density) and MRI (Magnetic Resonance Imaging, using the magnetic spin of water molecules to calculate fluid content) are able to provide detailed analyses of the body's entire anatomy, but are not specifically concerned with detailed imaging of the gut and therefore do not capture its dynamic nature.

The new medical technologies have counterpoised the association between seeing the interior spaces and death, and remind us of their life-giving functions since we live in an age of organ transplants, where liver and bowel transplants are now frequently used for the treatment of hereditary conditions such as cystic fibrosis.

The Living Body and the Gastrointestinal Tract

Despite its internal position in the body, the gastrointestinal tract may be considered an *internalised exterior* body space. That is to say, if you were to miniaturise yourself and coat your body with an enzyme resistant coating you would be able to walk from the lips to the anus of a friend without ever actually breaching the surface of the body. Having completed your journey, you would emerge, encased in faecal residue, from the anus (without having disturbed your friend's internal physiology or breached their body surface), certain in the knowledge that you had fully accessed this secret space.

The images that have been retrieved when artists have started journeys into these cavernous spaces have been reworked into many different works of art: film, installation and performance, revealing the artist's bizarre methods of exploration and their encounter with the equally alien landscapes.

The work of Linda Dement, an Australian multimedia artist, presents the female body as a series of monstrous shapes depicting forbidden internal anatomies as autonomous landscapes and valid sites for reinterpretation in her CD-ROM publications *Cyberflesh Girlmonster* and *Typhoid Mary*. Here, donations of images of female body spaces were animated and made interactive. When a viewer clicks on one of these 'monsters' the words attached to that body part may be heard or seen, another monster may appear, a digital video may play or medical information may be called-up. The user moves between these without a menu system or a clear controllable interface, giving the interpretations of the gastrointestinal orifices a different relationship to other body parts and creating a new hybrid language between the interior and exterior spaces.

The high quality video images now accessible as a result of the new digital flexible endoscopes, have attracted the attention of fine artists such as Mona Hatoum, a Palestinian artist who has been working with the issues of personal freedom and feminism. In *Corps Etranger*, an installation at the Tate Gallery 'Rites of Passage' exhibition in 1995, she used video footage of her rectum and anus as the texture for the floor of an immersive chamber. The gallery audience was invited to stand inside this chamber and enter her virtual body orifices, accompanied by sound recordings from these spaces; it is as if Mona Hatoum had literally eaten her audience. Hatoum's recreation of the intestinal space forces us to engage with and even experience the relationship that we have with our interior spaces and confront our fears and taboos about it.

Private or Public Space?

The gastrointestinal cavity has been used by smugglers and circus performers as a secret site, with the ultimate implication that it is unsuitable to show the anatomy full of refuse, or acting as a sanctuary for abomination or criminal activity. The performers in the Jim Rose Circus demonstrate snake-like contortions of the gut, accepting sharp, noxious and often impossibly dangerous objects, without any apparent harm to the gastrointestinal system, to exploit the audience's associations with a sinister and cannibalistic interior space.

> The stomach area was carefully flapped open and the intestines removed, disentangled and reknitted as it were, into a small net or web and hung between the pillars of the murder location ... It was definitely murder – but was it art?[4]

This particular taboo is revealed in Peter Greenaway's film *The Cook, the Thief, his Wife and her Lover*, a tragedy set in a restaurant. The garish interior design of the eating space, mimics the chambers of the human gut: red for the restaurant/stomach; green for the kitchen/small intestine and dark brown for the refuse yard/anus. In these settings, he explores base human drives and needs: eating, drinking, defecating copulating belching, vomiting, nakedness and blood. In mimicking the interior of the gut, Greenaway postulates a literal theatrical production within our digestive system:

> RICHARD: . . . It says more about death than eating and more about living than cooking.
> GEORGINA: Does it mention Cannibalism?
> RICHARD: (smiling) I believe it does.[5]

This theatrical possibility of acting in the gastrointestinal tract has been explored in the work of Ron Athey, a Los Angeles based, HIV positive performance artist, who has used his mouth, anus and rectum, without seeking collaboration or medical assistance, in his sadomasochistic performances.

During *Deliverance*, at the Institute of Contemporary Art, London, 1995, Athey used enemas and erotic objects which he inserted into his rectal space as an integral part of the narrative of his performance, drawing attention to the contamination and abject nature of the body-object. This extreme use of his body space degrades the 'creativity' of the flesh and inverts the prevailing power relationship between the gut and his decaying, mortal flesh. Athey reminds us that the gastrointestinal tract is designed to accept and expel human waste and is the ideal body space in which to communicate his performance agenda.

Stelarc has collaborated with medical professionals to go deeper into this terrain in his *Stomach Sculpture* performances. Stelarc constructed a sculpture that was collapsible into a capsule which could then be swallowed, and using a cable release, could be re-extended in the stomach space. Performing at Ars Electronica in Lin, 1992, Stelarc employed an interactive video setup where the body was able to switch between six cameras, one of which provided internal images of the inside of his stomach:

> I had to swallow an 80 centimetres long endoscope into the stomach. The pictures began, really, with the mouth at the

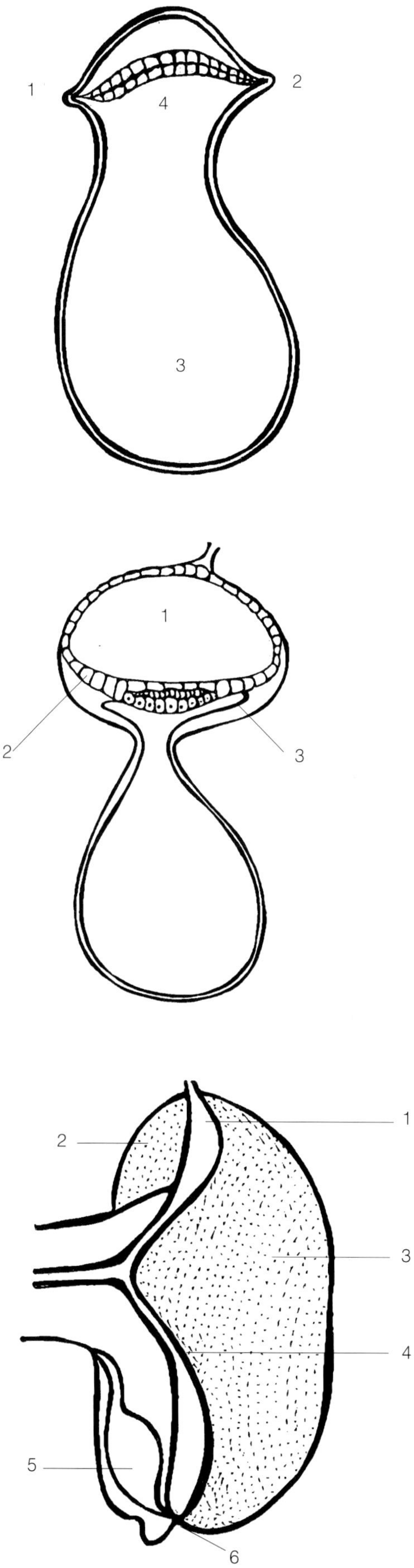

The three stages of embryonic development, ABOVE: (1) head (2) tail (3) yolk sac (4) embryonic plate consisting of ectoderm and endoderm; CENTRE: (1) amniotic sac (2) buccal membrane (3) cloacal membrane; BELOW: (1) stomach (2) rectal mesentry (3) dorsal mesentry (4) midgut hindgut (5) urogenital sinus (bladder) (6) proctodaeum

> opening and then the images of going down the throat, past the epiglottis and finally into the stomach. The images were quite interesting and I think, being able to switch using sensors on the different parts of the body: arms, head, legs, being able to alternate between the eternal images of the body and the inside of the stomach was quite intriguing. It was a real challenge to do this live. It took me five attempts to get the endoscope down and keep it down. It was very uncomfortable and you want to expel the thing. It's not simply that it hurts. It's involuntary. You've got involuntary stomach and throat actions going on that try to force that thing out.[6]

The sculpture was exhibited as part of the fifth Australian Sculpture Triennial at the National Gallery of Victoria, having been surgically inserted and then removed in a doctor's surgery prior to its display.

The aesthetic results of these experiments led Stelarc to explore more complex possibilities of performance in the stomach space, where the sculptural technology functioned within his curator/gallery body, not as a prosthetic replacement, but as an aesthetic adornment, and where the hollow body was a host, not for a self or a soul, but simply for a sculpture: 'One no longer looks at art, nor performs art, but contains art . . .'[7]

In 1995, Stelarc repeated the experiment in London, this time using a sedative and atropine to dry up his body fluids. The artwork was inserted as three separate capsules which would be reconstructed on site and when assembled, would be driven by a raw earth magnet creating a symphony of light, sound and vibration. The whole process was to be captured on film in a medical clinic, but owing to legal difficulties, the performance was abandoned. This technical feat would have been the first autonomous performance given by an assembled sculpture created in the body of a host artist-gallery.

Viewing the Inside From Outside

Access to the deepest areas of the gastrointestinal tract is still problematic, even with the collaboration of medical professionals. However, non-invasive medical imaging techniques are possible, the most sophisticated being ultrasound which has traditionally been used to scan for gallstones in the liver. Gallstones are common and often produce no symptoms, but on a scan, the nuclei appear as white shadows against a black gall bladder and spread white radii in this cavity. These monochrome images are initially incomprehensible, however, with explanation from a trained eye, offer interesting, abstract, low-resolution pictures for artistic or architectural analysis.

The Gut as a Sensory Organ and Musical Instrument

The gut has been used as the site of sound production and has inspired composers of ambient music to use sampled sounds in their projects. Reworking intestinal recordings from a bowel operation, Robin Rimbaud (aka Scanner) relocated them into a virtual environment designed as a training tool for consultant anaesthetists to investigate the properties of a new class of opiate. By using a joystick and headset to navigate the environment, users can play the sounds conceaed within the space like a three-dimensional instrument. Another property of long wavelength ultrasound vibrations engages the dynamic nature of the gastrointestinal tract. The muscular structure has been shown to be directly responsive to low frequency oscillations which verge on those signals employed by riot control police. Zbigniew Karkowski, a musician who works with low ultrasound frequencies, creates gestural performance pieces which possess and invade the inner recesses of the body, collapsing the specific and unique function of the ear as a sensory organ and allowing the gut to become part of an extended conductive hearing-device:

> In reality, all sounds are nothing else but the result of vibration of materials. Sound is a presence of energy vibrating through space. Music must become aware of the subtleties of its effects. There is no doubt that the body's metabolism functions via a combination of electrical frequencies, pulse rates and biochemical hormones. The brain is dependent on it. There is nothing else but sound, all that exists is vibration.[8]

Population and Colonisation

The gastrointestinal tract is responsive to its external environment and contains symbiotic bacteria which have colonised this space at birth and which assist in its digestive and absorptive functions. These microscopic inhabitants are regarded by some artists as those inhabitants which will, by techniques of recombinant genetic engineering, enhance the design, aesthetics and physiology of our exterior bodies.

Orlan, a French performance artist who has been working with her own body as a site for public debate about important issues of our time, in particular the use of aesthetic surgery and genetic engineering, considers the skin as a costume which is made for alteration or for redesigning. Orlan has already considered collaboration with genetic engineers to design bacteria which would be able to produce a pigment to change the colour of her skin when she eats a certain food. Different strains of bacteria could create various pigmented colourations so that, like a chameleon, her skin could change in relationship to her environ-

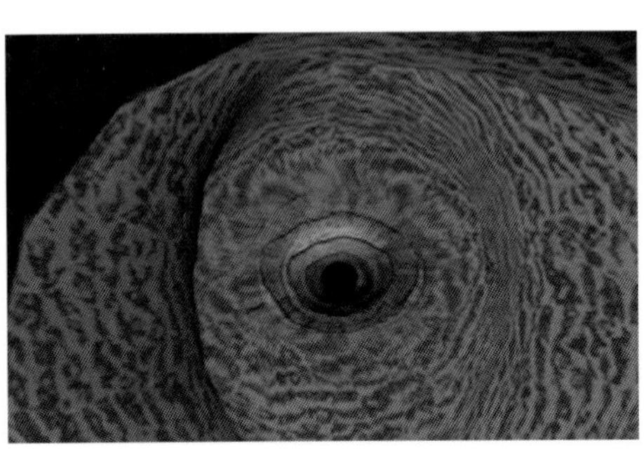

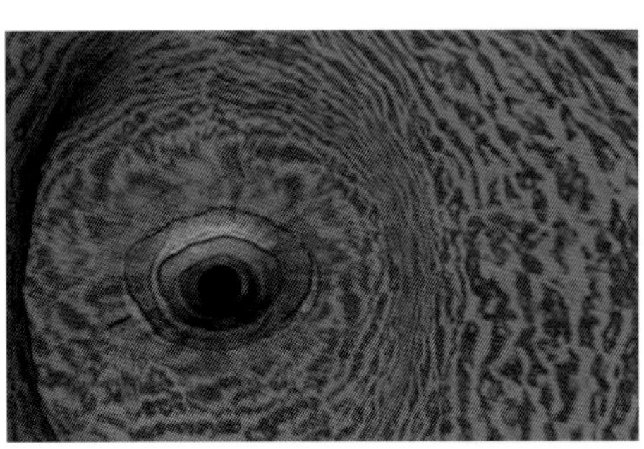

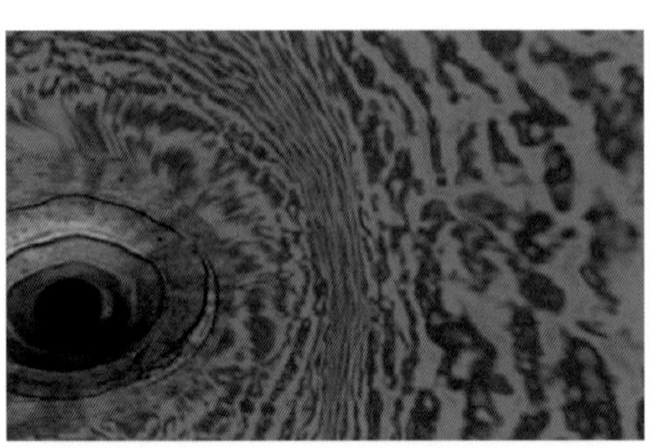

ment or aesthetic preferences.

> What can the common monster, tattooed ambidextrous, hermaphrodite and crossbred, show to us right now under his skin? Yes, blood and flesh. Science talks of function, cells and molecules to acknowledge that it is high time that one stopped talking of life in the laboratories, but science never utters the word flesh which, quite precisely, points out the mixtures in given place of the body, here and now, of muscle and blood, of skin and hair, of bones, nerves and of the various functions and which hence mixes up that which is analysed by the discerning knowledge . . . [9]

The ability to change the exterior through inner processes for fashionable purposes has already been speculated upon by some of the Cyberpunk authors, such as Pat Caddigan, who in the novel *Fools*, has the character Coney change his skin colour to orange by virtue of genetically engineered bacteria.

More direct integration of colour, design and sculpture on the gut surface may be accomplished by the invention of gels and lubricants that could facilitate the insertion of longer and more robust viewing objects into the rectum. Invited audiences or intimate partners would be able to view the inscribed symbol, object or tattoo with the appropriate equipment. These markings could be considered as a distinctive part of our identity.

Decorating the Gut

Once artists and architects have free access to the intestinal spaces they will be able to take advantage of some of the natural phenomena and create some adornments of their own. Fashions such as crystal growing may become fashionable. Gallstones, found by ultrasonic probes, take on a variety of various forms and may be cultured in the same way that oysters are encouraged to produce pearls! Other solutions which precipitate change in the gut could provide us with the capabilities of creating our own crystal gardens in our intestines or stomach.

Sociology of the Gut

The future holds the advent of autonomous artificial life forms and nanotechnology. Nanotechnology was first described by K Eric Drexler as molecules operating in groups to become more complex machines, or 'assemblers'. These preprogrammed automata would be capable of operating remotely in many sites of the body and could colonise the gut. Together with artificially designed life forms, these microminiature machines would be performing physiological functions, such as the removal of toxins from the absorptive surface, and may also offer a means of building decorative conformations which we would be able to view with flexible endoscopes, ultrasound or future medical imaging technologies. We would be able to take snapshots of our personalised sculptures and consider them as self portraits. The aesthetic design of the gastrointestinal tract could, therefore, provide a personalised fingerprint and become an essential component of our identity.

Harmless encapsulated implants could be swallowed to act as remotely activated keys, to provide identity markers, communication signals, tracking devices, telecommunication links and other personalised signals which could operate a sensitive environment. The gastrointestinal tract markers and identifiers could be changed almost daily to evade criminal activity attempting to copy a personal code.

Once documentation of access to the images is possible, they will be developed and socialised by autonomous workers outside the medical profession, giving them a popular identity and even, eventually, an aesthetic appeal. The development of the gastrointestinal space will be dependent on our bodily relationship to it and on the way in which we evolve with the coming biotechnological and mechanical residents.

> 'Change for the machines,' she sighed heavily. 'That's all we've ever done is change for the machines. But this is the last time. We've finally changed enough that the machines will be making the changes from now on'.[10]

Notes

1 Jayne Parker (artist), 1989, *Body as Membrane*, Catalogue, Nordic Arts Centre, Finland, 1996.
2 From *Gulliver's Travels* by Jonathan Swift, in *The Cyborg Handbook*, Routledge (London), 1995, p180.
3 Quotations from Antoin Artaud cited by Deleuze and Guattari, *Anti-Oedipus: Capitalism and Schizophrenia, The Desiring Machines*, Athlone Press (3rd ed) (London), 1994, p8.
4 From *Outside* album cover, David Bowie, 1996.
5 Extract from *The Cook, the Thief, his Wife and her Lover*, Peter Greenaway, Dis Voir, 1992 (Paris), p84.
6 Interview with Stelarc, 'Gotham City Gossip', Radio 3RRR-FM, Melbourne, 18 July, 1992.
7 Stelarc, interview with the artist, Internet web site http://www.merlin.ac.au/stelarc, 1995.
8 Artist's statement, quoted in *Enhanced Gesture/Remote Desire: Post Evolutionary Strategies*, accompanying CD Stelarc, Anckarstrom, Goteborg, 1992.
9 Michel Serres, quotation from the 1996 Orlan Conference, Institute of Contemporary Art, London, April, 1996.
10 Pat Cadigan, *Synners*, Harper Collins, 1991, p 334.

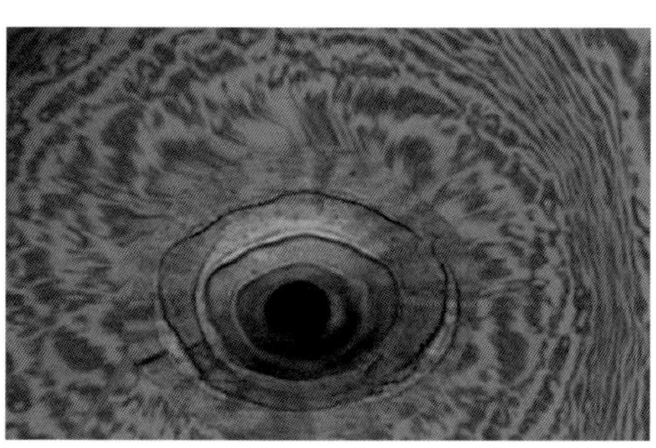

OPPOSITE, FROM L to R: Schematic representation of how the gut might appear in medical textbooks or in cultural/aesthetic discourses of the future. The stomach may become a site for aesthetic adornment or as a gallery, the intestines as site for their own decoration by crystals, sculptures or coding devices and the entire gastrointestinal system may be populated by genetically manipulated bacteria and/or nanotechnology

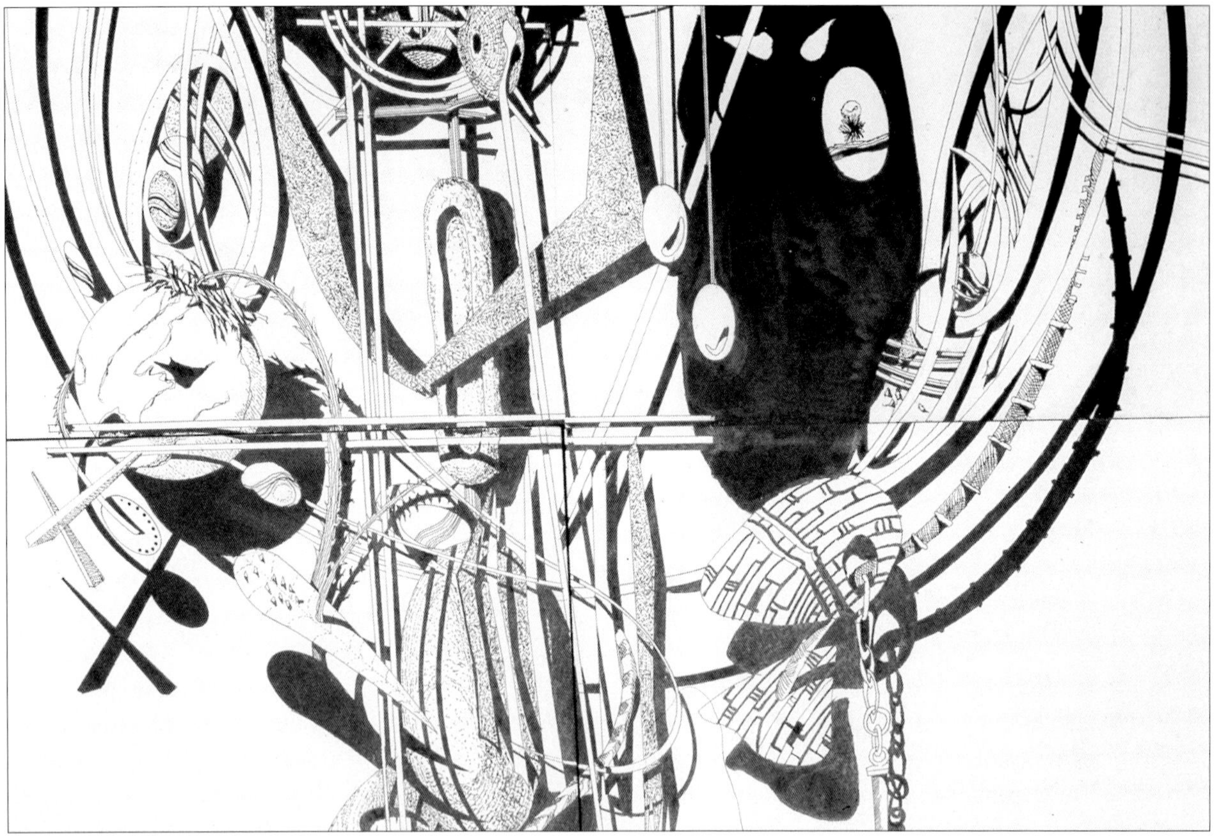

ABOVE: The Owl and Rotten Fruit, *1996 – Hieronymus Bosch was the most surreal painter of medieval religous cosmology. He used a variety of symbolic techniques to communicate his beliefs. One of his symbols for the Devil was the owl, silently watching over the debauchery of the world. It has been postulated that Bosch was a Cathar. The Cathars were a religious sect, persecuted by the Inquisition, who believed that the Earth was Hell and all matter was the Work of the Devil. There are many parallels between Cathar beliefs and the proponents of the 'New Flesh'; BELOW:* The Devil Ripped and Torn, *1996 – In Bosch's* The Garden of Earthly Delights, *Satan is represented as a 'hollow monster'. The pleasures of the world have become torments. The 'hollow monster' supports the whole composition yet is also pierced by it. Here the Devil is the body, its flesh cage impaled on the sharp scalpels of technology*

NEIL SPILLER

LEAVING NADIR

Cyborgian Mutation and Architecture

mindbody meatbody deathbody stinking sagging shitting foetus bursting organs hanging buried alive in a coffin of blood oh god not me don't let it be me got to get out of this bucket of tripe it's sucking me down throwing me up take it away this pulsing writing spurting spinning body-go-round, BODY.[1]

The Changing Carcass

The architectural subject is changing (by 'subject', both the body and practice is meant). Traditional notions of architectural enclosure are unable to respond to the growing range and virtuosity of the body, and this is an escalating problem. Architectural theory has been slow, if not frighteningly inert in understanding and facilitating the metamorphosis of its own subject, both spatially and biologically. Our spacescape and our bodies are two interacting fields: as the spacescape is transcribed by the constantly mutating body, it changes accordingly. The observer changes the spacescape simply by the act of operating within these fields. Much has been written in post-modern literature on the concept of the cyborg: the machine and flesh hybrid that contemporary technology has made, and continues to make of the body. The evolving symbiotic relationship between the cyborg and the spacescape is crucial to the development of such a preindustrial discipline as architecture. We need to explore and record some of the various states of the spatially transcribing biomechanical structure that we refer to as the body; and also postulate on its impact on the architectural spacescape.

There are many flesh chauvinists, and whilst one does not want to call into question the undeniable pleasures of inhabiting the body, these flesh Luddites seem unwilling to recognise that the integrity of the body is in shreds – torn, ripped and cut by technologies that have steadily multiplied in effect and number through the 20th century. The body is imploding and exploding all at once, and therefore so must architecture. However, the transition from states of implosion and explosion and *vice versa* is smooth and lacks a jolted boundary. Perception now swings both ways. With medical technology we look internally and with media technology we look outwards. It is conceivable that as the ontological distinctions between 'mechanical' and 'biological' disappear, then so too will concepts of distance.

Grow Your Own

The body is so precious and intimate to us, and so much an area of human culture that is fraught with hysterical gibbering about the sanctity of the flesh cage. Therefore it is perhaps wise to draw upon opinions from the medical profession, which is relatively untainted by the ongoing distrust of professional structures in other disciplines such as architecture and law. The mystical power of medical technology and methodology offer us the conceptual escape route that responds to a yearning for longevity – some respite or insurance against the death taboo. The first medical opinion we will consult is that of Robert Langer and Joseph P Vacanti, who assure us that in the near future, the growing of artificial organs and limbs will be of as little medical consequence as the giving of blood is now. In their essay entitled *Artificial Organs*,[2] they lead us through the techniques that will be employed in creating an artificial hand and arm which would be grown around biodegradable plastic:

> The structure of each system – muscle, bone, blood vessels, skin and so on – would be duplicated in biodegradable plastic. These 'scaffolds' would then be seeded with cells of relevant tissues. The cells divide and the plastic degrades, finally only coherent tissue remains. A mechanical pump would provide nutrients and remove wastes until the arm, which would take roughly six weeks to grow, can be attached to the body. Most of this technology is already in place. The remaining hurdle is the regeneration of nerve tissue . . .

Human skin grown on polymer substrates has already been used to help burns victims and other sufferers of skin complaints such as ulcers. In the same article, they also promote the use of microchips, or 'visionchips', to cure certain blinding diseases that attack the retinal surface but leave the nervous infrastructure of the eye intact. They also see artificial wombs as near future possibilities. This forthcoming ability of humanity to create flesh and organs outside the evolutionary equipped womb could well lead to a flesh fecundity – the prolific growing and use of artificial flesh.

Another medical physician, Dr Rachel Armstrong, in her essay *Post-human Evolution*[3] reminds us:

> Genes operate randomly by the process of Natural Selection and produce mutations through methods over which we have very little control. With current advances in biotechnology and intelligent systems, the ability for humans to be instrumental in directing their own evolutionary strategies is now possible. We are able to make designer mutants, beings who could not exist without considerable intervention.

Armstrong is a medical consultant to Orlan, a performance artist, of whom we will hear more later.

Visceral Escapology

Let us for the moment, leave the question of Matter and the New Flesh, and consider the body's shadow: the Cyberspatial Cyborg which can only be sustained, in its many split and shared forms, in virtual worlds. The body and its cyberspatial agents, are but differing manifestations and versions of the same distributed Self in different sectors of the Cyborgian spacescape. It is also foreseeable that these entities could eventually become amalgamations of virtual and vital intelligences. This potential of intelligence melding has been explored in many fictional scenarios, for example (in 'real' space) by Star Trek; The Next Generation's Borg:

> The Borg travel through the reaches of far space in their/its space cube habitat, searching for consumables . . . The ship appears a maze of machines where the humanoid Borg

components plug themselves in . . . [There is a] . . . confusion about whether The Borg is a single functioning unit or made up of separate parts – an 'it' or a 'they'.[4]

We will be drawing heavily on science fiction narratives where such visceral escapology has been examined frequently and extensively. The virtual persona of the cyborg is complex and difficult to define, its capacities and relationship to its fleshed self will be fluctuating and varied. The virtual world is one of anthropocentric invisibility, of consensual hallucination, of Artificial Life, of Artificial Intelligence, of alias, copy, version and mental upload. It is a domain of ecstatic emergences, flowering and mating genetic algorithms, self replication, hyperstructures and recursion. These are the *prima materia* of its architectures.

Whilst the Cyberspatial Cyborg can be the progeny of its fleshed partner, both offspring and lover; the virtual cyborg does not necessarily have to have a monogamous relationship with a fleshed wet spouse. Virtual sustainability of 'unreal' lifeforms need not be linked to some sort of 'feeder' umbilical cord which transverses the blurred boundary between virtual, vital and viral. They can become self determining; we can play God and give them free will.

In the book *Permutation City* by Greg Egan, many of the familiar notions of the role and nature of the Cyberspatial Cyborg are explored, set within a fairly straightforward survival plot. This plot revolves around a series of software personality copies. Each copy is a version of someone still alive (in real terms and time) or someone dead or copies of copies. Each software configuration then develops independently of its original creating versions with shared and part shared familial memory. These are all characters in the life and construction of a new virtual world which is used as a place of refuge from the terrors of software erasure whether by sabotage or mistake. The fear of erasure takes over from the fear of death. Egan makes us realise that the lot of a copy might not be all its cracked up to be, not all immortality and roses:

> People reacted badly to waking up as Copies. Paul knew the statistics. Ninety-eight per cent of Copies made were of the very old or the terminally ill. People for whom it was the last resort – most of whom had spent millions beforehand, exhausting all the traditional medical options; some of whom had even died between the taking of the scan and the time the Copy itself was run. Despite this, fifteen percent decided on awakening – usually in a matter of hours – that they couldn't face living this way.[5]

Whilst Egan refers to the process of up or downloading of consciousness (or software copying of wet neural networks into cyberspace) as 'scanning', Hans Moravec, a scientist specialising in robotics, has a much more invasive process in mind to achieve this aim: 'a futuristic robot surgeon peels away the brain of a conscious patient, using sensors to analyse and simulate the function in every slice'. As described by Moravec:

> Eventually your skull is empty, and the surgeon's hand rests deep in your brainstem. Though you haven't lost consciousness, your mind has been removed from the brain and transferred to a machine.[6]

In Egan's world order, other Cyberspatial Cyborgian entities will be various software gophers and daemons acting out relatively complex tasks: siphoning mail, sorting information and working creatively to explore new ideas and data bases and educate themselves and their fleshed counterparts. Egan's narrative also features 'the Lambertians', which are purely software-evolved, insect-like intelligences whose virtual world is Egan's Autoverse; his alternative copy environment, a hidden software utopia/Valhalla. He recognises that evolutionary procedures and their genetic algorithmic programmes are already hugely important in the continuing researches into Artificial Life and Artificial Intelligence. The Lambertians put food under their wings in an external wet sack and are described thus:

> It was no insect by the terrestrial definition; there were four legs, not six, and the body was clearly divided into five segments: the head; sections bearing the forelegs, wings and hind legs; and the tail . . . The head was blunt, not quite flat, with two large eyes – if they were eyes, shiny bluish discs, with no apparent structure. The rest of the head was coated in fine hairs, lined up in a complex, symmetrical pattern which reminded Maria of Maori facial tattoos. Sensors for vibration – or scent?[7]

So we see that in Egan's world, the Cyberspatial Cyborgian may evolve into forms that are alien, varying fundamentally from the Fleshed Cyborg which will still be dependent on wet engineering and gravity for sometime to come. Much has been made of the 'Aesthetics of Disappearance', as Virilio has called it,[8] and these observations are due to the ubiquity, ease of transmission and 'lightness' of information, and the ability to swiftly restructure and recalculate modifications in the virtual worlds. This disappearance has also had an impact on the wetware world of the body as technologies such as nanotechnology, which, through its claims of manipulating material atom by atom, makes death and ageing a simple menu option. Deleuze and Guattari have written of the Body without Organs (BwO), but as Bukatman claims, 'BwO is opposed not to the organs but the organisation of the organism'.[9] One is not, here anyway, arguing for a disappeared, disembodied organism, but a fleshed, wet intelligence; in effect, a Body with extra Organs (BwxO), where flesh has become even more abundant, hypersensitive and not despised.

You Thing Rike Jelly Fish Pretty Soon

Let us return to the fleshed body, the Realspatial Cyborg, and consider technologies of genetics and other bioengineering procedures of the future that will allow it to continue its existence and flourish. Already, even at their genesis, these technologies are rectifying some aspects of the defective rubbish of the born body. Currently, the gene therapied (or bioengineered body) looks no different to us, but it will not always be so. These changes to the body will change the way we calibrate the Universe. What happens when the ruler stretches, morphs, liquefies and disappears, or when its here and there simultaneously? As Manly P Hall makes us aware:

> The religious world of today is almost totally ignorant of the fact that the science of biology is the fountainhead of its doctrines and tenets. Many of the codes and laws believed by modern divines to have been direct revelations from Divinity are in reality the fruitage of ages of patient delving into the intricacies of the human constitution and the infinite wonders revealed by such a study.[10]

As the body changes so will religion, as we shall see. But first, let us examine one aspect of the liberating and potentially devastating technology of nanoengineering. Nano holds the key to the alchemic transmutation of matter, a potential that – should it be fully achievable – will assure its incredible influence not only on the inert and concrete but on the body itself. One of its more outrageous claims is that of a type of telepathy between organisms. Here, I quote K Eric Drexler:

> Authors have written of the direct sharing of thoughts and emotions from mind to mind. Nanotechnology seems likely to make possible some form of this by linking neural structures via transducers and electromagnetic signals. Though limited to the speed of light, this sort of telepathy seems as possible as telephony.[11]

So, the Fleshed Cyborg will be telepathic – probably across a variety of scales – having a much enhanced awareness of itself and 'others'.

A technology such as genetic engineering, once perfected, encourages a concept of genetic cross-pollination between species. Hybrids could be created and eugenically engineered to establish organisms with maximised sensitivity gleaned from a variety of disparate organic and non-organic sources. This theme has been picked up by the author Jeff Noon in his novel *Pollen*. The characters are Dogmen, Dogbitches, Robodogs, Shadows, Zombies and other genetic hybrids, set against a Manchester of the near future, and prone to the 'Vurt', a feather-induced drug that is inhaled or swallowed. As we can see, Mr Noon has a great imagination, and has much fun with us, as the following shows:

> She was a young woman, almost out of college, studying bio-plastics and *Hardwere*, those twin foundations of robotic canine life. Christina was genetically perfect, with a crystal clear intelligence and her tutors at the University of Manchester had praised the 'objective' eye she had brought to her studies of metadogology.[12]

In *Pollen,* hybrids were bred during a great 'Fecundity'; it seems as if we are on the verge of a real fecundity, the Flesh Fecundity. Other authors such as Vernor Vinge have expressed this notion:

> When a race succeeds in making creatures that are smarter than it is, then all the rules changed. And from the standpoint of that race, you've gone through a singularity . . . Their Art would not be art that you or I at this time could understand.[13]

Or to paraphrase, their architecture would not be understandable to us at this time. Perhaps the William Burrough's quote, 'You Thing Rike Jelly Fish Pretty Soon',[14] should be seen as a call to arms or a call to flesh; not a hymn to disappearance, but a psalm to fleshiness. Our bodily destiny is perhaps not to escape or to trash the flesh cage, but to pad it with permeable, sensitive additional flesh. This hyperfleshiness, augmented by the amplified advantages of our distributed virtual agents and selves, is one of our potential evolutionary destinies. Much cyberliterature has been perplexed by the limitation of current virtual reality soft and hardware, where full bodily immersion in cyberspace is a hellish world of experiential inertia and clunky prosthetics, the use of hypersensitised flesh could well provide another avenue out of the tyranny of datasuits and head mounted displays. We are perhaps closer than we think to making visually manifest what is already in existence, our cybernetised metaconsciousness: the flow of information at ever increasing bit speed through a global networked series of flesh components. Greg Bear's novel *Blood Music* explores some of these notions of networked intelligence and the role of the subsumed individual within such a structure:

> Bernard had lost his human form in the early morning. The cameras had recorded the transformation. Now, a grey and brown mass lay on his bed, portions extending to the floor on two sides. The mass moved fitfully, sometimes experiencing a short, violent shudder.[15]

Such smart biological structures might evolve, complemented by cyberspaces. These cyberspaces might be contained, not in silicon hardware, but in the biocomputable microbe, bacteria and enzymes of the secretions and cell structures of the new flesh. We return to Bear's narrative:

> I can go off in a million directions, lead a million lives (and not just in the *blood music* – in a universe of Thought, Imagination, Fantasy!) and then gather my selves together, hold a conference and start all over again, Narcissism beyond pride, propinquitous, far grander than simply living forever . . .[16]

The Stone Christ is Hiding

Orlan, the performance artist mentioned earlier, questions our bodily compliance with Nature and the genetic programme. She considers her work blasphemous. She subjects herself to a series of operations/performances that readjust her face, through the Euphrenic process of surgery.[17] Her work is confirmation that humankind now has dominion over the flesh. One of Orlan's future performances is to have the largest nose capable of being sustained by her lungs and facial structure. The successful completion of this performance will be dependent on a series of bone and skin stretching preliminaries.

What we are witnessing is the death throes of the Western God. Humankind has invested omnipotence and divine knowledge in the Deity, and has been willing to trust in His judgement for a variety of occurrences, particularly ageing, debilitating accidents and the moment of death. As we have seen, the cyberspatial half of the cyborg has been liberated already, immortality, serial and parallel selves, resurrection, evolution and omnipotence are all within its programming. In his book, *The Metaphysics of Virtual Reality,* Michael Heim describes this human craving for omniscience: 'What better way, then, to emulate God's Knowledge than to generate a virtual world constituted by bits of information? To such a cyberworld human beings could enjoy a God-like instant access'.[18]

The digital bit is immortal, instantly redefinable and easily reproduced. Thus, in the ether of cyberspace, the Cyber Cyborg's future is assured. But what of the Fleshed Cyborg as it again craves for the God-like status of omnipresence, immortality and resurrection, out here in the 'real' world and not in the there of the virtual world? Could our technologies, such as biotechnology, nanotechnology and other Euphrenic processes liberate us sufficiently to join the realm of the Gods, as we virtually can in cyberspace? Michael Heim also refers to the Russian, Nikolai Fedorovich Fedorov who, in the latter half of the nineteenth century, believed that the domination of Nature by technology was the ultimate altruistic goal, and that the resurrection of our ancestors was the fundamental altruist gesture.

According to Christian belief, the dead will rise again so that Christ, in a final judgement, will reorganise and completely redeem the world. The bodies of all human beings will one day rise again, and this resurrection, according to Fedorov, will take place through the work of human beings who carry out the divine plan. The long range goal of human cooperation must be to discover the laws of Nature to such a depth that we can eventually reconstitute the bodies of past human beings from their remaining physical particles still floating about in the universe.[19]

We can perceive echoes of this stance with Greg Bear's omnipresent Oneness of (the) *Blood Music*. While Fedorov's vision seems off beat, we have the theoretical ability to go far

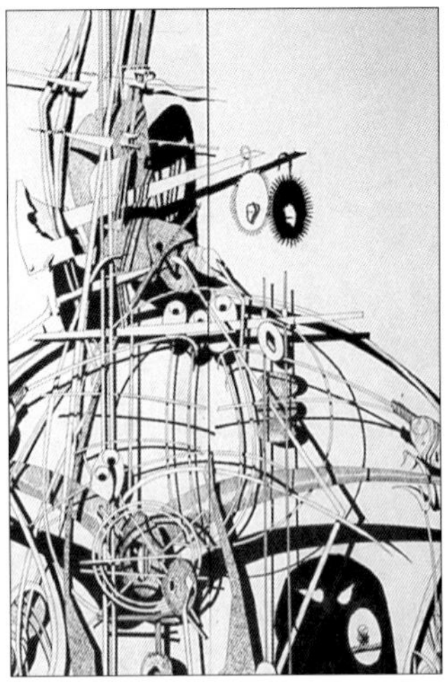

The Ship of Fools, *1996* – The Ship of Fools *is another of Bosch's symbols and is the place where 'souls succumb to the temptations of the world'. Our ship is perched on top of the holey globe, manned by fools who understand little of the inability of their heavy stone and spiked craft to float and glide in the ether of cybernetic connectedness*

Corrupt Seed, *1996 – The symbolism of the seed, fruit and grain symbolises Incarnation, Satan's way of trapping the 'soul' in the matter of a sick and inert world. NB, the theory that Bosch was a cathar is excellently framed in Lynda Harris'* The Secret Heresy of Hieronymus Bosch

beyond it. We may have the ability to not only animate past life forms but also, previously inanimate forms. Handy gives us a spiritual view: 'When humanity has completed its physical evolution, the empty shell of materiality left behind will be used by other *life waves* [my italics] as stepping stones to their own liberation.'[20] Again, we look to Greg Bear for inspiration in his short story, *Petra*:

> They saw the stone ornaments of the Cathedral come alive. With someone to see and believe, in a universe lacking another foundation, my ancestors shook off stone and become flesh. Centuries of rock celibacy weighed upon them.[21]

The Stone Christ had gone missing from the cathedral, but was in fact hiding in one of the dark recesses of the cathedral. The teller of the story encounters Him: 'I'd have to come from their midst, anonymous and that is clearly impossible. No, leave them alone for a while. They'll make Me over again, perhaps, or better still, forget about Me. About us. We don't have any place there.'[22]

Hans Moravec perceives the future as the domain of miniaturised machines, with humanity as a pampered menagerie illustrating the machine's evolutionary history. This is a future of supersmart robotised intelligences and not a fleshed fecundity. He also has a vision of God; an interviewer describes his view:

> And Moravec's vision of a supremely powerful artificial intelligence that will love humanity enough to recreate it is basically a vision of God – the only difference being that in his scheme of things, we create God version 1.0 after which it builds its own enhancements.[23]

Interestingly, the issues that gave Fedorov a moral and philosophical base for his promotion of the benefits of science and technology also appear in one of Moravec's scenarios:

> Assuming the artificial intelligences now have truly overwhelming processing power, they should be able to reconstruct human society in every detail by tracing atomic events backwards in time. 'It will cost them very little to preserve us this way,' he points out. 'They will in fact, be able to recreate a model of our entire civilisation, with everything and everyone in it, down to the atomic level, simulating our atoms with machinery which is largely subatomic'.[24]

Arguably, this event could have already taken place, how do we know one way or the other? Resurrection may have already occurred. Whilst we are killing the One God, we are pushing ourselves into a god-like role, a future where we take on the Deity's mantle and become the Many Gods. Human kind has taken both Christ's and God's job. We know that Godliness is next to wetness as well as 'bittyness'. The Christ of architecture, the body, has influenced architecture since humankind first sheltered from the rain and predators. It is hiding, unsure whether it will need architecture again. The architecture of the future will be homogeneous, networked, highly sensitised, telepathic, moist, dry, digital and biological. Few of our architectural tactics of today will be of any use in these central, but also peripheral locations in the spacescape. Vernor Vinge's Singularity may well be coming, and architecture may be torn apart.

Notes

1 David Skals, 'Antibodies', *Isaac Asimov Presents, (*ed) Gardiner Dozois, New York, 1988.
2 Robert Langer and Joseph P Vacanti, 'Artificial Organs' in *Scientific American – Key Technologies of the 21st Century,* September 1995.
3 Dr Rachel Armstrong, 'Post Human Evolution', *Artifice*, Bartlett School of Architecture, University College London, 1995.
4 Lynda H Schneekloth, 'Notions of the Inhabited', *Ordering Space – Types in Architecture and Design,* (eds) Karen A Franck and Lynda H Schneekloth, Van Nostrand Reinhold (New York), 1994, p47.
5 Greg Egan, *Permutation City*, Millennium (London), 1995, p5.
6 Charles Platt, 'Super Humanism', interview with Hans Moravec, *Wired,* October, 1995.
7 Egan, op cit, pp221.
8 P Virilio, *The Aesthetics of Disappearance,* Semiotext(e) (New York), 1991.
9 Scott Bukhatmen, *Terminal Identity,* Duke University Press, 1993, p328.
10 Manly P Hall, *The Secret Teachings of All Ages,* The Philosophical Society Inc (Los Angeles), 1988.
11 K Eric Drexler, *Engines of Creation,* Oxford University Press (Oxford), 1992, pp234.
12 Jeff Noon, *Pollen,* Ringpull Press Ltd, London, 1995.
13 Vernor Vinge, *Mondo 2000 – A Users Guide to The New Edge,* Thames and Hudson (London), 1992, p103.
14 William Burroughs, ibid.
15 Greg Bear, *Blood Music,* Legend (London), 1985, p237.
16 Bear, ibid, p239.
17 Armstrong, op cit, Euphrenic processes are ones that use unnatural surgical intervention in human biology.
18 Michael Heim, *The Metaphysics of Virtual Reality,* Oxford University Press (Oxford), 1993.
19 Heim, ibid, p120.
20 Hall, op cit.
21 Greg Bear, 'Petra', *Mirrorshades,* (ed) Bruce Stirling, Paladin (Boulder, CO), 1988.
22 Bear, ibid.
23 Platt, op cit.
24 Platt, op cit.

Neil Spiller is a partner of Spiller Farmer Architects and author of the forthcoming book Digital Dreams *to be published by Ellipsis in autumn 1996.*